Lord Morley's
Tryumphes of Fraunces Petrarcke

Drawing of Henry Parker, Lord Morley, by Albrecht Dürer, 1523

Lord Morley's

Tryumphes of Fraunces Petrarcke

The First English Translation of the *Trionfi*

Edited by D. D. Carnicelli

Harvard University Press
Cambridge, Massachusetts
1971

In Memoriam
Antonio Carnicelli

d'ogni laude degno
pien di filosofia la lingua e 'l petto

Preface

This edition of Lord Morley's sixteenth-century translation of Petrarch's *Trionfi* is presented for two distinct reasons. The first is to provide a critical, annotated text of Morley's rare and virtually inaccessible book. Those readers interested in tracing the fascinating byways of sixteenth-century Petrarchism represented by Morley's rendering of the *Trionfi* have hitherto had to consult one of the five extant copies of the work in rare-book rooms in England and the United States, or an inaccurate transcription of 1887 (which has itself become a rare book), or a brief selection from "The Tryumphe of Love" in Eleanor Prescott Hammond's *English Verse Between Chaucer and Surrey* (London, 1927).

The second aim is to make certain inquiries into an aspect of sixteenth-century Petrarchism which has never been given adequate attention. Though most students of English Renaissance literature are at least slightly familiar with Petrarch's *Trionfi* and with triumphal pageants that appear in the poetry and drama of the period, none has given serious consideration to English interest in the *Trionfi* or to Roger Ascham's complaint that Italianate Englishmen "have in more reverence the triumphes of Petrarche than the Genesis of Moses"; none has attempted to determine how much of Ascham's statement is attributable to his inveterate xenophobia and how much represents an objection to what he might have considered the excessive popularity of Petrarch's *Trionfi*. That popularity cannot be overestimated, because the *Trionfi* was what Ernest Hatch Wilkins called "the most triumphant poem of the early Renaissance," a poem whose popularity outshone both Petrarch's sonnets and Dante's *Divine Comedy* for a hundred years or more. Unfortunately, in recent years the poem has been eclipsed by the critical attention paid to the *Canzoniere*, but its importance is nonetheless undeniable, and the subtle changes it worked on the reading habits, on the literature, iconography, and pageantry of the Renaissance attest to the range and intensity of its influence. That influence is sometimes exaggerated and often completely misunderstood, but it was strong and so deserves careful attention and study. If my introductory remarks serve only to revive interest in the *Trionfi* and to remind readers that definitions of Petrarchism must take into account interest in the *Trionfi* as well as the *Canzoniere*, they will have served a useful purpose.

These then are the larger goals of the present work, but the reader is asked not to lose sight of the fact that the primary focus throughout is the impress of the *Trionfi* on the literature of the English Renaissance. Even when self-imposed, such restrictions are dangerous: what we must eventually have is a comprehensive study of the place of the *Trionfi* in the literature of the Renaissance, a study that takes into account how Italian, French, and Spanish, as well as English, poets read and imitated the *Trionfi*. Some historical groundwork for such a study was laid as early as the turn of the century by Melodia, Bertoni, and Farinelli, and in later years Sapegno, Calcaterra, Wilkins, and others made valuable contributions. The basic plan of my introduction is to bring together much of that historical criticism and thus achieve a clearer understanding of the fortunes of the *Trionfi* in England.

The brief account of Lord Morley's life and literary interests is designed to place him in historical and literary perspective. I owe much to the excellent biographical sketch found in Herbert G. Wright's introduction to his edition of Morley's translation of Boccaccio's *De claris mulieribus*. In addition, I have reexamined Morley's manuscripts at the British Museum and at the Bodleian Library.

The discussions of the contents of the original poem and of its place in the history of Petrarchism are intended for those not familiar with the Italian original or with its relation to the remainder of the Petrarchan canon. I trust that these discussions will be of use to English readers, though I suspect that to Italian scholars they will appear to be superfluous.

What appears to be a long digression on Renaissance editions of the *Trionfi* and the tradition of allegorical exegesis of the poem may need a word of justification here. The fifteenth and sixteenth centuries saw the appearance of a rush of editions of the *Trionfi*, most of which were shored and buttressed by richly detailed exegetical commentaries. These editions and commentaries required attention both because they were the cause of and the response to the Renaissance vogue for the *Trionfi* and because no scholar has treated them seriously, though Carlo Calcaterra and one or two of his predecessors mentioned them in passing. Moreover, Lord Morley's own argument in the dedicatory epistle to the translation is that in the poem's "manye devyne sentences" there are revealed "theologicall secretes"; such a statement is strong proof that he himself was aware of the long-standing tradition of allegorical exegesis of the *Trionfi* and that he invited his readers to read the translation as a complex allegory.

No writer on the *Trionfi* can ignore another indication of the poem's widespread popularity—its influence on Renaissance iconography— and I have not considered myself exempted from that obligation. I make no claim to presenting anything approaching a full analysis of that fascinating subject; my main concern is to sketch an outline for the literary scholar and to indicate the deep affinities between poetry and painting in the Renaissance. Art historians will find that I have left much undone, but they will be the first to admit that the subject begs for fresh treatment by their own profession. The fullest treatment of the subject, Victor Massena d'Essling's and Eugene Müntz's *Pétrarque, ses études d'art, son influence sur les artistes, ses portraits, et ceux de Laure,* however excellent, is now badly dated and needs to be revised in the light of recent discoveries.

Editorial procedures and the scholarly apparatus are explained in detail in the closing pages of the introduction. The bibliography is selective, included only to provide a guide to the editions, translations, and studies which I have found most useful and pertinent. The bibliography and notes are preceded by a bibliographical history of Lord Morley's *Tryumphes* and followed by a glossary and an index of the proper names in the translation.

The experience and advice of many persons has gone into the making of this book: I should like to express my gratitude to as many of them as possible. William Nelson of Columbia University first called my attention to the need for an edition of Lord Morley's translation and a study of the *Trionfi,* and under his expert guidance this edition was prepared as a Columbia doctoral dissertation between 1963 and 1966. Maurice Valency and John C. Nelson read the original draft and made valuable suggestions; Allen T. Hazen and Elizabeth Story Donno assisted with editorial and bibliographical problems. James G. McManaway of the Folger Library and Katherine Pantzer of the Houghton Library at Harvard brought the Sion College Library copy of the *Tryumphes* to my attention. In my requests to examine rare

Preface

books and manuscripts in libraries in this country and in England and France, I have had the full and courteous cooperation of the staffs of many libraries, and I must single out the Columbia University Library, the Willard Fiske Petrarch Collection at Cornell University, the Pierpont Morgan Library, the British Museum, the Bodleian Library, the Victoria and Albert Museum, Hampton Court, the Bibliothèque Nationale, and the Bibliothèque de l'Arsenal.

The material on Bernardo Illicino and the Renaissance commentaries on the *Trionfi* appeared in slightly different form in the August 1969 issue of *Romance Philology* and is reprinted here with the kind permission of the editor of that journal, Yakov Malkiel. I am also grateful to the University of Chicago Press for permission to quote from Ernest Hatch Wilkins, *The Triumphs of Petrarch*.

My brother, A. W. Carnicelli, and my wife, Joan Vogel Carnicelli, assisted in transcribing and checking Morley's text. Lastly, thanks to Danica Deutsch for a thousand personal kindnesses and encouragements.

D. D. C.

New York
July 14, 1970

Contents

Contents

xii

Illustrations

Frontispiece. Drawing of Henry Parker, Lord Morley, by Albrecht Dürer, 1523. Courtesy of the Trustees of the British Museum.

Following page 50

1. *Cassone*, Victoria and Albert Museum, no. 4639–1858. Reproduced by permission of the Victoria and Albert Museum.
2. *Desco da parto*, Victoria and Albert Museum, no. 398–1890. Courtesy of the Victoria and Albert Museum.
3. Luca Signorelli, *The Triumph of Chastity*, The National Gallery, London, no. 910. Reproduced by courtesy of the Trustees, The National Gallery, London.
4. Glass cup, Slade Collection, British Museum. Courtesy of the Trustees of the British Museum.
5. Psalter belonging to Alfonso of Aragon, British Museum, MS. 28962, fol. 378ᵛ. Courtesy of the Trustees of the British Museum.
6. Majolica dish, Victoria and Albert Museum. Courtesy of the Victoria and Albert Museum.
7. Tapestry, *The Triumph of Death over Chastity*, Hampton Court, no. 1031. Copyright reserved to H.M. the Queen; courtesy of the Lord Chamberlain.
8. Tapestry, *The Triumph of Fame over Death*, Hampton Court, no. 1032. Copyright reserved to H.M. the Queen; courtesy of the Lord Chamberlain.
9. Tapestry, *The Triumph of Time over Fame*, Hampton Court, no. 1033. Copyright reserved to H.M. the Queen; courtesy of the Lord Chamberlain.
10. Tapestry, *The Triumph of Chastity over Love*, Victoria and Albert Museum, no. 440–1883. Courtesy of the Victoria and Albert Museum.
11. Tapestry, *The Three Fates Triumphing over Chastity*, Victoria and Albert Museum, no. 441–1883. Courtesy of the Victoria and Albert Museum.
12. Miniature of the triumph of Love, Fonds français, no. 22541, fol. 1ʳ, Bibliothèque Nationale. Courtesy of the Bibliothèque Nationale.
13. Miniature of the triumphs of Fame, Death, and Chastity, Fonds français, no. 594, fol. 178ᵛ, Bibliothèque Nationale. Courtesy of the Bibliothèque Nationale.
14. Miniature of the triumph of Fame, Fonds français, no. 594, fol. 179ʳ, Bibliothèque Nationale. Courtesy of the Bibliothèque Nationale.

Illustrations

Introduction

The Life of Lord Morley

What little is known of the life of Henry Parker, Lord Morley, the first English translator of Petrarch's *Trionfi*, is enough to single him out as a minor but important public and literary figure in the early Tudor court. In the course of a long life Morley played so many roles—courtier, scholar, poet, diplomat, public official, confidant and kinsman to royalty—that his life would be of special interest to the social and political historian of the Tudor era even if he did not hold the distinction of being at the forefront of English interest in Petrarch in the sixteenth century. As a translator of Latin as well as Italian works, Morley is a noteworthy figure in English literary history, one of the main links between Caxton and the great Elizabethan translators.[1] As a "courtly maker" in the court of Henry VIII, he wrote lyrics that invite comparison with the work of major figures such as Wyatt and Surrey and minor ones such as Robert Fairfax, George Boleyn, and Thomas Chaloner.

Henry Parker was born in 1476 and died in 1556.[2] His mother was Alice Lovel, through whom we can trace one of his two distant family connections with English royalty: Morley's maternal uncle, Henry Lovel, was the husband of Elizabeth de la Pole, who was the sister of Edward IV and Richard III.[3] His father, William Parker, appears to have been a faithful servant of the Plantagenets; he was reputed to have been in great favor with both Edward IV and Richard III, and he was knighted for his bravery in an expedition against Scotland in 1482 or 1483. When Richard seized the throne in 1483, Sir William was appointed Privy Counselor and Standard Bearer to the new king. His fortunes had already prospered by his marriage to Alice Lovel, who had brought him a considerable amount of property in Norfolk, Buckinghamshire, and Herefordshire, as well as the manor of Great Hallingbury in Essex, where many years later Morley was to write a reflective poem to posterity.[4] Alice Lovel increased the wealth of the Parker family even more when in 1489 she inherited the baronies of Morley, Marshall, Hengham, and Rhie after the death without issue of her brother Henry at the Battle of Dixmude.

But more important to the young Parker than the position and wealth his family enjoyed was the opportunity for daily contact with prominent people of the Tudor court. As a young boy he served as page in the household of Margaret Beaufort, Countess of Richmond and mother of Henry VII. The Countess was famous for her piety and for her love of learning; she had encouraged both Caxton and de Worde, and she was the founder of St. John's College and Christ College, Cambridge. Her own piety and learning and the pious and scholarly habits she inspired in those around her made a deep impression on her young servant, for Morley's later recollections of his service to Margaret in his youth and his memories of the lady's great generosity were vivid and warm.[5]

Little is known of Morley's education or his early literary activities other than Anthony à Wood's hazy statement that "he was educated in most kinds of literature in the University of Oxford and in his youth was occupied with all kinds of superficial learning."[6] Indeed we know virtually nothing about the first half of his life; his name does not appear in public records until 1516, when he was in his fortieth year. Thereafter, it is possible to follow his public and diplomatic career over a period of some forty years, from 1516 to the year of his death, 1556. The incomplete portrait of Morley which emerges from public records is one of a courtier serving three successive sovereigns faithfully and well; it is also the portrait of a seasoned politician treading lightly in troubled times, shifting allegiances nimbly, and, by virtue of these talents, surviving all political and religious upheavals to die quietly in bed at the age of eighty.

Morley's appointment as gentleman usher to the king occasioned his first appearance in the public records, at the time his infant son Henry became a page of the royal chamber. Later, in June of 1520, Morley attended Henry VIII at his meeting with Francis I at the field of the Cloth of Gold; he was also present at Henry's meetings with Charles V in the same month. On April 15, 1523, he was summoned to the House of Lords as Lord Morley in the right of his maternal grandmother, and he was to occupy this seat with regularity until 1547. Some months later, in the late summer of 1523, he was despatched to the Low Countries and to Germany to present the Order of the Garter to Ferdinand, Archduke of Austria and brother to Charles V, for his efforts in suppressing Lutheran doctrines in Germany. A papal ban had been pronounced on Luther at the Diet of Worms two years earlier, and when Morley arrived as emissary of the king of England Luther was busily engaged in writing polemical treatises against the papacy. As head of the diplomatic mission, which included Edward Lee, Archdeacon of Colchester and Almoner to the king, Sir William Hussey, and Sir Thomas Wriothesley, Morley despatched a series of four communiqués to London in which he gave detailed accounts of the progress of the mission.[7] The first letter was addressed to Wolsey; after some flattering overtures to the prelate, Morley goes on to describe how the party entered Flanders, passed through Dunkirk and Bruges, and entered Antwerp on September 20; he also gives an account of the party's passage to Mechlin, where he was presented to Lady Margaret of Savoy. The second letter, written from Cologne, is addressed to Henry VIII and reports the death of Hadrian VI, the controversy between Ulrich von Hutten and Erasmus, and Luther's enormous popularity in Germany. In the third letter Morley tells Wolsey almost exactly what he had told Henry, but he uses the occasion to flatter the cardinal by reminding him of his great popularity and influence abroad. The last letter is also addressed to Wolsey; dated November 19, it reports the arrival of the mission in Nurnberg and the expected arrival of the Archduke Ferdinand, as well as the continued popularity of Luther. The Order of the Garter was bestowed on the Archduke Ferdinand on December 8; by February of 1524 Morley and his party were back in England.

But before leaving Germany, probably in October of 1523, Morley sat for Albrecht Dürer.[8] In many respects Dürer's drawing gives a clearer insight into the character of the man than all the public records. Dürer was not given to idealized portraiture, and we can therefore assume that his drawing is a faithful representation of Morley's physical features. The man depicted by Dürer is well dressed in richly flowered robes and a fur collar; he wears the chains of office, his left hand is thrust into his robe, and his right hand, powerful and massive, holds a pomegranate, symbol of the unity of the church and of resurrection and hope in immortality. The face is lean and handsome, extremely youthful in appearance considering Morley's forty-seven years, and its angular and elongated features suggest that Morley was a tall man. In the eyes is an abstracted look in which one critic has seen "that expression of disinterestedness or momentary distraction which is not merely an individual or national characteristic, but part of the professional mask of the diplomat."[9]

From the time of his mission to Germany, Morley appears to have been in the good graces of every reigning monarch, and the public records indicate that he supported and served those monarchs selflessly for the remainder of his life. In 1526, as a reward for his faithful service to the Tudor house, he was awarded the manor of Hasilbach, near Derby. On July 13, 1530, Morley was one of the signatories to a letter from the peers of England to Clement VII urging the pontiff to grant Henry a divorce from Catherine of Aragon. He served regularly in Parliament from 1529 to 1547, and in the course of that long career he was witness to events of great moment. He was present at the trials of a series of noblemen who had offended Henry VIII—Lord Dacre, Lord Darcy, Lord Hussey, Lord Montague, and the Marquis of Exeter. But in May of 1536 came what must have been the most painful of all these trials: it was then that Morley was one of the judges at the trial of Anne Boleyn and her brother, George Boleyn, Viscount Rochford, both of whom were personally close to him. He had long been on cordial terms with Anne, to whom, when she was Marchioness of Pembroke, he had dedicated a translation.[10] George Boleyn was even more closely connected with Morley: he had married Morley's daughter Joan. In June of 1536, less than two months after the trial and execution of Anne and George Boleyn, Morley was granted the offices of "chief steward of the manor or lordship, master of the hunt of deer of the whole forest, and keeper of the park at Hatfield Regis." (Whether there is a connection between this mark of Henry's favor and the role Morley played in the Boleyns' trial, as Herbert G. Wright suggests,[11] is impossible to establish at this remove.)

Although Morley appeared at two ceremonial functions in 1537, first the christening of Prince Edward, at which he was instructed to help carry Princess Elizabeth "for her tender age," and then the funeral of Jane Seymour, at some time after the trial of Anne and George Boleyn he seems to have withdrawn from the court to lead the life of a country gentleman at Mark Hall and Hallingbury Place, his residences in Essex. However, he visited the court on special occasions, such as the official welcome of Anne of Cleves at Rochester on New Year's Day of 1540 (when he formed part of a procession of gentlemen who preceded the king) and the entertainment of the Lord Admiral of France at Greenwich in 1546.

But retirement and advancing age did not curtail Morley's efforts to further his fortunes. The year 1537 shows Morley exploiting his connections with persons in high places for the purpose of acquiring church lands available as a result of Henry's dissolution of the monasteries. Morley made two separate attempts at landgrabbing. The first was a successful attempt to secure lands belonging to a priory at Aldeby. Having obtained the lands, Morley found it difficult to dislodge the monks and take possession. He appealed to Cromwell for assistance, but even the Lord Chancellor's power and influence could not bring him success. However, Morley's persistence, and perhaps some additional pressure from Cromwell, eventually brought the property to him, for in a document dated 1547 the lands of the priory are listed as his.

Morley also attempted to repossess property which he himself had earlier awarded to the church. At some unspecified time, perhaps during his early days at court, Morley had founded a priory at Beeston in Norfolk, and in 1537, at a time of great religious and political turmoil, he was determined to regain his property before it fell into the hands of others. He appealed once more to Cromwell for assistance, this time addressing him as "my specyall good Lorde" and acknowledging that "there will be inoughe that will be agaynst me, but God and youe with me, I fere no enemys." Despite the fact that Morley was requesting to have his own property restored to him and despite his appeal to the Lord Chancellor, the following year the property was awarded not to Morley but to a certain John Travers.

Save for an occasional visit to court, Morley seems to have spent the remainder of his life in easeful retirement in Essex, though there are signs that he took care to maintain his connections at court, particularly with Cromwell. In 1539 he sent Cromwell a gift of Machiavelli's *Istorie Fiorentine* and *Il Principe*, the former carefully annotated and marked with precedents the king might use in his quarrel with the pope. In the same year he published *The Exposition and Declaration of the Psalme, Deus Ultionum Dominus*,[12] dedicated to Henry VIII, noting in the dedicatory epistle that Henry's "Empire mooste triumphant hath been wrongfully kept as tributarie unto the Babylonicall seate of the Romyshe byshop."

In Essex he faithfully carried out the administrative assignments inevitably assigned by the crown to one of his rank, and he appears in the public records as a nobleman charged with a wide variety of duties. In 1539 he was appointed one of the commissioners in Hertfordshire to deal with musters; from 1540 to 1543 he was one of the noblemen responsible for the drainage of Essex and Hertfordshire counties. In 1545 he was one of the collectors of "benevolences" for the French war, and in the following year he was charged with the responsibility of collecting other "loving contributions" for the French war. In 1546 there fell to Morley still another duty connected with Henry's war against France, that of raising levies of from four to six hundred footmen from Essex and Hertfordshire, equipping them, and conducting them to Dover for embarkation to France. In 1547, the year of Henry's death, he was listed as one of the commissioners of the peace, a post he had occupied since 1530. In the troubled reign of Edward VI his loyalty to the crown was undiminished; in 1549, despite his advanced age, he was called upon to provide protection for Edward VI when the young king was thought to be in danger at the hands of the Duke of Somerset. In 1549–1550, when the country found itself in a serious financial crisis, and Parliament was forced to pass new taxes on sheep, wool, and personal income, Morley was appointed one of the commissioners in Essex and Hertfordshire to collect the "relief," as the tax was called. A year later, during the same financial crisis, he was called upon to look into price fixing in Essex and Hertfordshire and to report his findings to the Privy Council.

One final manuscript, addressed to Queen Mary shortly before Morley's death, contains a collection of "miracles" of the Holy Sacrament and a brief life of Richard III and provides some additional biographical material, mostly about Morley's boyhood.[13]

Morley's long life, which spanned seven reigns of English monarchs and eighty years of turbulent English history, came to an end in November of 1556, just two years before the accession of Elizabeth. He was buried in the church of Great Hallingbury in Essex, according to the account of Arthur Machyn, with all the splendor and magnificence usually accorded a gentleman of his rank: "The iij of Desember was bered in [Essex] Lord Morley, with iij harolds, Master Garter and odur [harolds, a] standard and a banor of ys armes, and iiij bane[rs . . .] and iiij baners of emages and elmett and cott[-armour,] targett and sword and viij dossen of skochyon[s], . . . dosen of torchys and ij whytt branchys [and many] mornars, and after the masse a grett dener."[14]

Morley as Writer and Scholar

Since Morley's age had no "professional" class of writers (as we understand that term), his literary interests were naturally those of the cultivated sixteenth-century courtier who, following the ideal described in Castiglione's *Il Cortegiano*, often sought to combine the profession of arms with a lively interest in letters. As a gentleman Morley was expected to carry out his duties as counselor, diplomat, and public official, but he was also expected to be familiar with the major texts of classical and medieval literature, particularly those with a strongly moral cast; he was expected to be able to write passable occasional verses, perhaps even a reflective poem or two; and he was expected to be able to produce a readable translation from Latin, French, or Italian. If then we are to do justice to him as a writer, he must be compared with the minor "courtly makers" of Henry VIII's court—with aristocratic amateur poets such as Nicholas Vaux, George Boleyn, Robert Fairfax, and the courtly contributors to *Tottel's Miscellany*—not with gifted exceptions such as Skelton, Wyatt, and Surrey. Nevertheless, Morley's literary interests were wide and varied, and their nature and scope are readily displayed in his printed works, in manuscripts containing translations he sent as gifts to eminent persons at the Tudor court, in contemporary references to his lost works, and finally in numerous references to his reading found in his own printed works and manuscripts.

The Printed Works. There are two printed works which were published in Morley's own lifetime. The first is *The Exposition and Declaration of the Psalme, Deus Ultionum Dominus*,[1] dedicated to Henry VIII and printed by Thomas Berthelet in 1539. There is some justification for the attack on the short treatise as a "pious lucubration,"[2] but from another point of view the work may be seen as an excellent example of sixteenth-century polemical literature.[3] As the title indicates, it purports to be a commentary on the ninety-fourth psalm, but it is in fact a bitter and sometimes brilliantly impassioned defense of Henry's policies and of his position as "supreme head immediatly under Christe of the Church of Englonde." Perhaps in gratitude for grants of land and other favors which had been accorded him, Morley was a staunch defender of the crown in "the King's Great Matter," and he

9

made his position abundantly clear in *The Exposition and Declaration*. Overlooking Henry's brutal treatment of those who opposed his wishes, Morley argued that the church was guilty of countless murders in the name of orthodoxy and that only by fomenting political agitation among secular rulers could that corrupt institution thrive; moreover, argued Morley, the church could sustain itself only by maintaining false doctrines, idolatries, and superstitious distortions of the Bible. Given the seriousness of the situation, he continued, only two solutions were possible—unlimited access to the Scriptures for all people and the unification of the secular princes of Europe against the pope. God had chosen Henry VIII "to espie out the peryllous doctryne of the byshop of Rome," and it was through Henry that "the worde of god, that in tyme paste was cloked and hyd to the elders of the realme, is nowe manyfest to chylderne, that ceasse not to prayse with their mouthes, god, and his holy worde."[4]

The second printed work is Morley's translation of Petrarch's *Trionfi*, originally translated for Henry VIII but dedicated in its published version to young Henry Fitzalan, Lord Maltravers, son of Henry, twelfth Earl of Arundel. Lord Maltravers, who was born in 1538, knighted in February 1547, and matriculated at Queen's College, Cambridge, in May 1549, was an embodiment of the Renaissance ideal of gentlemanly courtesy and learning, as we know from Roger Ascham's remark that "two noble primroses of nobility, the young Duke of Suffolk and Lord Henry Matrevers, were two such examples to the court for learning, as our time may rather wish than look for again."[5] In April 1555 he was married to Anne Wentworth, and in April of the following year, while on a mission to the king of Bohemia, he died of a fever at Brussels.

Because in the dedicatory epistle of the *Tryumphes* Morley speaks of Lord Maltravers as though he were still alive and because the printer, John Cawood, signed himself in the colophon as "Prynter to the Quenes hyghnes" (a title granted him in 1553), it is clear that the book must have been printed between 1553 and 1556, the year of the young man's death. It is impossible to establish the year when Morley translated the poem; in the dedicatory epistle to Maltravers Morley makes it clear that the work he is presenting to the young nobleman had been presented to the king in his lifetime and that it had been well received. Since Henry died on January 28, 1547, the very latest date we can set for the execution of the translation is December 1546.[6] It seems likely that Morley made it some time after his retirement to Essex in 1536 or 1537, during the years when his interest in Italian literature prompted him to read and annotate Machiavelli's *Istorie Fiorentine* and *Il Principe* and send them to Cromwell as gifts.

Appended to the translation of the *Trionfi* is a poem of sixty-four lines by Morley, "Vyrgyll in his Epigrames of Cupide and Dronkenesse." The Virgilian epigrams to which Morley alludes in the title are those disputed or pseudo-Virgilian verses which were often included in sixteenth-century editions of Virgil. Some—the "Culex," the "Ciris," the "Copa," the "Moretum," the "Dirae," the "Lydia," the "Priapea," and the "Catalepton" (or "Catalecta")—are so Virgilian in style that they are still included in modern editions of Virgil; but others—"De livore," "De litera et carmen," "De musarum inventis," "Vir bonis," and "De venere"—are so transparently non-Virgilian that they are categorically excluded by modern editors. In the sixteenth century the first group was usually printed, but the second was sometimes excluded from the Virgilian canon. Thus the epigram entitled "De venere," the first line of which provided Morley with the epigraph for his "Vyrgyll in his Epigrames," can be found in an edition of Virgil printed in Lyons in 1529 and in another edition printed in Basel in 1561, but it does not appear in an edition printed in Paris by Robert Etienne in 1532. Morley's poem is not a translation of the epigram but rather an *amplificatio* on the subject of the epigram, excess in drink and sexual matters. It consists of eight eight-line stanzas in the ballade form and provides an excellent example of Morley's technical competence when he was not constrained to follow too closely the sense of a foreign text.[7]

Neither *The Exposition and Declaration* nor *The Tryumphes of Fraunces Petrarcke* generated enough interest to warrant second editions in the sixteenth century, and Morley's name sank into relative obscurity shortly after his death. Nevertheless, he continued to enjoy a certain reputation among antiquarians and bibliophiles, and largely through the efforts of such scholars more of his work was later published. Thus his translation of Boccaccio's *De claris mulieribus* was first printed by the eighteenth-century antiquarian F. G. Waldron,[8] and his two short meditative poems caught the attention of nineteenth-century antiquarians and as a result were subsequently printed.[9]

Introduction

Morley's Work in Manuscript. No complete picture of Morley's literary interests can be achieved without some attention to the manuscripts containing the bulk, and in some respects the most important and most interesting part, of his work. Seventeen in number, they contain, for the most part, translations which Morley sent as gifts to eminent persons connected with the early Tudor court. Taken together, these manuscripts provide what is probably the very best picture of the breadth of Morley's literary interests; through them, we see his concern with authors ranging from ancients such as Cicero, Seneca, and Plutarch to patristic writers such as St. Anselm and St. Athanasius to contemporaries such as Erasmus, Maffeo Veggio, and Masuccio Salernitano. Fifteen of these manuscripts are preserved at the British Museum; one, his translation of Plutarch's life of Paulus Aemilius, at the Bodleian Library;[10] and one, his translation of Boccaccio's *De claris mulieribus*, at Chatsworth.[11]

Manuscripts Dedicated to Henry VIII. Morley sent a total of six manuscripts to Henry VIII: three translations from Plutarch, two translations from contemporary Italian authors, and one translation from Boccaccio's Latin. The translations from Plutarch mark Morley as one of the first Englishmen of the sixteenth century to show interest in Plutarch, preceding those of Sir Thomas North by some thirty years. The first, probably sent to Henry at some time before 1534, consisted of Plutarch's lives of Scipio and Hannibal,[12] translated from the Latin version by Donatus Acciaiolus, which Morley probably found in an edition of Plutarch printed in Venice in 1491. Of the other two, the first, the life of Theseus, probably translated some time after 1534, has the distinction of containing Morley's sole reference to America; in the preface he refers to "these barberus pepyll of the late fownde contres, that be more lyke in maner to beastes then men but that they have the shap of men, withe owte eny knowledge of thinges paste or thinges to cum at all."[13] The second is a translation of the life of Paulus Aemilius,[14] which must be assigned to the period 1537–1547. Plutarch was no doubt intended to appeal to the king's love of learning, and Morley's choice of lives of warriors and lovers of learning like Scipio and Paulus Aemilius was also intended to provide the king with "mirrors for magistrates," portraits of behavior that any king might do well to emulate.

Also addressed to Henry were translations of two Italian works, the forty-ninth novella of Masuccio Salernitano's *Il Novellino*[15] and Paolo Giovio's *Commentario delle Cose de' Turchi*.[16] Masuccio's novella is a fiercely antipapal tale of the treachery of "that false Antecryste Alexander iiij" against the Emperor Frederick.[17] Presumably the translation was made after 1534 because the preface compares Frederick's treatment at the hands of the pope to Henry's at the hands of Pope Paul. Henry, noted Morley, had been treated "unfaithefully, unjustly and falsely by dyvers and sundry tymes by Paule, Bysshope of Rome, with all fraude possible."[18] Morley's translation of Paolo Giovio's general treatise on the history and habits of the Turks was addressed to Henry at some indeterminate time between 1539 and 1547. The preface calls on Henry to put himself in the front ranks of Christian defenders of Europe against the constant threats of Turkish invasion.[19] These two translations demonstrate Morley's strong antipapal and pro-English tone, as well as his continued interest in Italian literature.

The last of the manuscripts addressed to Henry VIII is the Chatsworth manuscript of Morley's translation of Boccaccio's *De claris mulieribus*. The Latin original contained one hundred and four short biographies, beginning with Eve and closing with Joanna, queen of Naples, but Morley translated only the first forty-six, breaking off with the life of Lucrece. He used an edition printed in Louvain in 1487 by Egidius van der Heerstraten, completing and presenting the translation to Henry some time between 1534 and 1544.

Manuscripts Dedicated to Princess Mary. Morley sent eight manuscripts to Mary, and (with one exception) all these were addressed to her while she was still princess. They may have been Christmas or New Year's gifts, for it was typical of him to choose as gifts to his royal patrons learned works rather than the more traditional gifts of jewelry and finery. Six of the manuscripts contain translations of works by classical moralists, medieval theologians, and Renaissance humanists. These are English versions of Cicero's "Somnium Scipionis" from Book VI of the *De republica*;[20] Seneca's ninety-first and one hundred and twentieth epistles;[21] St. Anselm's "The Stature and forme and lyfe of ouer blessed Lady and of ouer Savior Criste Jesu," together with St. Thomas's "Angelicall Salutation";[22] Angelo Poliziano's Latin preface to St. Athanasius's "Prologue to the Psalms";[23] Erasmus's hymn to the Virgin Mary, "Paean Virgini matri dicendus";[24] and an exposition of Psalm 26 by the Spanish humanist Juan de Torquemada, to which is appended the Latin text and English translation of a poem by the early fifteenth-century Italian humanist Maffeo Veggio, which Morley noted he had translated into "an Italion Ryme called Soneto."[25] Morley's use of the sonnet form in his translation of Maffeo Veggio's poem is of special interest since it coincides almost exactly with Wyatt's and Surrey's use of the Petrarchan form.

The other two manuscripts dedicated to Mary cannot be called translations in any sense of the word. One contains a Latin commentary on the psalms by an unknown hand, as well as extensive comments on some Old Testament canticles, probably by Richard Rolle of Hampole.[26] Morley's only contribution to this manuscript was a preface and a dedicatory letter to Lady Mary written some time between 1537 and 1547. The other manuscript is a collection of miracles connected with the Holy Sacrament.[27] Morley's account of these miracles is interwoven with personal reminiscences about the piety and generosity of Lady Margaret Beaufort, Mary's grandmother, and includes a description of a "miracle" connected with Henry VII and Richard III at the Battle of Bosworth:

> But God gevyng victory to the king your grauntfather, and King Richarde slayne by the verye devine punishment of God, Bigott [a gentleman in the court of Henry VII] sayde that Kyng Richard callyd in the mornyng for to have had masse sayd before hym, but when his chappelyne had one thing ready, evermore they wanted another; when they had wyne they lacked breade, and ever one thing was myssing. In the meane season King Henry romyng on a pace, King Rychard was constrayned to go to the battayle, wher God showed His puissaunce, that the noble king your grauntfather having but a fewe, vanquished hym that had thre men for one, and King Richard layde upon a horse nakid was caryed through the felde with shame infynyte. I tell this bycause I thinke God wolde not that same day that he shulde se the blyssed sacrament of the aulter, nor heare the holy masse, for his horrible offence comytted against his brothers children.[28]

Manuscripts Dedicated to Anne Boleyn, Thomas Cromwell, and Edward Seymour, Duke of Somerset. Morley also sent gifts of manuscripts to three other members of the Tudor court. "The Pistellis and Gospelles for the .lij Sondayes in the yere"[29] is an extraordinarily beautiful manuscript in which each Gospel is given in French, with an English "exhortation" and commentary following. Herbert G. Wright argued that Morley presented it to Anne Boleyn,[30] but this is doubtful since Morley's name is not mentioned at any point in the preface. The only evidence that Morley was in fact the donor of the manuscript is the notice in the preface that a "bond of blood" exists between the donor and Anne. Three persons are likely candidates for such a relationship— John Bourchier, Lord Berners, who had married Anne's maternal grandfather's half sister; Henry Howard, Earl of Surrey, who was Anne's first cousin and sixteen years of age in 1532, the year in which the manuscript was sent to her; and Morley, whose daughter Joan had married Anne's brother George. Lord Berners can be ruled out because his relationship with Anne was far too distant to allow him to speak of any "bond of blood." That phrase hardly describes Morley's relationship either, and because the donor speaks of himself as Anne's "moost lovyng and fryndely brother," it seems reasonable to ascribe the donation of the manuscript to Henry Howard, Earl of Surrey, rather than to Morley.

Between July 9, 1536, when Cromwell was made a baron, and July 28, 1540, when he was executed, Morley dedicated a translation of Plutarch's life of Agesilaus to the Lord Chancellor. The translation was probably made from a Latin translation by Antonius Tudartinus, which Morley might easily have found in an edition of Plutarch printed in 1491. Morley's manuscript was formerly part of the Phillipps Collection, but it is now missing.[31]

During the period of his protectorship the Duke of Somerset was the recipient of a manuscript containing Morley's commentary on the Book of Ecclesiastes.[32] That commentary, written between Morley's sixty-first and seventy-first years, is probably the fullest and maturest exposition of his views on life; to set forth those views Morley was able to find a prose style both graceful and mellow. For example, rejecting the ascetic ideals of the monastic life and insisting that man accept with joy both the goods and evils which God sends him, Morley felicitously notes:

> Yf the Lorde shall geve the meate, eate yt; yf He shall geve the fast, forbeare yt; yf He shall call the to honor, take yt; yf He shall

sende the losse, suffre yt; yf He shall caste the in preson, take yt
paciently . . . for thoos that wilbe taken in very deade for the
trewe contemptors of this worlde must take all thinges paciently
and use all thinges with thankesgevinge when they be present,
and abstayne from the same willinglye, when the Lorde shall
withdrawe them.[33]

By his insistence that man must resign himself to fate, that he is an
insignificant creature who must learn that true happiness lies in learning
to control his wishes, and by his firm belief that man should make the
best of a highly imperfect world, Morley reveals himself as an expe-
rienced and stoical courtier who had achieved much wisdom.

Lost Works. There is good reason to believe that Morley wrote
considerably more than the works which have survived in printed
form and in manuscript. John Bale, Bishop of Ossory and an important
figure in the history of Tudor drama, noted in a catalog of the writings
of the major British authors of his day[34] that Morley was the author
of several comedies and tragedies in English. Bale's similar description
of Sir Thomas More as a writer of comedies in his youth[35] suggests
that both More and Morley dabbled to some extent in drama and are
perhaps to be linked with the group of playwrights who flourished
in the early Tudor court, a group comprised of Henry Medwall,
John Rastell, and John Heywood. Like Morley, all three playwrights
were closely connected with the Tudor court—Medwall as chaplain
to Cardinal Morton (Archbishop of Canterbury under Henry VII);
Rastell as printer and deviser of pageants for the court; and Heywood
as court musician from 1519 to 1528.[36] We can only conjecture about
Morley's lost comedies and tragedies and about his connection with
this "school" of early Tudor writers of interludes, but if his comedies
and tragedies resembled theirs in any way, then Morley would have
been part of what Frederick S. Boas described as "a group of play-
wrights who, though scholarly and showing the stamp of the new
learning, formed what may be truly called a native English dramatic
school. They were indebted to foreign sources for part of their material,
but their technique and methods of characterization were their own."[37]
Though it is difficult to imagine sage and sober Morley as the author
of frothy interludes like Heywood's *John John* and *The Pardoner and
the Friar*, he would have been attracted to the interlude because it was

a splendid vehicle for the discussion of philosophical and political subjects, as is evidenced by Medwall's *Fulgens and Lucrece*, which takes up the Ciceronian question of the nature of true nobility. Furthermore, the medieval morality tradition was continued in the work of several of these playwrights, and there was a heavily political cast to interludes such as Skelton's *Magnificence* and Bale's *King John*. If Morley was in fact the author of comedies and tragedies, the probability is strong that his tragedies resembled the medieval moralities and that his comedies had all the earmarks of the New Learning.

Morley's Reading and Learning. Other valuable sources of information about Morley's reading and scholarship are his own numerous references. Of course these references should not be interpreted as proof of profound or thorough scholarship, but they do serve as a valuable index to the range of his literary interests. After all the necessary allowances have been made for name-dropping and the Renaissance habit of bolstering every argument with a series of *exempla* from the *auctores*, Morley still stands as a well-read man by Renaissance standards. For instance, he mentions and gives evidence of having at least a passing acquaintance with a number of the most important classical authors, Aristotle and Epicurus among the Greeks and Terence, Plautus, Ovid, Cicero, Martial, and Quintilian among the Latin writers. It was probably from Seneca that he learned the stoical view of life that allowed him to survive the turbulent political events of his age. He was particularly interested in devotional literature, and his writings give evidence that he had thorough knowledge of the Old and New Testaments, that he was particularly fond of the psalms, and that he was well read in the church fathers, especially St. Augustine, St. Gregory, St. Thomas, St. Jerome, and St. Anselm. The writings also show his familiarity with the principal events in church history, from the Donation of Constantine to the role played in that history by the major figures of his own day—Alexander VII, Julius II, Leo X, Clement VII, and Paul III. His references to secular history show especially close reading of Livy and Roman history, and he was not unfamiliar with the history of non-European peoples such as the Assyrians, the Medes, and the Persians. The history of his own country he seems to have gathered from Higden, William of Malmesbury, and Polydore Vergil. How much he knew of English literature is impossible to determine because his only reference to literature in his own language is a disparaging remark in the dedicatory epistle of the *Tryumphes* about the popularity of "dongehyll matter" such as the tales of Robin Hood. There is no question that of the vernacular literatures of the early Renaissance Morley definitely preferred the Italian, and he could probably read that language with greater facility than French and even Latin. I have already noted his interest in Machiavelli, Masuccio Salernitano, and the recently imported sonnet; of even greater importance was his concern with the great triumvirate of Italian literature—Dante, Petrarch, and Boccaccio. His translation of Boccaccio's *De claris mulieribus* contains the first account in English of these three masters:

> In the tyme of the flowre and honour of prynces, Kynge Edwarde the thyrde of that name . . . there sprange in Italy three excellente clerkes. The fyrst was Dante, for hys greate learnynge in his mother tunge surnamyde dyvyne Dante . . . The next unto thys Dante was Frauncis Petrak, that not onely in the Latyne tunge, but also in swete ryme, is so estemyde that unto thys present tyme unnethe is ther any noble prynce in Italy, nor gentle man, withoute havynge in hys handes hys sonnetes and hys "tryhumphes" or hys other rymes. And he wrote also in the Latyne tunge certeyn eglogges in versys and another booke namede "Affrica" and "Of the Remedyes of bothe Fortunes," with dyvers epistles and other wourkes . . . The last of thies three . . . was John Bocas of Certaldo, whiche in lyke wyse as the tother twayne, Dante and Petrarcha, wer moste exellent in the vulgare ryme, so thys Bocas was above all others in prose, as it apperythe by his hundrith tayles and many other notable workes. Nor he was no lesse elegaunte in the prose of his oune tunge then he was in the Latyne tunge, wherin, as Petrak dyd wryte clerkly certayn volumes in the Latyne tunge, so dyd thys clerke. And fyrst "Of the Fall of Prynces," "Of the Genoelogye of the Goddes," and emonge other thys booke namede "De preclaris."[38]

Clearly Morley was familiar with Petrarch's sonnets and with Boccaccio's *Decameron*; yet he chose to turn to the *Trionfi* and to the *De claris mulieribus* instead. The eagerness with which he did so does not reflect solely his predilection for didactic literature; it reflects also the taste of his generation, a taste which preferred to view both Petrarch and Boccaccio as "clerkes," sage humanists and writers of works of high seriousness, rather than as creators of love poetry and indecorous tales.

Petrarch's *Trionfi*

To the modern reader accustomed to think of English Petrarchism simply as a convenient label for describing the process by which the Italian sonnet was anglicized in the course of the sixteenth century, Morley's decision to translate the long allegorical poem rather than the *Canzoniere* may well seem strange. That choice may seem even more unusual if the reader reflects that Wyatt and Surrey were Morley's contemporaries at the Tudor court and that the sonneteering vogue was receiving its original impetus from those poets at almost the very time when Morley set out to translate the *Trionfi*. But Wyatt and Surrey were young men and their taste was that of a generation which admired collections of courtly verse such as *Tottel's Miscellany* (1557) and *The Paradise of Dainty Devices* (1576); to a great extent their verse was what we today would call "experimental," and it might well have evoked that most favorite of sixteenth-century adjectives, "newfangled." Morley was in his early sixties when they were setting the new fashion for Petrarchan poetry, and his tastes were understandably more sedate and conventional than those of the younger poets; his generation believed that the primary function of poetry should be to instruct and improve man. Younger men might attitudinize and sing of "Petrarch's long-deceased woes / With newborn sighs and denizened wit" (as Sidney was to phrase it); for Morley to strike the Petrarchan pose would have been, quite simply, indecorous and ludicrous. It is not surprising, then, that he chose not the sonnets but Petrarch's long allegorical poem tracing the progress of the soul from its youthful concern with the carnal to its mature quest for salvation and eternal life, just as it is not surprising that he passed over the human comedy contained in the *Decameron* for the series of biographies of virtuous ladies in the *De claris mulieribus*.

Moreover, in turning to the *Trionfi* Morley was in fact turning to the most popular and the most widely read of all the works in the Petrarchan canon. Those for whom Petrarch is synonymous with introspective love lyrics and mannered poetic diction may find it difficult to connect his name with an allegorical, "medieval" poem such as the *Trionfi*; those who have read the *Trionfi* and who have been both delighted by its occasional moments of pathos and annoyed by its tedious, pedantic catalogs of classical and medieval notables may find it even more difficult to accept Ernest Hatch Wilkins's judgment that it was "the most triumphant poem of the early Renaissance" and that for a hundred years or more it outshone both Petrarch's sonnets and Dante's *Divine Comedy*. But popular it certainly was, and almost from the time of Petrarch's death its popularity grew, sustained and extended first by a spate of widely disseminated annotated editions, all designed to make of it an epic of the progress of the soul, and then by an inexplicably strong tendency on the part of medieval and Renaissance artists to "illustrate" the poem and draw themes from it. Before examining these important manifestations of popularity, it may be useful to glance at the *Trionfi* proper and to consider the circumstances surrounding its composition, its contents, and its place in the Petrarchan canon.

In 1338, when Petrarch was thirty-four, he acquired a house in the lovely hamlet of Vaucluse, not far from the papal seat of Avignon; there he led a life of solitude and contemplation, confining himself to a few close friends such as Dionigi da Borgo San Sepolcro and Pierre Bersuire and working on the *Canzoniere* and on the *De viris illustribus*, *Africa*, and the *Epistolae metricae*.[1] It was in this period of his life, too, that he began work on a series of "triumphs," Italian poems in terza rima whose basic metaphor Petrarch had probably drawn from descriptions of triumphal pageants in the works of classical authors such as Ovid and Lactantius and from the Roman triumph itself. The first of these *trionfi*, a triumph of love, he subdivided into four *capitoli*, or chapters, the first three of which were written during this first stay at Vaucluse and the last of which was composed somewhat later. The first capitolo presents the triumphant figure of Cupid riding atop a chariot drawn by four white horses and surrounded by a series of captives. This first group of captives consists of figures from classical history and mythology, and it includes Venus, Jupiter, Paris, Helen, Aeneas, and Caesar. This long catalog overlaps into the next capitolo, though the emphasis there is on the story of Massinissa and Sophonisba, and then into the third capitolo, where there is a biblical series and a medieval series which includes the foremost lovers of the literature of the middle ages—Lancelot and Guinevere, Tristan and Isolde, and Paolo and Francesca. At the close of the third capitolo Laura appears to the poet and, vanquished by her beauty, he joins Cupid's thralls.

In May 1341, the month after Petrarch's coronation as poet laureate in Rome, the poet accepted an invitation to spend the summer in Parma. His host was Azzo da Correggio, who with his three brothers had just led a successful popular revolt against the tyrant of Parma, Mastino della Scala. In Parma Petrarch enjoyed tranquillity and the opportunity to study and write, and in fact he was so contented with the city that he remained until the following January, working on his Latin epic, the *Africa*, and on a number of *canzoni*. It was probably in this period, or during the second stay at Vaucluse and Avignon that followed, that he added a fourth and final capitolo to the "Triumph of Love." Here the thralls of love are all poets, and Petrarch, true to the pattern he employed in other catalogs, starts with figures from classical literature and proceeds chronologically until he reaches the poets of his own generation. Thus, after alluding to Alcaeus, Pindar, Anacreon, Virgil, Ovid, and other Greek and Roman poets, he mentions eminent contemporaries such as Dante, Cino da Pistoia, Arnaut Daniel, and other troubadours, as well as his recently deceased friend Tommaso Caloiro and his two old friends "Socrates" and "Laelius," Ludwig van Kampen and Lello di Pietro Stefano dei Tosetti, respectively. It was probably during this period, too, that Petrarch decided to write a palinode to the "Triumph of Love," a "Triumph of Chastity" in which he would show the tyrannical Cupid defeated by the power of chaste love. At this point, the two poems were probably conceived as companion pieces, but there is no reason to believe that Petrarch had yet envisaged the full series of six trionfi as beginning with the "Triumph of Love" and concluding with the "Triumph of Eternity."

In December 1343 Petrarch found himself once more in Parma, once more at the invitation of Azzo da Correggio, and the two years in Parma that followed (1343–1345) proved to be the most prolific of his life: he worked on the *Africa*, on his metrical epistles, on a number of Italian poems, the most important of which were the canzoni "Io vo pensando" and "Italia mia"; he even found time to engage in a literary feud with Brizio Visconti, a son of Luchino Visconti, the tyrant of Milan. It was in this period that he completed the "Triumph of Chastity," in which he describes how Laura, with the aid of a host of allegorical personifications such as Honesty, Shame, and Courtesy, defeats and binds Cupid. The vanquished god of Love is then made part of a triumphal procession, led by Laura, who is surrounded by a throng of chaste women, including Lucrece, Penelope, and Virginia. The procession starts on the southern shore of the Bay of Naples and proceeds to Linterno, where Scipio Africanus joins the group, and then goes on to Rome, where Cupid is deposited at the Temple of Patrician Chastity.[2]

In 1348 Petrarch must have been particularly conscious of the power of death; it was the year of the Black Death and the year in which death claimed three of his closest friends: in May he received word of the death of his friend and kinsman Franceschino degl'Albizzi; on May 19 came the shattering news of the death of his beloved Laura; and in July he learned of the death of his old friend and patron Cardinal Giovanni Colonna. It is little wonder, then, that thoughts of death seem to have obsessed Petrarch in this terrible year, and that the little poetry he wrote reflects that concern. Three of Petrarch's twelve eclogues were completed in that year, and all three are directly or indirectly about death; in the ninth eclogue, a shepherd laments the effects of the pestilence on shepherds and their flocks; in the tenth eclogue, the Black Death is presented allegorically as a windstorm that has the power to destroy the laurel tree, which represents both poetry and Laura; and the eleventh eclogue is a lament on the death of Laura. Before the end of 1348 Petrarch added a capitolo of the "Triumph of Death" to his two earlier trionfi. Here the processional aspect of the two earlier trionfi is continued, but there are no catalogs naming the illustrious dead. Instead, Petrarch describes a throng of unnamed dead and a group of living ladies who have come to witness the serene death of Laura.

In the following year, probably still distraught by the loss of his closest friends and stunned by the ravages of the Black Death, Petrarch completed the second capitolo of the "Triumph of Death," a description of a vision of Laura on the night following her death. In the course of an imagined conversation that is perhaps the high point of the poem, the poet elicits from her a confession that she in fact loved him as deeply as he loved her and that she kept her love from him to keep his ardor from becoming uncontrollable.

In this same period (1349–1350) Petrarch conceived of a fourth triumph, one of "Fame over Death," and he completed a capitolo ("Nel cor pien d'amarissima dolcezza") in which he presented the figure of Fame leading a procession of more than a hundred figures from classical and biblical literature. This capitolo, however, was later discarded, and its contents were redistributed among two other capitoli written to replace it.

In the spring and summer of 1352 Petrarch was once again in Vaucluse, working on a collection of his letters, adding to *De viris illustribus*, and completing two more capitoli of the "Triumph of Fame" to replace the original "Nel cor" that he had written in Parma. The first of these capitoli, "Da poi che Morte triumphò," is devoted for the most part to Roman heroes; among those who figure most prominently are Julius Caesar, Scipio Africanus, and Vespasian; the second, "Pien d'infinita e nobil meraviglia," is devoted largely to famous foreigners —Greeks, Trojans, Persians, Hebrews, and Assyrians—and famous women of antiquity, but included too are six moderns: Godfrey of Boulogne, Saladin, Ruggiero di Lauria, Henry, Duke of Lancaster, King Robert of Sicily, and Stefano Colonna the Elder. A third capitolo of the "Triumph of Fame," "Io non sapea da tal vista levarme," was probably also written at this time, but apparently Petrarch was dissatisfied with it, and he planned to replace it with a capitolo beginning with the line "Poi che la bella e gloriosa donna." However, "Poi che la bella" was never completed, and most modern editions give "Io non sapea" as the third capitolo of the "Triumph of Fame."

There is ample evidence that at various times between September 1356 and September 1360 Petrarch revised, retouched, or recopied the "Triumph of Love." By 1370 he had completed, and revised, apparently to his satisfaction at that time, four triumphs, those of Love, Chastity, Death, and Fame. Petrarch probably thought of these four trionfi as a logically unified series, though there is no reason to believe that before 1370 he had thought of completing the series by adding the "Triumph of Time" and the "Triumph of Eternity." Nevertheless, at some time between 1370 and 1374 Petrarch completed a relatively short "Triumph of Time" in which he depicted the defeat of Fame at the hands of Time; in the course of the trionfo the poet realizes with great sadness that Fame is as fragile and evanescent as the human body itself and that the quest for Fame is the greatest of human vanities. The final "Triumph of Eternity," written between January and February 1374, describes how the poet finally places faith in God's mercy and aspires to eternal salvation. The old world disappears, and before him appears the vision of a new world in which Time itself has no meaning and in which those who have placed their faith in God will enjoy perennial bliss. At the Resurrection, concludes Petrarch, Laura will appear to him in all her splendor and he will love her even more than when she was alive.

What Petrarch conceived the final form of the *Trionfi* to be we will of course never know; indeed it is likely that he had no final plan for the work and that the various capitoli merely suggested themselves to him as he grew older and matured intellectually. In this respect the poem was a living organism that, like the *Canterbury Tales*, grew and matured with its author and reflected the breadth of his experience and learning. What is certain, however, is that Petrarch thought of the poem as one of the most important of his literary creations, one that was every bit as important as the *Canzoniere* and perhaps even as important as his epic *Africa*; he therefore returned to the work with regularity from 1338 until his death in 1374. For the modern reader, the *Trionfi* remains precisely what the medieval and Renaissance exegetes claimed it to be: an intellectual and spiritual autobiography in which the poet's private joys and sufferings are fused with his scholarly experiences to produce a panoramic view of the growth of the poet's—and Everyman's—soul from youthful obsession with love to the mature search for salvation.

This, then, is the poem that fascinated the Middle Ages and had such an important impact on the literature and art of the Renaissance. Through one of those unfortunate quirks of literary history, its importance has been overshadowed since the Renaissance (especially in the twentieth century) by the great scholarly attention paid to the *Canzoniere* and to the effects of that collection on European poetry. When we restore the *Trionfi* to its rightful place of importance in the Petrarchan canon, it becomes clear that it is very inaccurate to speak of Petrarchism as a self-contained entity and that it is a vastly more complicated literary phenomenon than has hitherto been imagined.

Petrarch's works, it should be remembered, fall into three distinct categories, and when talking about "Petrarchism" we must account for the influence of each of these categories.

It is often forgotten that Petrarch considered himself first and foremost a Latin humanist and that his Latin works make up the largest (and perhaps the most important) part of his work. On these Latin poems and prose pieces he lavished a lifetime of attention. There are three works in verse: the *Africa*, an epic of the Punic War; the *Bucolicum carmen*, a collection of twelve allegorical pastoral eclogues; and the *Epistolae metricae*, imitations of Horace. In prose there are three didactic treatises: the *De remediis utriusque fortunae*, the *De vita solitaria*, and the *De otio religioso*; two collections of historical anecdotes: *Rerum memorandarum libri* and *De viris illustribus*; the *Secretum* (a dialogue between the author and St. Augustine); four controversial pamphlets: *Invectiva contra medicum*, *Invectiva contra eum qui maledixit Italie*, *De sui ipsius et multorum ignorantia*, and *Invectiva contra quendam magni status hominem*; three collections of letters: the *Familiares*, the *Seniles*, and the *Sine nomine*; seven penitential psalms in prose; six orations; and a Latin guidebook to the west coast of Italy, the *Itinerarium syriacum*.[3] The *Trionfi* and the *Canzoniere* make up the second and third categories.

Beginning in Petrarch's own lifetime, each of these three categories generated overlapping waves of influence, the Latin works exerting their influence first, the *Trionfi* next, and the *Canzoniere* last. As Ernest Hatch Wilkins pointed out, in Italy "the wave from the Latin works reached its peak in the fourteenth and early fifteenth centuries, diminished thereafter, and virtually disappeared in the seventeenth century. The wave from the *Triumphs* reached its peak in the fifteenth century, diminished thereafter, and virtually disappeared in the sixteenth century. The wave from the *Canzoniere*, of lesser strength, until the latter part of the fifteenth century, than the wave from the *Triumphs*, thereafter gained strength swiftly, rose to a tremendous peak in the sixteenth century, and has diminished gradually since that time, though occasionally resurgent and still existent."[4]

The pattern of Petrarchan influence in other European countries was, generally speaking, very similar to that in Italy, and what I have noted about Italian Petrarchism may be applied with equal validity to Petrarchism in the English Renaissance. Important Petrarchan influences on English literature may be detected as early as the time of

Chaucer. We know that Chaucer was familiar with at least one of Petrarch's Italian poems: the "Canticus Troili" of the *Troilus and Criseyde* (I, 400–420) is in actuality a rather close translation of Sonnet 132 of the *Canzoniere*.[5] Chaucer may have known other poems from the *Canzoniere*, and he may even have known the *Trionfi*, but there are no clear signs in his poetry that this is so.[6] On the contrary, his other references to Petrarch show that he saw the Italian poet not as a vernacular poet or as an anatomist of love but rather as an *auctor*, as a "clerk" whose Latin works in the "heigh stile" were of far greater importance than his Italian poems. When Chaucer's clerk prepares to tell Boccaccio's tale of the Patient Griselda from Petrarch's Latin version of the work,[7] he notes with considerable pride that it is a tale he has learned "at Padowe of a worthy clerk," and he goes on to describe Petrarch as a humanist and as a neoclassical poet:

> Fraunceys Petrak, the lauriat poete,
> Highte this clerk, whos rethorike sweete
> Enlumyned al Ytaille of poetrie,
> As Lynyan dide of philosophie,
> Or lawe, or oother art particuler;
> But deeth, that wol nat suffre us dwellen heer,
> But as it were a twynklyng of an ye,
> Hem bothe hath slayn, and alle shul dye.[8]

In the fifteenth century, when the second wave of Petrarchism was already under way in Italy and on the Continent, this view of Petrarch as humanist and neoclassical poet persisted in England. In John Lydgate's *Fall of Princes*, for example, Petrarch is mentioned six separate times,[9] and not one of these references describes him as the author of works in the vernacular. Lydgate's attention had been drawn to Petrarch's Latin works by Humphrey, Duke of Gloucester, whose personal library contained several of Petrarch's Latin works, including a copy of "Franciscus de remediis fortuitorum," which Gloucester was to present to Oxford University in 1439.[10] Lydgate refers to Petrarch as "laureate poete," and links his name with those of Ovid, Seneca, Cicero ("cheeff welle of eloquence"), "my maistir Chaucer," and Boccaccio. On one occasion Lydgate even provides a catalog of Petrarch's Latin works which is virtually complete, but he does not include the *Canzoniere* or the *Trionfi*.

Petrarch's name also appears in a catalog of authors in Benedict Burgh's fifteenth-century "Letter to Lydgate," in which Petrarch is listed with Cicero and Quintilian as a master of the "crafte of speche."[11] This view of Petrarch as Latinist, humanist, and rhetorician persisted well into the sixteenth century: as late as 1523, not too many years before Morley's translation of the *Trionfi* and Wyatt's and Surrey's popularization of the sonnet form, Skelton referred to the Italian poet in his *Garland of Laurel* and included him in a long catalog of classical rhetoricians and contemporary humanists.[12] It is to Morley's great credit that he was perhaps the first Englishman to appreciate Petrarch's importance as an Italian as well as a Latin author. After reading many conventionalized descriptions of Petrarch's accomplishments as an author of Latin works, it is refreshing to read Morley's statement that Petrarch was proficient "not onely in the Latyne tunge, but also in swete ryme" and that "unnethe is ther any noble prynce in Italy, nor gentle man, withoute havynge in hys handes hys sonnetes and hys Tryhumphes or hys other rymes."[13]

The second wave of Petrarchism in England, the vogue for the *Trionfi*, was the weakest and the least enduring of all three insofar as its permanent effect on literature was concerned. Though it is true that some traces of the *Trionfi* are to be found in the poetry of the early sixteenth century, principally in the work of More, Hawes, Skelton, and Surrey, and though there are isolated examples of interest in the poem later in the century, no appreciable body of poetry comparable to the sonnet sequences generated by the *Canzoniere* seems to have been inspired by the *Trionfi*. It is therefore perhaps not excessive to claim Morley's translation itself as the most important representative of the second wave of Petrarchism in England. But though the poem had inspired few imitations when Morley turned to it, it had been enjoying great popularity for many years both in England and on the Continent. The first sign of that popularity was the appearance in Morley's lifetime of a great number of annotated editions of Petrarch's vernacular poetry with extensive commentaries on the *Trionfi* as well as the *Canzoniere*. These editions, and those that followed later in the century, circulated widely throughout Europe, and they soon became the raw material, so to speak, of European Petrarchism. Their immediate effect was to generate deep and widespread interest in Petrarch's vernacular poetry; there then followed a series of translations of the sonnets and the *Trionfi* into the major vernaculars of Europe, including English. Almost all of these editions carried prefaces and exegetical commentaries which underscored the allegorical content of the work. Morley's preface to his translation is no exception to this general rule; in his dedicatory remarks to Lord Maltravers he notes that in the *Trionfi* is "comprehended al morall vertue, all Phylosophye, all storyall matters, and briefely in many devyne sentences theologicall secretes declared." To understand the significance of Morley's statement and the long tradition to which his interpretation belonged, it is necessary to turn to those editions and translations.

Renaissance Editions and Translations of the *Trionfi*

Both the *Trionfi* and the *Canzoniere* circulated widely in manuscript long before their first printing in 1470,[1] and judging from the greater number of manuscripts of the *Trionfi*, fifteenth-century readers distinctly preferred that poem; that preference was continuous from the year of Petrarch's death (1374) on, and there are no signs that it diminished when the vernacular poems were finally printed in 1470. Of the twenty-five editions of the Italian poems printed between 1470 and 1500, for example, nine were separate editions of the *Trionfi*.[2] It would thus appear that there was a strong demand for the *Trionfi* in the late fifteenth century and that early printers were aware of the commercial value of the poem.

Of even greater interest than the first editions of the *Trionfi* are the first annotated editions of the poem, all of which interpreted the work as an allegory of the progress of the human soul. The first of these were little more than halfhearted attempts at explicating the poem and at sketching the biographical and historical background of the work: Antonio da Tempo's edition of 1471 included the first published biography of Petrarch and some light annotations, and an anonymous commentary of 1473 was so incomplete that it was never reprinted.

In 1475 there appeared what proved to be by far the most influential of the early annotated editions of the *Trionfi*. This edition carried the commentaries of a Bernardo da Pietro Lapini da Montalcino, about whom we know virtually nothing. His name appears in later editions of the *Trionfi* as "Glicino" or, more often, "Illicino"; the little we do know about him comes from an edition of the *Trionfi* printed in 1488 by Bernardino da Novara. In the dedicatory epistle of that edition Bernardo identifies himself as "Bernardi Ilicini medicinae," and the printer notes tantalizingly in the colophon that he is "il prestantissimo philosopho Misser Bernardo da Monte Illicinio da Siena" but adds nothing else.[3]

In the 1475 edition and in subsequent editions the *Trionfi* and Bernardo's commentaries were bound together with the *Canzoniere*, which itself bore the commentaries of Girolamo Squarciafico and of the noted humanist and translator of Xenophon's *Cyropaedia*, Francesco Filelfo. Bernardo's commentary on the *Trionfi* is a massive affair amounting to some fifteen or twenty words of exegesis for every word of text, and it deserves close scrutiny because it became the model for virtually all the subsequent Renaissance commentaries on the *Trionfi*. From Jacopo Poggio's commentary on the "Trionfo della Fama"[4] at the close of the fifteenth century to the sixteenth-century editions of Petrarch's Italian poetry prepared by Giovanni Andrea Gesualdo,[5] Bernardino Daniello,[6] Francesco Alunno,[7] and Alessandro Velutello,[8] there are echoes in one form or another of the elaborate allegorical interpretations first set forth in Bernardo's commentary. Curiously, even prefaces and commentaries accompanying sixteenth-century translations into French, German, Spanish, Portuguese, and English tend to parrot Bernardo's interpretation and vocabulary. As late as 1826 Giacomo Leopardi set forth an interpretation of the *Trionfi* which differed little in substance and wording from that proposed by Bernardo almost four centuries earlier.[9]

From the outset it is clear that Bernardo reads the *Trionfi* as an allegory of the growth and progress of the soul and that his approach is not very different from that of other allegorizers such as Petrarch's friend Pierre Bersuire, author of the *Ovide moralisé*,[10] and Giovanni Boccaccio.[11] Under the guise of a fabulous narrative,[12] Bernardo says, Petrarch has taken as his theme the ancient injunction *nosce teipsum*, and using the triumphal pageant as his starting point, he has created a continuous and unified allegory of the fate of the soul. The role of the commentator on Petrarch's poem, he continues, is simply to ferret out the "admiranda doctrina in essa interclusa," but he promises not to do so by following the excessively elaborate methods of the "antichi & optimi expositori," because doing so would obfuscate the text rather than clarify it. While availing himself of the techniques of "Servio honorato al principio de la opera & delucidatione di Vergilio" and the techniques of Averroës in his commentaries on Aristotle, he will confine his commentaries to the explanation of four important aspects of the poem: its intention and subject, its usefulness, its title, and its structure. Servius, however, had listed in his commentary on the *Aeneid* not four but seven separate items: the author's life, the title of the work, its genre, the author's intention, the number of books, their order, and finally an explanation of the work; and in actuality, Bernardo's simplified plan of exegesis is closer to the method advocated by Boethius, who called on the exegete to concern himself with the intention of the poem, its profitableness, its arrangement or structure, and the division of philosophy to which it could be assigned.[13]

The subject of the *Trionfi* is the human soul itself, its progress and variety, seen in its relation to human action and human reason,[14] and in order to illustrate this point Bernardo invokes the authority of appropriate classical and Christian thinkers. Both Aristotle (*Nichomachean Ethics*) and Cicero (*Offices*, Book I), reasons Bernardo, recognized two contrasting principles at work in the soul, the rational and the sensual, and both believed that all human behavior could be explained by the dominance of one or the other of these principles. In Christian theology, adds Bernardo, St. Paul was the first to assert the endless conflict between these two principles.[15]

Bernardo then argues that the soul may be divided into "due generali parti cioe in ioventu & vechieza," the young soul being given over to the sensual appetite and the old soul to the rational faculty. At long last he establishes the connection between his detailed analysis of the nature of the soul and Petrarch's Triumphs of Fame, Time, and Eternity. Fame is the remembrance of good works which were performed when the body and the soul were one;[16] Time is the agent which destroys all good works, including Fame;[17] and Eternity is the soul's measuring of its own Time against a sempiternal infinity to which it will be conducted, an infinity in which human intellect is infinitesimal.[18]

After reminding the reader that the *utilità* of the poem lies in its ability to lead men to the virtuous life[19] and pointing to the fact that the Roman triumphal pageant provided the title for the poem, Bernardo analyzes the structure of the work, explaining that Petrarch divided it into six parts to represent six consecutive states of the soul. The first Triumph (of Love) shows the soul dominated by the sensual appetite; the second (of Chastity) dramatizes the triumph of reason over sensuality; the third (of Death) analyzes the process by which the body and the soul are separated; the fourth (of Fame) is concerned with man's remembrance of the soul after the death of the body; the fifth (of Time) illustrates the defeat of this memory by Time; and the sixth (of Eternity) shows the soul subject to universal divine justice.[20]

How completely and effectively Bernardo's commentary established a "standard" allegorical reading of the *Trionfi* for Renaissance readers becomes clear when one examines the commentaries prepared by his successors in the sixteenth century. Most of them drew extensively on Bernardo's edition: some were wholesale borrowings from his commentary, often repeating his very vocabulary and phrasing, and sometimes misconstruing his arguments; others were clumsy abridgments of his commentary by editors eager to satisfy the popular demand for editions of Petrarch's Italian poetry.

Bernardo's influence is perhaps best seen in the most popular and most widely disseminated of all the sixteenth-century editions of Petrarch, that by Alessandro Velutello, which first appeared in 1525 and which underwent no less than twenty-seven editions between that date and 1585. Velutello is not mentioned by Morley, but it is very likely that he knew Velutello's work, because it was the most popular of all editions of Petrarch and because Morley's fellow-courtier, Sir Thomas Wyatt, used Velutello's commentaries when preparing his translations of Petrarch's sonnets.[21]

Velutello's edition was based on the text established by Pietro Bembo in the first Aldine edition of 1501, but Velutello emended what he believed to be corrupt readings.[22] His interests were clearly editorial and historical rather than literary, and his preface shows clearly his concern with scientific investigation of the text of the poems and with the biographical and historical data surrounding them. There is a detailed biography of Petrarch and Laura, a description of a personal visit to Vaucluse, even a map of Vaucluse and its environs.[23] Velutello seems to have gone directly to Bernardo for his explication of the "Soggetto de' Triomphi," and the interpretation and the language of the commentary are strongly reminiscent of his fifteenth-century predecessor: The *Trionfi*, Velutello writes, are an analysis of the growth of the soul; Petrarch's intention was to present the "vari stati" of the rational soul. The poem begins with the analysis of the soul "ne la sua nova eta" (in its youth), for which the metaphor is the Triumph of Love; in the Triumph of Chastity Petrarch goes on to consider the more mature soul in which reason has gained the ascendancy. In the Triumph of Death the soul is separated from the body, and so it can be dominated neither by the flesh nor by reason. Fame, or the remembrance of good works, triumphs over Death, and in turn is vanquished by Time. Finally, knowing that Time is finite and that all human hopes are vain, Petrarch allows Eternity to triumph over all, "a darne ad intendere che solo in Dio eterno e infinito dobbiamo ogni nostra fede e speranza porre" (to have us understand that we must place all our faith and hope in Almighty God). Love, Velutello concludes in his sole departure from Bernardo, figures most prominently in the poem, for it provides the occasion in the first trionfo for describing how the poet, disdained and suffering from the effects of unrequited love, locks himself in his room, where he has a vision of Love on a fiery chariot.[24]

Apart from Velutello's edition, three other major editions of Petrarch's Italian poems appeared in Morley's lifetime: Giovanni Andrea Gesualdo's (1541), Bernardino Daniello da Lucca's (1541 and 1549), and Francesco Alunno's (1550). Not one of these offers anything even approaching a fresh reading of the poem; each merely repeats the substance of Bernardo's exegesis, one underlining one aspect of that interpretation, another stressing some other. Gesualdo, for example, opens with the now familiar explanation that the subject of the poem is the "vari stati" of man's soul. He goes on to speak of the two potentials of the soul, of the tendency for the sensual element to prevail in youth and the rational in old age, and in one relatively minor departure from Bernardo he discusses the relationship between Petrarch's triumph metaphor and the triumphal pageants found in the writings of Valerius Maximus, Livy, and Lactantius.[25] All in all, however, his commentary is little more than Bernardo in sixteenth-century dress.

The influence of Bernardo's commentary on the sixteenth-century view of the poem is also apparent in commentaries accompanying translations of the *Trionfi* into the various European vernaculars. The

Trionfi enjoyed enormous success not only in Italy and England, but in France, Spain, Portugal, and Germany as well. In France, for example, the poem was so popular that it was translated by at least four different persons in the course of the century, and some of these translations were so successful commercially that they attained second, third, and even fourth editions.[26] Two of them appeared early enough in the century to have come to Morley's attention, though his reading of the poem along the allegorical lines set down by Bernardo could not have derived from his reading of either translation, because they both appeared without commentaries. The first of these was a prose translation, Georges de la Forge's *Les triumphes messire francoys petrarcque*; this was first published in Paris in 1536, and it became so popular that it was reprinted in 1538, 1545, and 1554. The other, a verse translation by Jean Meynier d'Opède, *Les Triumphes Petrarques*, appeared in 1538 but was never reprinted. We know for certain that Morley had seen at least one of these translations and that it had inspired him to translate the *Trionfi* into English.[27]

Of greater interest than these two early translations are two later translations by Vasquin Philieul[28] and Philippe de Maldeghem,[29] both of which carry prefaces with interpretations of the poem that are strikingly similar to Bernardo's. Vasquin Philieul's translation, for instance, contains all the cardinal points of the allegorical reading I have been tracing back to Bernardo—the "vari stati," the two aspects of the soul, the final triumph of reason and eternity over the carnal and the temporal:

> Nostre tres moral Poete en sa presente divine oeuvre ha voulu monstrer divers estas de l'ame raisonnable, soubz nom de ses six Triomphes icy descris. Dont considerant que l'homme sur son Printemps est naturellement presque seigneurise de l'appetit sensitif, introduict, soubz le nom d'Amour, que l'appetit surdict triomphe de luy. Au second estat fainct, en personne de M. D. Laure, & soubz nom de Chastete, que la Raison, venant l'home plus neuf en age, triomphe... & estre maistresse d'Amour: c'est a dire de l'appetit. Au troisieme estat... fainct que la Mort triomphe de l'homme, & par consequent de l'appetit, & de la Raison. Au quatrieme, fainct que Renomee triomphe, & eit maistresse de la Mort... Au cinquieme estat... fainct que le

temps triomphe de Renomee. Au sixieme & dernier lieu ...
introduict l'Eternite, ou Divinite triompher du Temps, & de
toute aultre chose: pour nous donner a entendre que seulement
en Dieu eternel & infiny devons toute nostre foy & esperance
mettre.[30]

In this excellent work our moral poet intended to show the
various states of the rational soul by presenting them as six triumphs.
Therefore, since man in his youth is virtually ruled by the sensual
appetite, the poet, using the figure of Love, demonstrates how
sensuality triumphs over man. In the second triumph he shows, in
the person of Laura and under the name of Chastity, how Reason,
coming even to the youngest of men, triumphs over Love or
sensuality. In the third triumph he shows how Death triumphs
over man, sensuality, and Reason. In the fourth triumph he shows
how Fame triumphs and masters Death, and in the fifth he shows
Time triumphing over Fame. In the sixth and last triumph he
presents Eternity, or Divinity, triumphing over Time, and every-
thing else, to teach us that we should place our faith and hope
only in Almighty God.

The commentaries accompanying Spanish, Portuguese, and German
translations show the same echoing of Bernardo. The commentary
in Antonio de Obregon's Spanish translation opens with the statement
that "Escrive aqui micer Francisco Petrarca el sensitivo dominio
fingendo a cupido triumphar delos hombres en esta forma"[31] (Here
Petrarch writes of the power of sensuality by depicting Cupid trium-
phing over men), and the remainder of the commentary does little
more than paraphrase Bernardo. Hernando Hozes's edition[32] promises
a "nueva glosa" and acknowledges familiarity with Bernardo and
Velutello by noting that the commentary will be "no tan breve como
el de Alexandro Velutello, ni tan largo en muchas cosas, como el
de Bernardo Illicinio" (neither as brief as Alessandro Velutello's
nor as extensive as Bernardo Illicino's), but what follows is a skillful
distillation of the best features of Bernardo's exegesis, with particular
emphasis on the "diversos estados del anima racional," the various
states of the rational soul. A Portuguese translation that may well have

been the work of the poet Luis de Camoens (though the evidence is far from conclusive) repeats the substance and language of Bernardo, as does an interesting German translation by one Peter Perna.[33] Even a late sixteenth-century translation by the Scotsman William Fowler,[34] the only other complete English translation in that century, carries a preface highly reminiscent of Bernardo's exegesis.

It is difficult to avoid the conclusion that, for the better part of the sixteenth century, translators regarded Bernardo's commentary as an integral part of the work and that they consequently did not scruple to translate it along with the poem proper.[35]

Not until the high tide of Petrarchism had passed in Italy were there any significantly different approaches to the *Trionfi*. Thus Ludovico Castelvetro's edition of Petrarch's Italian poetry (1582) is a milestone, for it was the first virtually to ignore the allegorical interpretation of the *Trionfi* that had been current for more than a century. Castelvetro reduced ethical considerations to the simple statement that "lo 'ntendimento suo e convertimento a Dio, & pentimento de' predetti desideri"[36] (his intention is to convert to God and to repent for the aforesaid desires). He focused instead on the contents and structure of the poem and on its place in the Petrarchan canon, and he was the very first to attempt to prove that the *Trionfi* was meant to be a "continuation" of the sonnets, that is, a fuller and more extensive treatment of the themes of love and salvation which Petrarch had discussed in the *Canzoniere*. In 1592 there appeared a radically new interpretation of the *Trionfi*: during the surge of interest in the epic which had already produced the *Orlando Furioso*, the *Gerusalemme Liberata*, the *Faerie Queene*, and several discourses on epic theory, the Neapolitan Tomaso Costo stretched and tugged at the *Trionfi* in an attempt to force it into the epic mold as it was conceived by the Renaissance theorizers. After finishing the sonnets and the canzoni, Costo argued, Petrarch sought the amplitude of the epic; if one sets aside "il senso allegorico, che in essi Trionfi s'asconde, come dottamente da gli espositori vien dimostrato" (the allegorical meaning hidden in the *Trionfi*, as the exegetes have so learnedly shown), it is clear that the subject matter, action, characters, diction, and unity of the *Trionfi* all point to Petrarch's intention to write an epic. Costo's absolute conviction of the validity of his interpretation prompted him to write a closing paragraph in which he was swept away by the tide of his own rhetoric:

Ne i quali versi, ed in tutti gli altri allegati, se voi conoscerete essere quella perfetta locuzione, que'colori e lumi rettorici... quelle metafore, quella purità e proprietà di lingua, quell'armonia, quella gravità, quell'altezza, quella veemenza, quella energia, ed in somma tutti que'meriti del nome Eroico, che a me pare di conoscere ed in essi, ed in tutto il rimanente di que'maravigliosi Trionfi, sarà segno, ch'io habbia saputo spiegarvi l'intenzion mia.[37]

If in these and all the other verses you are able to recognize the perfect diction, colors and flowers of rhetoric, metaphors, linguistic purity and decorum, verbal harmony, seriousness, elevation of style, force, power, in short, all the virtues of the epic poem that I detect there and in the rest of the marvelous *Trionfi*, it will be a sign that I have been successful in explaining my intention.

In applying Aristotelian criteria of unity, action, diction, and structure both Castelvetro and Costo were instrumental in bringing to an end the tradition of allegorical exegesis first established by Bernardo Illicino.

While sixteenth-century Italian editors and commentators were establishing fresh ways of reading the *Trionfi*, in England interest in the poem continued unabated, as we can see in the many attempts to translate the poem either in part or in its entirety. The first of these translations probably precedes the work of Castelvetro and Costo by some two decades, and it is of very special interest because it came from the hand of Elizabeth I herself. In the Arundel Harington Manuscript, first printed by Ruth Hughey in 1960,[38] is Elizabeth's translation of the first ninety lines of Petrarch's "Triumph of Eternity"; the translation, which may have been executed in the early years of her reign or even earlier as an exercise for one of her tutors,[39] is extremely accurate and felicitous, perhaps the very best of her six translations of Italian, Latin, and Greek verse. In 1585, about forty-five years after Morley's translation, Sir Edward Dyer published a translation of twenty lines of the "Trionfo della Morte" in a passage on the vanity of worldly goods in his *Prayse of Nothing*. The translation is a very modest effort in unrhymed hexameters and is attributed by the author to "an unlearned translator," perhaps Dyer himself.[40] In the mid-1580's Mary Sidney, Countess of Pembroke, also tried her hand at the *Trionfi*, and hers is a more ambitious undertaking which renders all of the first and second capitoli of the "Trionfo della Morte" with remarkable accuracy and grace.[41] Her translation also has the distinction of being the only English version of the *Trionfi* successfully to employ and sustain the terza rima, a verse form which every other English translator of the poem from Morley to Ernest Hatch Wilkins has conceded he has not been able to render satisfactorily. In 1587 William Fowler, a Scotsman, dedicated a manuscript translation of the entire poem to Lady Jean Fleming; in plodding fourteeners, it opens with wordy praise of Petrarch's poem for its

> statelye verse with morall sentences, godlye sayings, brawe discoursis, proper and pithie arguments, and with a store of sindrie sort of historeis, enbelleshed and inbroudered with the curious pasmentis of poesie and golden freinzeis of Eloquence, I was spurred thairby and pricked fordward incontinent be translatioun to make thame sum what more populare then they ar in thair Italian originall; and especiallye when as I perceawed, bothe in Frenche and Inglish traductionis, this work not onelie traduced, but evin as it war mangled, and in everie member miserablie maimed and dismembered, besydis the barbar grosnes of boyth thair translationis, whiche I culd sett down by privif . . . in twoe hundreth passages and moe.[42]

Fowler's reference to the "morall sentences" contained in the *Trionfi* points to his debt to Bernardo and the Renaissance tradition of allegorical exegesis of the poem. The French translations to which he alludes are probably those by Jean Meynier d'Opède and Georges de la Forge, and, though he speaks disparagingly about the "barbar grosnes" of English translations as well, his own version, which is the only other complete sixteenth-century translation of the poem into English, is prolix and inaccurate and hardly improves on Morley's. Given the spate of editions and commentaries in Italy and the ensuing translations of the poem into all the major European vernaculars, it appears unlikely that Fowler's translation could have made the *Trionfi* any more popular than it already was.[43]

The *Trionfi* and Renaissance Iconography

Another sign of the popularity of the poem was the extraordinarily far-reaching impact it had on European art during the Renaissance: an enormous number of paintings, frescoes, miniatures, tapestries, faïences, enamels, and medals were based wholly or in part on the *Trionfi*, and a great many prominent artists—Mantegna, Signorelli, and Titian among them—turned to the *Trionfi* for inspiration.[1] It is of course no accident that the Petrarchan editions and translations (Morley's among them) appeared at the very time when artists were turning to the poem for subject matter; Renaissance critical theorists were fond of making analogies between the arts of poetry and painting, and the deep affinities between these "sister arts" are nowhere more clearly seen than in the eagerness with which the Renaissance artist turned to the *Trionfi*.[2]

For reasons unknown to us, the methods of the medieval and Renaissance artists who illustrated the *Trionfi* became crystallized as early as the late fourteenth century and remained substantially unchanged for some two hundred years. The conventional illustrations of the *Trionfi* depict the six triumphs described in Petrarch's poem, but, with the exception of the first triumph, the details of the illustrations have virtually nothing to do with the contents of the poem. Several explanations for this disparity have been advanced, but all of them are either unsatisfactory or unconvincing. D'Essling and Müntz were the first to be puzzled by the "entente internationale entre les illustrateurs," and they suggested the possibility that a commentary, now lost, was published between the first appearance of the poem and the first appearance of its illustrations and that the commentator established the conventional representations of the poem.[3] One critic suggested that the illustrators had in mind actual pageants of the *Trionfi* by living men and women and that the iconography of the poem became fixed in this way;[4] another argued cleverly but unconvincingly that Renaissance copies of Roman coins on which were depicted Roman triumphs of various sorts offer the best explanation of how the traditional iconography of the poem became established.[5] However, another explanation suggests itself: Petrarch had introduced the triumphal chariot drawn by beasts only in the first trionfo, but the illustrators conceived each of the six trionfi as a cortège with a central figure seated on a chariot drawn by a beast. Since these beasts are not mentioned in Petrarch's text, it seems likely that the illustrators followed the medieval bestiaries rather than the poem for their animal symbolism.[6] In any case, it is clear that the illustrators took from Petrarch's poem little more than the titles of individual trionfi and the allegorical figures; none of the illustrations are attempts to render graphically and realistically the actual characters and incidents of the poem.[7]

Whatever the reason for the "entente internationale" among the illustrators of the *Trionfi*, it is certain that the process began early. The first examples of illustrations of the *Trionfi* that we have are watercolors and woodcuts accompanying the fifteenth-century manuscripts of the poem. The techniques and conventions established by these first illustrators were soon copied and improved upon by craftsmen in other fields of the arts. By the fifteenth century, a completely symmetrical form had been given to the representations: each trionfo was assigned a chariot, each depicted an allegorical figure sitting atop that chariot, and each included throngs of victims surrounding the chariot. Though all six trionfi were illustrated, some were more popular than others, and illustrators distinctly preferred the triumphs of Love, Chastity, and Fame to the triumphs of Death, Time, and Eternity. This preference seems to have been shared by Morley: the trionfi he most painstakingly translated were those of Love, Chastity, and Fame. Also in the fifteenth century a number of innovations not based on Petrarch's text were introduced: one representation of the triumph of Love, for example, contained the figure of Adam, depicted as an old man wearing a tiara resembling that of the pope; in one triumph of Fame, there appeared two nude men, one young and the other old, whose hands are tied behind their backs to symbolize the two vices of Inertia and Laziness (or Prodigality and Madness) being conquered by Fame.[8]

In the fifteenth and sixteenth centuries the poem—or, to speak more precisely, its subject matter—pervaded virtually all areas of the graphic arts. In many of these representations the iconography is highly standardized and differs little from its predecessors; in many others there are minor but interesting variations on the standard iconography of the poem. The museums of Europe preserve thousands of paintings, drawings, miniatures, and assorted objets d'art whose subject matter was drawn from the themes of the poem. England is extraordinarily rich in such art, and the major museums of that country offer a wealth of examples of works of art based on these themes. The Victoria and Albert Museum, for example, houses two unusually beautiful cassoni that depict scenes from the *Trionfi*. One of these marriage coffers (Fig. 1) dates to the second quarter of the fifteenth century; on a single, continuous front panel are portrayed the triumphs of Love, Chastity, and Death, and on the side panels are representations of Pyramus, Thisbe, and Narcissus. The three triumphs show the artist's use of the traditional Renaissance iconography of the *Trionfi*—chariot, allegorical figure, beasts, and throng—and in many respects they differ little from hundreds of other fifteenth- and sixteenth-century renderings of the poem. But conventional though it is, the coffer is remarkable for its exquisitely fine human figures and for its unique combination of three separate trionfi in a single representation. The other cassone was made in Siena in the last quarter of the fifteenth century, probably by Francesco di Giorgio, who drew much of the subject matter for the cassone from the story of Solomon and the Queen of Sheba, combining it with the iconography of the *Trionfi* to produce an illustration which is an interesting blend of the biblical story and the "Triumph of Love."

Also at the Victoria and Albert Museum are three wooden birthtrays decorated with illustrations from the *Trionfi*. The birthtray, or *desco da parto*, was used to bring food and refreshment to women in labor, and the most appropriate trionfo for such a tray was naturally the "Triumph of Love" (see Fig. 2). The iconography of the decorations on the birthtrays at the Victoria and Albert Museum is highly conventional, but all three bear at the bottom an additional interesting scene, one not found in other Renaissance representations of the "Triumph of Love": Delilah cutting the hair of a naked, sleeping Sampson and a man reduced by love to the level of a beast being ridden by a woman. This, and other innovations introduced by Renaissance illustrators of the *Trionfi*, indicates that the illustrators of the poem considered themselves bound to follow certain universally accepted methods of depicting the poem but that they also felt free to add as many individual touches as pleased them.

In the National Gallery in London are two fifteenth-century paintings illustrating the theme of the "Triumph of Chastity." Luca Signorelli's rendering (Fig. 3) introduced another minor but important variation of the traditional iconography of the poem; it used all the conventional devices but placed them all in the background rather than in the center. The painting depicts three separate stages of the "Triumph of Chastity": in the background and to the right is the chariot, bearing the personifications of Chastity and the enslaved Cupid; slightly below and to the left is the second stage, in which Chastity and her followers struggle with the winged god; finally, in the foreground, occupying the largest space of the painting, is the binding of Cupid by Chastity, who is surrounded by two armed warriors and by a throng of chaste women holding Cupid's wings and his broken shafts.

The other painting at the National Gallery in London is *The Combat of Love and Chastity* by an unknown painter of the Florentine School of the fifteenth century. This painting is particularly interesting because it illustrates the "Triumph of Chastity" without using any of the conventional devices of such representations. There are no chariots, no crowds of victims, no symbolic beasts; all these have been discarded and attention is focused on the two personifications: the naked god of love stands on one foot and shoots his arrows at the figure of Chastity, who wards off the attack with her shield.

There are a great number of minor fifteenth-century representations on miscellaneous objets d'art, three of which are especially interesting. In the Slade Collection at the British Museum is preserved a glass cup (Fig. 4); on this are crudely depicted what appear to be two successive triumphs of Venus and Chastity, though it is impossible to say with certainty because the symbolic use of swans and alligators remains obscure. Also at the British Museum is a manuscript of a fifteenth-century psalter that belonged to Alfonso of Aragon.[9] It contains a miniature of the "Triumph of Death" (Fig. 5), a rather abbreviated rendering lacking the conventional chariot and with the throng represented by two figures that resemble a king and a pope. The illustrator did, however, use two conventional devices found in other illustrations of the *Trionfi*, the ghastly figure of Death and the bull, which often (along with the buffalo) is symbolic of Death. One of the loveliest of these minor representations of the *Trionfi* is a majolica dish preserved at the Victoria and Albert Museum (Fig. 6). The decoration seems to convey the "Triumph of Chastity," though again one cannot be certain because the symbolism is complex and obscure; the central figure carries the scales and sword of justice, but above her and to the left is prominently displayed the figure of the sun, regularly used in the Renaissance to depict the "Triumph of Time," and at the bottom of the dish are three naked figures resembling the figures traditionally included in illustrations of the "Triumph of Love."

Extensive though the influence of the *Trionfi* may have been on the artists of the fifteenth century, to the following century belong the most grandly conceived and executed of all representations of the poem: the magnificent triumph tapestries now preserved at Hampton Court Palace and at the Victoria and Albert Museum. Similar tapestries still hang at museums in Spain, Belgium, Austria, and the United States, but the sets at the two English museums are by far the richest and most finely executed of all.[10] In the Great Watching Chamber at Hampton Court are three enormous triumph tapestries, measuring some thirteen by twenty-seven feet each, depicting three consecutive triumphs, of Death over Chastity, Fame over Death, and Time over Fame.[11] These, like the tapestries at the Victoria and Albert Museum, were woven during the first quarter of the sixteenth century in Brussels, which was second only to Tournai as a center for tapestry weaving. The tapestries at Hampton Court Palace were originally part of a set of eight panels purchased by Cardinal Wolsey from the executors of the estate of the Bishop of Durham in about 1523, an extravagance that was promptly recorded for posterity in Skelton's *Colin Clout*.[12] Judging from the descriptions of the tapestries found in the poem, Skelton must have seen or heard about the complete set of eight, including the panel depicting the "Triumph of Love," which is now lost.

The chief features of these tapestries can of course be described, but the incredibly rich detail of every square inch of the panels must be seen to be appreciated. Each of the panels at Hampton Court Palace contains two triumphal cars, one for the victims at the left and another for the victors at the right. At the left of the panel devoted to the triumph of Death over Chastity (Fig. 7), one sees the chariot of Chastity and the central figure, labeled "Castitas," being stabbed by Atropos while Clotho stands by and Lachesis rides behind the other two Fates. The chariot is drawn by two unicorns, symbolic of Chastity, and beneath their feet is the figure of Venus. Cupid, naked and bound, is seated on the front of the chariot, which is surrounded by a number of chaste ladies, of whom only Lucrece, whose train is being carried by the figure of Bonvouloir, is identifiable. Alongside the chariot rides Scipio Africanus, and in front of it is an armed warrior named Grevance, who aims a long spear at the body of the fallen king. The chariot on the right of the panel shows Death, in the person of Atropos, riding triumphantly; and the defeated figure of Chastity now replaces the defeated figure of Cupid at the front of the chariot. The chariot is drawn by buffaloes, traditional symbols of Death, and towering above the multitude of figures are Fortitudio and Malheur.

The *Triumph of Fame over Death* at Hampton Court (Fig. 8) also consists of two central chariots around which are grouped scores of figures and realistic details. On the left of the panel four richly decorated bulls draw the chariot of Death, and above it a flying figure of Fame blows her trumpet, the sound of which is beginning to topple Atropos from her pedestal on the chariot. The figures of Clotho and Lachesis can be distinguished under the wheels of the chariot, and the figure of Chastity remains bound and overpowered on the chariot. At the right of the panel is the triumphal chariot of Lady Fame, who carries a trumpet and looks down at the vanquished figure of Atropos at her feet. Lady Fame's chariot is drawn by four elephants and is surrounded by crowds of ancient heroes. In the center of the panel are the dominant figures of a splendidly appareled queen and of Julius Caesar.

In the tapestry depicting the Triumph of Time over Fame (Fig. 9) the chariot at the left of the panel carries the slumping figure of Fame, her trumpet now rendered useless by Time. Four elephants draw her chariot, which is surrounded by multitudes; by contrast the chariot of Father Time at the right of the panel is drawn by winged horses and is attended only by the defeated figure of Fame at his feet.

At the Victoria and Albert Museum are preserved three panels of triumph tapestries: *The Triumph of Chastity over Love, The Triumph of Death over Chastity*, and *The Triumph of Fame over Death*. The last two of these are identical to the tapestries of the same name at Hampton Court Palace save for some extremely minor details in the floral borders, landscaping, and decoration; but the *Triumph of Chastity over Love* (Fig. 10) is not duplicated at Hampton Court Palace. Like all the triumph tapestries considered thus far, it depicts two chariots, around which are arranged a series of allegorical figures. At the left of the panel, attended by the figures of "Honestate," "Honte," and "Bonvouloir," is Chastity riding astride a unicorn;

above her head is the descriptive phrase "Laura pour raison," and she is shown pulling Cupid from his chariot. Around the chariot are grouped a number of famous victims of love, Caesar, Cleopatra, Penelope, Dido, Virginia, and Jacob among them. On the far right of the panel is a temple containing a statue of Diana; below the statue is the date 1507, though the date 1510 appears on the roof of the temple. Just below the temple, and slightly to the left of it, Chastity rides atop a chariot drawn by four unicorns; at her feet sits Cupid, bound and naked. Accompanying the procession is a band of chaste women and a lone male figure riding a horse.

Also at the Victoria and Albert Museum are two curious smaller tapestries, one of which is most certainly based on Petrarch's poem, though it incorporates none of the iconographic devices normally used to illustrate it, and the other of which makes use of most of those devices but does not illustrate a Petrarchan theme. The first of the two is a Flemish tapestry of the early sixteenth century (Fig. 11) which depicts the three Fates triumphing over Chastity. Clotho holds a distaff, while Lachesis spins the thread of life and Atropos cuts it. Beneath the feet of the Fates is the prostrate figure of a lovely young girl with a broken lily by her side. The tapestry is obviously a representation of the "Triumph of Death over Chastity," despite the absence of the traditional chariot and throng. Moreover, the content and composition of this tapestry are so remarkably similar to those of a pen and ink drawing (Fig. 15) found in a series of sixteenth-century French illustrations of the "Triumph of Death" now preserved at the Bibliothèque de l'Arsenal in Paris that there is virtually no doubt that the tapestry was intended to be a "Triumph of Death." The other tapestry is a fragment of a larger work executed at Tournai at the beginning of the sixteenth century, and it appears to represent the triumph of the Church over Death. The Tournai fragment shows Clotho, Lachesis, and the partial figure of Atropos being trampled by a chariot driven by a church father, who is accompanied by St. Jerome. This tapestry is an interesting example of the use of the iconographic conventions of the *Trionfi* to illustrate themes not directly connected with the poem, though from a certain point of view a triumph of the Church can easily be seen as a variation on the Petrarchan theme of the triumph of Eternity.

To the sixteenth century, too, belong a large number of less grandly conceived illustrations of the *Trionfi*, most of which made use of the same iconographic devices employed in the tapestries at Hampton Court Palace and at the Victoria and Albert Museum. The bulk of these illustrations accompanied Renaissance editions and translations of the *Trionfi*. One can select almost at random from the splendid collection of illustrated manuscripts of the *Trionfi* now housed at the Bibliothèque Nationale in Paris and find example after example of finely made yet highly conventional watercolor miniatures accompanying texts of the poem. One excellent example is a large folio volume containing the Italian text, a French commentary that gives every sign of being a translation of Bernardo Illicino's exegesis, and a series of miniatures (Fig. 12) that employs virtually every single iconographic device so far discussed.[13] Each illustration has its chariot, its allegorical beasts, its central figure, and its crowds of victims, and the illustrator has created a series of miniatures which differ little from hundreds of other illustrations of the *Trionfi*.

On the other hand, some sixteenth-century illustrators tried to vary the standard iconography of the *Trionfi* and to find more simple and more graceful ways of illustrating the poem. One of these innovations involved the attempt to portray the author himself, and there are two manuscripts which contain representations of the poet. One contains a miniature depicting the poet asleep and having the dream with which the "Triumph of Love" opens.[14] In the other manuscript the poet appears as a member of the triumphal procession of the victims of Love.[15] Still another departure from the conventional manner of representing the *Trionfi* was an attempt to exclude most of the paraphernalia of the trionfo and to concentrate instead on the members of the triumphal procession. Thus in one manuscript the illustrator of the "Triumph of Love" does away completely with the chariot, beasts, and allegorical figure and simply depicts famous pairs of lovers such as Paris and Helen, Medea and Jason, and Holofernes and Judith.[16] In the same manuscript, this illustrator introduced another interesting variation by providing not one but two separate illustrations for each of the six trionfi. In the "Triumph of Fame," for example, the first illustration combines the triumphs of Chastity, Death, and Fame and shows Fame defeating Death, which has in turn just defeated Chastity (Fig. 13); the second is a more conventional representation focusing on the figure of Fame (Fig. 14).

One of the most interesting variations on the traditional method of representing the *Trionfi* appears in a manuscript I have already mentioned: MS. 5066 at the Bibliothèque de l'Arsenal in Paris, which contains pen and ink illustrations of the poem. The illustrator of this manuscript completely excluded the conventional chariot, crowds, and allegorical beasts and portrayed instead the triumphant figure and its victims (Fig. 15). Although these illustrations, like so many others based on the Petrarchan trionfi, have little to do with the actual contents of the poem, they are nevertheless among the most gracefully executed of all the illustrations of the *Trionfi*.

I have reserved comment on one earlier influence of the *Trionfi* on European art because the phenomenon illustrated in that influence is central to an understanding of the relationship between poetry and painting in the Renaissance and, more specifically, to an understanding of how the *Trionfi* were understood and used by English writers of the sixteenth century. Some time after 1475, Lydgate translated a well-known French poem, *Danse Macabre*, into English.[17] The *Dance of Death* is particularly interesting because it strongly resembles the "Triumph of Death"; both poems describe a procession in which Death addresses a crowd of people and then asks them to follow his cortège. The *Dance of Death* enjoyed wide popularity in the fifteenth century, as we know from the numerous medieval manuscripts of the poem and from the many frescoes and tapestries in which the poem was illustrated and the text used as a running commentary on the illustrations. Lydgate said that he had seen the original of the *Dance of Death* "depict upon a walle" at the Eglise des Innocents in Paris. Often, as J. M. Clark has demonstrated,[18] the iconography of wall paintings such as those at the Eglise des Innocents or the Chiesa dei Disciplini at Clusone, or the great fresco of the Camposanto di Pisa, was achieved by conflating the Triumph of Death and the Dance of Death, the result being neither, strictly speaking, a Triumph of Death nor a Dance of Death. What is important about Lydgate's translation is that it is an excellent illustration of a practice that was to become widespread in the sixteenth century: that of drawing subject matter for poetry from a painting which in turn may have been originally inspired by a poem. To understand how the *Trionfi* entered English literature in the sixteenth century, it is necessary to keep in mind the ease and frequency with which this generous exchange between painter and poet took place.

The *Trionfi* and the Literature of the Early Tudor Period

Precisely such borrowing of material from the graphic arts as took place in the case of Lydgate's *Danse Macabre* no doubt took place in the composition of those three poems of the early sixteenth century which are said to have been inspired wholly or in part by Petrarch's *Trionfi*. Sir Thomas More's "Nyne Pageauntes," Stephen Hawes's concluding chapters to *The Pastime of Pleasure*, and John Skelton's *Colin Clout* were all written before Morley's translation of the *Trionfi*; and all three show that their authors were far more familiar with iconographical representations of the poem than they were with the poem itself.

Sir Thomas More was the first of the three to bring the *Trionfi* into English literature in this indirect manner. According to Rastell, More composed the "Nyne Pageauntes," which strongly resemble the *Trionfi*, in about 1503.[1] What is especially striking about these nine stanzas of rime royal is that they were written to accompany tapestries that More himself had designed for his father's house in London. The circumstances under which they were written were described by Rastell in the first edition of More's English works (1557):

> Mayster More, in his youth devysed in hys fathers house in London, a goodly hangyng of fyne paynted clothe, with nyne pageauntes: which verses expressed and declared, what the images in those pageauntes represented; and also in those pageauntes were paynted the thynges that the verses over them dyd (in effecte) declare, which verses here folowe.[2]

The nine stanzas that follow describe Youth, Manhood, Love, Age, Death, Fame, Time, Eternity, and, finally, the triumph of the Poet over all. When examined closely, these stanzas show both very great similarities to the *Trionfi* and decided differences from it. More's poem contains a curious combination of allegorical personifications, some of which can be found in Petrarch's text and others of which cannot. It seems very likely that More conflated some of the personifications from Petrarch's *Trionfi* and traditional figures used in representations of the theme of the four ages of man.[3] Thus he views man's life as a progression toward death and also as a series of "triumphs" that concludes with the triumph of Art (in the personification of the Poet) over all.

More's first triumph describes not Love but Youth, in the person of "a boy playing at the top and squyrge [scourge, whip]," and the second describes Manhood triumphing over Youth. More indicates that in the tapestry the figure of Manhood was "rydyng uppon a goodly horse, havynge an hawke on his fyste . . . and under the horses fete, was paynted the same boy, that in the fyrste pageaunte was playinge at the top and squyrge." This practice of depicting victor and vanquished together and of allowing the personification of a later stage of human development to triumph over an earlier one is especially Petrarchan, and was used repeatedly in the fifteenth-century illustrations of the *Trionfi*. When considered together with More's borrowing of the figures of Love, Death, Time, and Eternity, it underlines the debt More owed to Petrarch's *Trionfi*, even though the poem reached him by way of an iconographical intermediary.

In More's third pageant Manhood is defeated by Love; the young man is depicted lying on the ground, "And uppon hym stode Ladye Venus goodes of Love" with Cupid by her side. The fourth pageant, of Age, has no equivalent in the *Trionfi*, but More did use the Petrarchan devices of representing victor and vanquished in one description and of showing a mature personification triumphing over a younger one: "In the fourth pageant was paynted an old sage father sittynge in a chayre. And lyeing under his fete was painted the ymage of Venus and Cupyde, that were in the third pageant." The fifth, sixth, seventh, and eighth pageants, of Death, Fame, Time, and Eternity, follow the *Trionfi* rather closely: Death conquers all men; Fame triumphs over Death, Time over Fame, and Eternity over Time. The last of More's triumphs, which affirms the supremacy of the Poet over all, has no parallel in Petrarch's *Trionfi*.

A number of points about the composition of "Nyne Pageauntes" indicate that More made use of an iconographic intermediary rather than Petrarch's text itself. First, the fact that the verses were intended to accompany tapestries suggests the interesting possibility that More had seen triumph tapestries somewhere and that he was modeling his own designs on those. Second, as I have noted, by More's time the iconography of the *Trionfi* had become standardized so that the central figures were always depicted mounted on a triumphal chariot drawn by beasts, even though Petrarch's text mentioned neither the chariots nor the beasts except in the first trionfo. In More's verses the figures of Age, Death, Eternity, and the Poet are described as "sittynge in a chayre"; More's "chayre" was in all probability the triumphal chariot that appeared in virtually all the fifteenth- and early sixteenth-century representations of the *Trionfi*. It was these illustrations, and not Petrarch's poem itself, that provided much of the subject matter of More's "Nyne Pageauntes."

The presence of an iconographic intermediary is also apparent in the three concluding chapters of Hawes's *Pastime of Pleasure*,[4] in which there appear personifications of Fame, Time, and Eternity very similar to their Petrarchan counterparts. As in the Petrarchan *Trionfi*, Time conquers Fame and is then defeated in turn by Eternity. But here the resemblances end: Hawes's rich and detailed description of the three figures suggests that he followed some fifteenth- or early sixteenth-century illustrator of the *Trionfi* rather than Petrarch's text, which provides only the barest details about the appearance of the figures. Petrarch describes Lady Fame simply as "quella / Che trae l'uom del sepolcro e 'n vita il serba"[5] (the one who saves man from the tomb and gives him life), but Hawes says that she enters with "brennynge tongues," and the woodcut that accompanies Chapter XLII portrays her as a winged lady. Hawes's Lady Fame boasts of her ability to immortalize men—Hector, Joshua, Judas Maccabeus, David, Alexander, Julius Caesar, Arthur, Charlemagne, and Godfrey. Many of these figures appear in the catalogs of illustrious persons found in Petrarch's "Trionfo della Fama," but they may also have appeared in the "full manye bokes ryght delycyous" and "ryall bokes and Iestes hystoryall"[6] in which Hawes claimed he had read of their exploits, so that it is impossible to say with certainty that his model was the *Trionfi*.

Hawes's description of Time is even more concrete and explicit than his description of Fame, and to a great extent even further removed from Petrarch's figure. In the "Trionfo del Tempo" the wasteful effects of Time are presented through the traditional symbolism of the sun being drawn across the sky by mythological beasts; Hawes's Time is very different:

> Aged he was with a berde doubtless
> Of swalowes feders his wynges were longe
> His body fedred he was hye and stronge
>
> In his lefte hande he had an horology
> And in his ryght hande a fyre brennynge
> A swerde aboute hym gyrte full surely
> His legges armed clerely shynynge
> And on his noddle derkely flamynge
> Was sette Saturne pale as ony leed
> And Iupyter a myddes his forhed
>
> In the mouthe Mars and in his ryght wynge
> Was splendent Phebus with his golden beames
> And in his brest there was resplendysshynge
> The shynynge Venus with depured streames
> That all about dyde cast her fyry leames
> In his left wynge Mercury and aboue his wast
> Was horned Dyane her opposycyon past.[7]

Nor are there any discernible verbal similarities between Hawes's passages and the "Trionfo della Fama." Petrarch's trionfo is a laconic meditation on the vanity of human wishes, the ultimate moral of which is "beato chi non nasce," that it is a blessing not to have been born. This tone is completely absent in Hawes's *Pastime of Pleasure*, where the description of Time is used as a starting point for rehearsing the story of the fall of man, redemption through Christ, and the intercession of the Virgin. Hawes's ingenious invention, as Erwin Panofsky and Samuel Chew have shown,[8] resulted from the fusion of the image of Time developed by the medieval illustrators of Petrarch's *Trionfi* with the Visions of the Apocalypse. Hawes's description of Time is therefore, like Lydgate's *Danse Macabre* and More's "Nyne Pageauntes," a poem twice removed from its Petrarchan sources.

Finally, there are great differences between the "Trionfo dell' Eternità" and the portrait of Dame Eternitye that brings the *Pastime of Pleasure* to a close. In Petrarch's poem the meditative mood of the

1. *Cassone* with illustrations of the triumphs of Love, Chastity, and Death; Italian, second quarter of the fifteenth century

2. *Desco da parto* depicting a triumph of Love; Italian, fifteenth century

5. A representation of a triumph of Death, from a psalter belonging to Alfonso of Aragon; Spanish, fifteenth century

6. Majolica dish with representation of the triumph of Chastity; Italian, fifteenth century

7. Tapestry, *The Triumph of Death over Chastity*, Hampton Court; Flemish, sixteenth century; copyright reserved

8. Tapestry, *The Triumph of Fame over Death*, Hampton Court; Flemish, sixteenth century;

9. Tapestry, *The Triumph of Time over Fame*, Hampton Court; Flemish, sixteenth century; copyright reserved

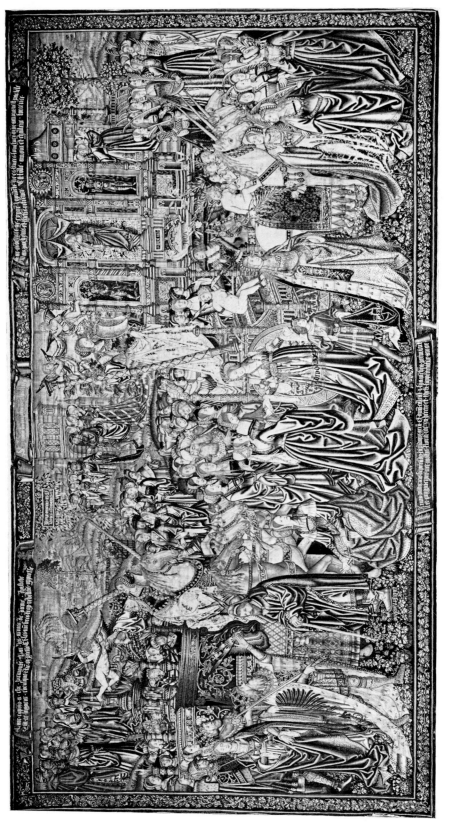

10. Tapestry, *The Triumph of Chastity over Love*, Victoria and Albert Museum; Flemish, sixteenth century

11. Tapestry, *The Three Fates Triumphing over Chastity*, Victoria and Albert Museum; Flemish, sixteenth century

12. Miniature of the triumph of Love; from a sixteenth-century French manuscript

13. Miniature of the triumphs of Fame, Death, and Chastity; from a sixteenth-century French manuscript

14. Miniature of the triumph of Fame; from a sixteenth-century French manuscript

Pen and ink drawing of the triumph of Death; from a sixteenth-century French manuscript

16. Bronze medals depicting triumphal chariots; Italian, sixteenth century

preceding trionfo is sustained and amplified; the machinery of allegory and personification is abandoned completely, and what follows is a vision of Eternity simple in spirit and diction:

Da poi che sotto 'l ciel cosa non vidi
Stabile e perma, tutto sbigottito
Mi volsi al cor e dissi, "In che ti fidi?"

Rispose: "Nel Signor, che mai fallito
Non a promessa a chi si fida in lui;
Ma ben veggio che 'l mondo m'a schernito

. . . .

Questo pensavo, e mentre più s'interna
La mente mia, veder mi parve un mondo
Novo, in etate immobile ed eterna.[9]

When I saw that nothing under heaven is stable and firm, in dismay I turned to my heart and said: "In what do you trust?" And it answered: "In the Lord, who has never failed those who have faith in Him, but I see full well that the world has scorned me . . ." So I thought, and as my mind reflected more deeply, I seemed to see a new world, changeless and eternal.

In this "mondo novo" Time itself will come to an end; past, present, and future will be reduced to a single term, and Death will become the door through which man will pass into a timeless existence. Petrarch will be reunited with Laura and with "color che sotto 'l freno / di modesta fortuna ebbero in uso / senza altra pompa di godersi in seno" (those who, beneath the check of modest fortune, lived contentedly and without ostentation); being beyond the pale of Time and Death, they will enjoy immortal beauty and eternal fame. The trionfo then closes with a quiet prayer to Laura.

No such flights of meditative verse are to be found in Hawes's description of Lady Eternitye:

And thus as tyme made his conclusyon
Eternitye in a fayre whyte vesture
To the temple came with hole affeccyon

> And on her hede a dyademe ryght pure
> With thre crownes of precyous treasure
> Eterne she sayde I am nowe doubtles
> Of heuen quene and of hell empres.[10]

After affirming her invincibility and man's incapacity to comprehend her until the Day of Judgment, she urges man to set aside worldly felicity and to look to the health of his soul. The poem then closes with a prayer to the Virgin for intercession on man's behalf.

John Skelton's *Colin Clout* also seems to have been chiefly inspired by a work of art rather than by Petrarch's original poem. How much of Petrarch's vernacular poetry Skelton had read is not certain; but his references to Petrarch in the *Garland of Laurel* suggest that, like other fifteenth-century English poets, he knew Petrarch primarily as a Latin humanist. Skelton's *Colin Clout*, probably written in 1522,[11] purports to be a general attack on the pomp and worldliness of clerics, but it is actually a pointed attack on the splendor of Cardinal Wolsey's residence at Hampton Court. In what appears to be a sweeping indictment of all worldly prelates, Skelton complains of those churchmen who build "royally / Theyr mancyons curyously / With turrettes and with toures, / With halles and with boures"; but the barbed allusions to "clothes of golde and palles / Arras of ryche aray, / Fresshe as flours in May" soon make it clear that what Skelton had in mind were the eight pieces of triumph tapestries that Wolsey had acquired from the executors of the estate of the Bishop of Durham. Skelton's sharpest satire is leveled at that part of the collection of tapestries at Hampton Court that he believed to be most inappropriate for a cardinal:

> Wyth dame Dyana naked;
> Howe lusty Venus quaked,
> And howe Cupyde shaked
> His darte, and bent his bowe
> For to shote a crowe
> At her tyrly tyrlowe;
> And howe Parys of Troy
> Daunced a lege de moy,
> Made lusty sporte and ioy
> With dame Helyn the quene.[12]

This is followed by a description of the panel of the triumph of Fame:

> With triumphes of Cesar
> And of Pempeyus war,
> Of renowne and of fame
> By them to get a name:
> Nowe all the worlde stares,
> How they ryde in goodly chares,
> Conueyed by olyphantes,
> With lauryat garlantes,
> And by vnycornes
> With their semely hornes;
> Vpon these beestes rydynge,
> Naked boyes strydynge,
> With wanton wenches winkyng.[13]

In a final thrust at Wolsey, Skelton notes that such tapestries provide "mete meditacyon / For prelates of estate, / Their courage to abate / From worldly wantonesse." In fairness to Wolsey, it should be noted that Skelton carefully avoided mentioning the panels depicting the triumph of Death and the triumph of Time, both of which would have been entirely appropriate for a churchman.

If these early examples of the use of the subject matter of the *Trionfi* can be traced to the presence of iconographic intermediaries rather than to direct imitation of the poem, to what extent was the poem read and used as a model by the poets of the first half of the sixteenth century? One might well expect to find wide familiarity with the poem and conscious imitation of it in the third, fourth, and fifth decades of the century, the period when the Petrarchan vogue was being given impetus by Wyatt and Surrey and by the dissemination of the editions of Petrarch's poetry. By 1527, the year of Wyatt's first visit to Italy, there had already appeared a number of editions of Petrarch's Italian poetry, almost all of which included the *Trionfi*. It is well known that these editions aroused a great deal of interest in Petrarchan poetry; what remains puzzling is the almost exclusive interest in the *Canzoniere* on the part of English Petrarchists. Wyatt and Surrey, for example, could hardly have been unaware of the existence of the *Trionfi*; yet the Petrarchan poems they chose as models for their poetry were all taken from the *Canzoniere*, with one minor exception in the poetry of Surrey. Of the twenty-seven poems in the Wyatt canon which show Petrarchan influence, not a single one can be traced to the *Trionfi*.[14] So too with Surrey's poetry: of the twelve poems by him that may be described as translations, adaptations, or imitations of Petrarchan poems, only one, "Suche waiwarde waies hath love," can be traced to the *Trionfi*.[15] It would appear, therefore, that after the middle of the century the poem ceased to be an important model for English poets, many of whom found the sonnet form more fashionable, and perhaps, judging from the torrent of sonnet sequences in the 1580's and 1590's, more lucrative as well. Nevertheless, the *Trionfi* must have continued to be popular among English readers, particularly those of an Italianate or scholarly bent. As late as 1570, for instance, it was popular enough for Ascham to complain that Italianate Englishmen had "in more reverence, the triumphes of Petrarche, than the Genesis of Moses."[16] Considering the popularity of Petrarchan poetry in general and the unremitting flow of Renaissance art based on the *Trionfi*, there is no reason to accuse him of exaggerating.

The Elizabethan Triumph

Despite the diminished interest in the *Trionfi* as a direct model for English poetry in the early Tudor period, the poem left its impress on Elizabethan literature in a highly complex and indirect manner. Like their fifteenth- and early sixteenth-century predecessors, Elizabethan artists found in the *Trionfi* an abundance of subject matter, and in turn their representations of the poem often provided inspiration for creators of triumphal pageants and processions. Some of these pageants were actually staged and, as forerunners of the court masque, achieved enormous popularity in the Elizabethan age. Others, such as those described in Sidney's *Arcadia* and in Spenser's *Faerie Queene*, formed part of major literary works, but they too were no doubt modeled on pageants actually observed.

In its various maifestations as pageant, procession, ceremonial entry, progress, and *tableau vivant*, the public spectacle was enormously popular in English life and literature between the twelfth and the eighteenth centuries,[1] but it was the sixteenth century that first fully appreciated the dramatic uses to which these paraliterary forms could be put.[2] So popular was this form of entertainment that by the 1580's, when the public spectacle reached a peak of popularity in England, the distinctions between its various forms had become so blurred that most public, dramatic, and literary spectacles were simply grouped together under the collective title of "triumph" or "triumphall." Though a few of these spectacles included distinctly Petrarchan themes—an interesting example is an entertainment of Queen Elizabeth (1578)[3] in which the figure of Chastity proved her strength over Cupid by ejecting him from her coach and claiming it for her own—most of these entries, processions, and progresses had little direct connection with Petrarch's *Trionfi*. Nevertheless, as was the case with the early Tudor poetry, Petrarchan themes and conventions such as the use of allegorical figures of Chastity and Fame and the introduction of the triumphal chariot and the throngs of followers made their way into these pageants by way of the artists and illustrators. The closer one looks at the Elizabethan use of the word "triumph," the clearer it becomes that the word did not suggest Petrarchan themes and that it was used either in a general sense to signify a victory or procession or in a slightly more specialized sense to mean a ceremonial celebration of any kind. The entries for "triumph" in the most popular Renaissance dictionaries—Cooper's,[4] Thomas's,[5] Barrett's,[6] and Florio's[7]—all indicate that a triumph was nothing more than "a solemne pompe or showe at the returne of a capitaine for a victory that he hath got," to use Florio's words.

Much to the embarassment of the critical essayists of the period, the triumphal pageant became so popular that it achieved the status of a genre, and it is as a genre that it is fully described in *The Arte of English Poesie* (1589). This essay, generally ascribed to George Puttenham, is a typical Renaissance literary treatise, highly dependent on classical and Italian treatments of the nature and scope of poetry and as such an excellent yardstick for measuring what the Renaissance understood the triumph to be. In Book I, which contains a discussion of the nature of poetry and an analysis of the poetic genres, there is a discussion of "poeticall rejoysings," among which is included the triumph:

And they be of diverse sorts and upon diverse occasions growne. One & the chiefe was for the publike peace of a countrie, the greatest of any other civill good ... An other is for a just and honourable victory atchieved against the forraine enemy. A third at solemne feasts and pompes of coronations and enstallments of honourable orders. An other at jollity at weddings and marriages. An other at the birth of Princes children ... And as these rejoysings tend to divers effects, so do they carry diverse formes and nominations; for those of victorie and peace are called *Triumphall,* whereof we ourselves have heretofore given some example by our *Triumphals,* written in honor of her majesties long peace.[8]

Apparently the popularity of these "triumphals" did not diminish at all in the seventeenth century. So popular were they, in fact, that Bacon felt obliged to acknowledge their existence in an essay, "On Masques and Triumphs," even though he personally held them in very great disdain. In that essay Bacon made quite clear how little he thought of triumphal spectacles and the verses recited at the appearance of allegorical figures, and he indicated that he would scarcely dignify them with the name of poetry were it not for the fact that aristocrats were so fond of them. Bacon does not mention Petrarch's poem, and in fact his discussion of chariots and beasts and other trappings of the Renaissance triumphal procession gives every indication that the originators of the spectacles modeled their work on paintings and tapestries, that, in short, the iconographers rather than Petrarch provided the inspiration:

> These things are but toys to come amongst such serious observations. But yet, since Princes will have such things, it is better they should be graced with elegance than daubed with cost ... For justs and tourneys and barriers, the glories of them are chiefly in the chariots, wherein the challengers make their entry; especially if they be drawn with strange beasts, as lions, bears, camels and the like; or in the devices of their liveries; or in the goodly furniture of their horses and armour. But enough of these toys.[9]

In the triumphal processions described in the works of the major Elizabethan writers—Sidney, Shakespeare, and Spenser—the triumph was nothing more than "a solemne pompe or showe," and the details of these poetic descriptions were drawn largely from graphic representations of the *Trionfi.* A triumph in Book I of Sidney's *Arcadia* provides a good illustration. After Pyrocles has disguised himself as Zelmane in order to be close to Philoclea, a young knight named Phalantus comes to King Basilius "to crave license . . . he might . . . defie all Arcadian knights in the behalfe of his mistresse," Artesia. Sidney's account of Phalantus's personal history soon makes it clear that the young man is no suffering Petrarchan lover; indeed, the passage has a singularly anti-Petrarchan ring to it. Unlike the Petrarchan lover, Phalantus is one of those who "will love for want of other businesse, not because they feel indeed that divine power, which makes the heart finde a reason in passion." Instead, "taking love unto him like a fashion, he courted Artesia," herself a parody of the Petrarchan lady: "For she, thinking she did wrong to her beautie if she were not prowde of it, called her disdaine of him chastitie."

The triumph of Artesia that takes up all of Chapter 16[10] is reminiscent, in its general outlines, of Petrarch's "Trionfo d'Amore," but Sidney's triumph is so saturated with broad parody of Petrarchan love conventions that it is unthinkable to call the *Trionfi* its model, except perhaps as a convenient framework for ridiculing the Petrarchan ideal in general. Artesia rides atop a "triumphant chariot" drawn by four winged horses with "artificiall flaming mouths"; she is followed by Phalantus and preceded by footmen who carry portraits of "conquered beauties," each of whom has a fault that makes her inferior to Artesia. The long muster of beauties conquered by Phalantus is of course reminiscent of the throngs of vanquished lovers described in Petrarch's "Trionfo d'Amore" and of the numerous Renaissance illustrations of that trionfo, but far from imitating the serious mood of the Italian original, Sidney's triumph sounds more like Leporello's catalog of Don Giovanni's conquests: Andromana has lost to Artesia not because she is older but because she has red hair and small eyes; Baccha is too corpulent, and her breasts are "over-familiarly laide open, with a mad countenance about her mouth, between simpering and smyling"; Leucippe is simple-minded and gullible; Laconia is simply a queen "and therefore beautyfull." So the triumph continues, and what emerges is not a triumph of Love but a triumph of Artifice and Hypocrisy, the main details of which appear to have been drawn from illustrations of the *Trionfi* or from actual triumphal pageants that Sidney had seen.

Though we cannot say with any degree of certainty that Shakespeare knew the *Trionfi* itself, it is inconceivable that he was unacquainted with the triumphal pageants and processions that had achieved such wide popularity in his own lifetime. The diction and imagery of several of his plays provide several indications that Shakespeare conceived of the triumph both in the general sense in which Puttenham described it and as a pageant or procession that had its origins in the iconographic representations of the *Trionfi*. The generalized sense of the word may be seen in *3 Henry VI*, in which the Duke of York complains as he is being arrested that "So triumph thieves upon their conquer'd beauty; / So true men yield, with robbers so o'ermatch'd" (I, iv, 63–64).[11] In *Richard II* the word is used to refer to what appears to be a "solemne showe or pompe": "My lord, some two days since I saw the Prince, / And told him of those triumphs held at Oxford" (V, iii, 13–14). And of course there are many cases in which it is extremely difficult to make a distinction between the literal and figurative use of the word, as in *Julius Caesar*: "But, indeed, sir, we make holiday, to see Caesar And to rejoice in his triumph" (I, i, 34–35).

More interesting, however, are the several cases in which Shakespeare uses the word with what appears to be full understanding of the themes, as well as the iconographic particulars, of the Petrarchan *Trionfi*. A good example is the opening passage of *Love's Labour's Lost*, in which King Ferdinand argues the necessity of a retreat from the world and the acceptance of a scholarly, quasi-monastic life of seclusion; here Shakespeare takes up no less than five of the six Petrarchan trionfi, a remarkable accomplishment considering that he did not resort to the word "triumph" or to the use of the iconographic conventions. Seclusion and study, argues Ferdinand, will give rise to a sort of triumph of Chastity in which "affections / And the huge army of the world's desires" will be defeated; having accomplished this, the young scholars will be guaranteed Fame, and Fame, "spite of cormorant, devouring Time," will make the young aristocrats "heirs of all eternity." Only the triumph of Love is lacking in this fascinating distillation of the Petrarchan trionfi:

> *King.* Let fame, that all hunt after in their lives,
> Live register'd upon our brazen tombs
> And then grace us in the disgrace of death;
> When, spite of cormorant, devouring Time,

Th' endeavor of this present breath may buy
That honour which shall bate his scythe's keen edge
And make us heirs of all eternity.
Therefore, brave conquerors,—for so you are,
That war against your own affections
And the huge army of the world's desires,—
Our late edict shall strongly stand in force.
Navarre shall be the wonder of the world:
Our court shall be a little Academe,
Still and contemplative in living art.

(I, i, 1–14)

Titus Andronicus opens with a "solemne showe or pompe," a triumphal pageant celebrating Titus's defeat of the Goths, and, more important, it contains a passage whose imagery reveals that Shakespeare was familiar with the iconographic conventions of the "Triumph of Love." At the outset of Act II Tamora's lover Aaron notes that his mistress's fortunes have risen, and that he will try to profit from her improved situation; in passing, he refers to their liaison, using the imagery of the "Triumph of Love":

Then, Aaron, arm thy heart, and fit thy thoughts,
To mount aloft with thy imperial mistress,
And mount her pitch, whom thou in triumph long
Hast prisoner held, fetter'd in amorous chains
And faster bound to Aaron's charming eyes
Than is Prometheus tied to Caucasus.

(II, i, 12–17)

It is in the Henry VI trilogy and in Richard III, however, that Shakespeare resorts most consciously and extensively to the iconographic devices associated with the Trionfi, using the "Triumph of Death" and adjusting the theme of that triumph to the recurrent themes of the history plays: the triumph of Fortune and the fall of princes. One instance of this occurs in 3 Henry VI, when the deposed Margaret mourns the loss of her throne:

3*

> I was, I must confess,
> Great Albion's queen in former golden days;
> But now mischance hath trod my title down
> And with dishonour laid me on the ground,
> Where I must take like seat unto my fortune
> And to my humble seat conform myself.
>
> (III, iii, 6–11)

When Lewis, the French king, tries to comfort her with the thought that she must stand firm against adversity, he describes Fortune as a form of triumphant Death, a figure that must be opposed with strength and equanimity:

> Yield not thy neck
> To fortune's yoke, but let thy dauntless mind
> Still ride in triumph over all mischance.
>
> (III, iii, 16–18)

The *Henry VI–Richard III* tetralogy is deeply saturated with the imagery of the triumph of Fortune, and it is far from accidental that the many references to Fortune in these plays go hand in hand with allusions to pageants and triumphs. In *2 Henry VI*, referring to the downfall of his ambitious wife, the Duke of Gloucester recalls how Fortune had smiled upon her in former days; his description makes deft use of two features of the iconographic representations of the *Trionfi*, the throngs and the symbolic chariot:

> Sweet Nell, ill can thy noble mind abrook
> The abject people gazing on thy face,
> With envious looks laughing at thy shame,
> That erst did follow thy proud chariot-wheels
> When thou didst ride in triumph through the streets.
>
> (II, iv, 10–14)

Earlier in the play the Duchess herself, describing her own role in history and the risks she might run at the hands of Fortune, conceives of herself as a participant in the triumph of Fortune:

Were I a man, a duke, and next of blood,
I would remove these tedious stumbling blocks
And smooth my way upon their headless necks;
And, being a woman, I will not be slack
To play my part in Fortune's pageant.

(I, ii, 63–67)

Another instance of the way in which Shakespeare uses the imagery of the triumphal pageant to express the *de casibus* theme is found in *3 Henry VI*: when the Duke of York is captured and humiliated by Margaret, the Lancastrian queen, he lashes out at her, describing her as a bestial creature that thrives on the unhappiness of those who have been cast down by Fortune:

She-wolf of France, but worse than wolves of France,
Whose tongue more poisons than the adder's tooth!
How ill-beseeming is it in thy sex
To triumph like an Amazonian trull,
Upon their woes whom fortune captivates!

(I, iv, 111–115)

But Fortune's wheel comes full turn when Margaret herself becomes another of her victims in the closing play of the tetralogy, *Richard III*; in bewailing her misfortunes at the hands of the goddess Fortuna, she appropriately resorts to the imagery of the triumphal pageant:

I call'd thee then vain flourish of my fortune;
I call'd thee then poor shadow, painted queen;
The presentation of but what I was;
The flattering index of a direful pageant;
One heav'd a-high, to be hurl'd down below.

(IV, iv, 82–86)

Marked as the imagery of triumphal pageantry is in these plays, the themes of the Petrarchan trionfi do not appear in any direct manner in either Shakespeare's narrative poems or in his sonnets, though the question of the alleged Petrarchan origins of these poems has generated a good deal of discussion, most of it unwarranted. Fairchild and others[12] suggested that Shakespeare derived the story of *The Rape of Lucrece* from tapestries of the triumph of Chastity designed by either Giulio Romano or Francesco Salviati. The popularity of these tapestries was very great, and, as we know from a cryptic reference to Giulio Romano (the designer of Hermione's statue in *The Winter's Tale*, V, ii, 105), Shakespeare either knew the artist's work or was familiar with his reputation. It is therefore possible that he had seen Romano's or some other artist's representations of Lucrece. Moreover, many of the sixteenth-century tapestries of the *Trionfi*, including those now at Hampton Court Palace and at the Victoria and Albert Museum, depicted Lucrece as one of the most important figures accompanying Chastity. But despite the popularity of these representations of the story of Lucrece, the principal sources of the tale were literary, and in fact sixteenth-century readers were familiar with it through Livy's *History of Rome* and Ovid's *Fasti* and, to a lesser extent, through Painter's *Palace of Pleasure* and Chaucer's *Legend of Good Women*. If Petrarch's "Triumph of Chastity" played any part in the many Renaissance poems containing the story of Lucrece, it was probably that of reinforcing a theme that had already gained currency through literary renditions.

Notable, and ingenious too, have been the attempts to establish Petrarchan origins for Shakespeare's treatment of the idea that Time triumphs over all human endeavors and is defeated only by procreation and artistic creation. The theme is of course almost an obsessive one with Shakespeare, appearing as it does sporadically in the plays and in more concentrated fashion in the sonnets and in the long digression on Time in *The Rape of Lucrece*.[13] Petrarch's "Trionfo del Tempo" merely reinforced a theme that had become a commonplace of medieval and Renaissance literature and iconography.[14] In the last analysis, the figure of Time as destroyer, revealer, nurse, breeder of all good and evil, and companion of Fortune and Occasion derives not from Petrarch but from the Greek figures of Kairos (Opportunity) and Kronos (Time). Certainly only one of Shakespeare's sonnets contains any imagery resembling the sharply-drawn triumph imagery in the dramas: Sonnet 77 contains one tantalizingly slim reference to "Time's thievish progress to eternity," but beyond this nothing links the sonnets on time to either the *Trionfi* or to the iconographic representations and pageants. It was clearly not to the *Trionfi* that Shakespeare turned when he sought another poetic treatment of time but to "the sweet witty soul of Ovid," to the *Metamorphoses* and the *Fasti*, and it was in these works that he found ample precedent for the idea that time is the great devourer.

The origins of the Petrarchan elements in Spenser's poetry are particularly difficult to trace, because by Spenser's time Petrarchan themes and diction, derived principally from the *Canzoniere* rather than from the *Trionfi*, had become so conventionalized that it is virtually impossible to distinguish direct imitation of Petrarch from the infusion of the Petrarchan mode of feeling into his poetry by way of the Pléiade or by way of Ariosto, who were themselves to a limited extent Petrarchan in spirit and outlook. Thus the *Complaints* volume (1591) derived its Petrarchism chiefly from Du Bellay, and the *Amoretti* (1595) show the influence of the Pléiade and of Ariosto and Tasso. The *Complaints* volume also indicates the extent to which Petrarchism and the *Canzoniere* were probably synonymous to Spenser. Compiled by Ponsonby, who was perhaps attempting to capitalize on the interest in Spenser's poetry generated by the appearance of the first installment of *The Faerie Queene*, the volume was made up largely of translations of the work of French Petrarchists, although two of Spenser's most original poems, "Mother Huberd's Tale" and "Muiopotmos," were included. "The Ruines of Time" and "The Ruines of Rome" were modeled on Du Bellay's *Antiquitez de Rome*, a series of Petrarchan sonnets; and the two short collections of sonnets entitled "The Visions of Bellay" and "The Visions of Petrarch" were translated respectively from Du Bellay's *Songe* (which was appended to the *Antiquitez de Rome*) and from Marot's translation of Petrarch's canzone "Standomi un giorno," which had become the source of much of the emblematic poetry of the Renaissance.[15] Because both Du Bellay's and Marot's poems were translations from the *Canzoniere* and not from the *Trionfi*, it seems clear that the *Trionfi* did not enter Spenser's minor poetry by way of the French Petrarchists.

In *The Faerie Queene*, however, Spenser exhibits a conception of the triumph that is practically identical with those of Sidney and Shakespeare In this poem the word "triumph" is used several times to describe either a victory or a procession,[16] and there are other instances in which the word is used to describe a formal, grandly conceived pageant or procession. The marriage of the Medway and the Thames in Book IV is conceived of as a triumphal procession led by Neptune and his wife Amphitrate. The pageant is heralded by Triton, who sounds his trumpet "For goodly triumph and for great iollyment," and though the word "triumph" appears here, as it does in the triumph of Adicia over Prince Arthur in the following book (V, viii, 51), both episodes lack the traditional paraphernalia of the Petrarchan triumph.

But *The Faerie Queene* does contain three fully-developed triumphal pageants that give every indication of having been modeled either upon actual processions or upon artistic renderings of the *Trionfi*. In Book I there is a triumphal procession of the Seven Deadly Sins from the House of Pride (I, iv, 16–37). Lucifera calls for her "coche," a splendid triumphal chariot "Adorned all with gold, and girlonds gay, / That seemed as fresh as Flora in her prime, / And stroue to match, in royall rich array, / Great Iunoes golden chaire"; and the chariot leaves the House of Pride, drawn by six symbolic beasts on which are mounted personifications of the other six deadly sins. Idleness rides an ass, Gluttony a swine, Lechery a goat, Avarice a camel, Envy a wolf, and Wrath a lion. Atop the chariot, accompanying Lucifera and Duessa, rides Satan, whipping the entire team. In its details, the passage is extremely reminiscent of the illustrations which accompanied fifteenth- and sixteenth-century editions of the *Trionfi*:

> Huge routs of people did about them band,
> Showting for ioy, and still before their way
> A foggy mist had couered all the land;
> And vnderneath their feet, all scattered lay
> Dead sculs and bones of men, whose life had gone astray.
>
> (I, iv, 36, 5–9)

The Masque of Cupid which brings Book III to a close was also evidently conceived as a triumphal procession, one which celebrates the seeming invincibility of Cupid. There are few similarities of detail between the Petrarchan trionfo and the Spenserian masque, yet the themes of both, the triumph of Love and its attendant personifications of Ease, Fancy, and Desire, are virtually identical. Spenser may indeed have had the Petrarchan trionfo in mind, but he no doubt drew from other sources as well, from Ovid's *Amores*[17] and possibly from his own earlier *Court of Cupid*; and, as so often happens in Spenser's poetry, what emerges is derivative and highly individual at the same time. This originality arising out of eclecticism is also seen in his description of a series of tapestries adorning the House of Busirane (III, xi, 28–35). Here the similarity to the Petrarchan theme of Love the Conqueror is even stronger than in the details of the Masque of Cupid, yet some important details of the *Trionfi*, the triumphal chariot and the allegorical beasts, are missing. There are other analogues: the passage is also vaguely reminiscent of Ariosto's description of the tapestries Bradamante sees in the Rocca di Tristano;[18] and there are deep affinities with the illustrations of the "Triumph of Love," for images of war, conflict, defeat, and triumph predominate. But however much the passage may be indebted to Petrarch, Ariosto, or the illustrators of the *Trionfi*, the result is uniquely Spenserian:

And in those Tapets weren fashioned
    Many faire pourtraicts, and many a faire feate,
    And all of loue, and all of lusty-hed,
    As seemed by their semblaunt did entreat;
    And eke all *Cupids* warres they did repeate,
    And cruell battels, which he whilome fought
    Gainst all the Gods, to make his empire great;
    Besides the huge massacres, which he wrought
On mighty kings and kesars, into thraldome brought.

                          (III, xi, 29)

    The Procession of the Seasons at the conclusion of the Mutability Cantos is as complex in its literary and iconographic origins as are the triumphal pageants: two of Spenser's sources, Ovid's *Fasti*[19] and his *Metamorphoses*,[20] were also powerful influences on Petrarch's conception of Time; and the Procession of the Seasons or the Zodiac was an important element in Renaissance iconology in general[21] as well as in representations of the triumph of Time. The tapestry of the triumph of Time at Hampton Court Palace, for example, contains precisely such a procession of the seasons (Fig. 9). All that can be said with certainty is that the theme of the power of Time over human life was a recurrent one in Spenser's poetry, as it was in the writings of Petrarch, and that Spenser shares common ideas on the subject with sixteenth-century illustrators of the *Trionfi*.

In sum, Renaissance poets often took up themes from the *Trionfi*, themes that were in effect among the most prominent in the history of European ideas, without awareness that these themes were particularly "Petrarchan" or that the forms in which those themes were conveyed, the pageant and procession, were Petrarchan as well. The Renaissance poet's mind was omnivorous and he took his content and form from whatever quarter he could find it, caring far less for "sources" than we do; we can therefore safely assume that, with very few exceptions, the authors of Elizabethan literary triumphs had little idea how much they owed to Petrarch.

The Triumph: Late Renaissance and After

By the late sixteenth century, then, the triumphal pageant had become so popular that its Petrarchan origins were thoroughly obscured. Still, some late Renaissance and post-Renaissance works do reflect a substantial thematic or formal connection with the *Trionfi*. The plague pamphleteers and religious poets of the late sixteenth and early seventeenth century often used the Petrarchan metaphors of the triumph of Death or the triumph of Eternity in their triumphal pageants. Nashe, for example, introduces the triumphant figure of Death in *Christ's Tears Over Jerusalem* (1594)[1] to exhort his contemporaries to the moral life, and John Davies of Hereford presents a personification of Despair that "like a Conqueror in Triumph rides" in his *Triumph of Death* (1609),[2] though in both cases it would be inaccurate to describe Petrarch's "Trionfo della Morte" as a model. Similarly, two of the four books of Giles Fletcher the Younger's *Christ's Victory in Heaven* (1610)[3] bear titles—"Christ's Triumph over Death" and "Christ's Triumph after Death"—that suggest a connection with the Petrarchan *Trionfi*; but though they take up the matter of redemption and salvation through Christ and are therefore closely tied thematically to Petrarch's triumphs of Death, Time, and Eternity, the author's choice of Petrarchan subtitles seems to be wholly fortuitous. Moreover, it is quite impossible to distinguish which part of Fletcher's description of the ascent from the carnal to the eternal comes from traditional Christian theology and which part comes from the treatment of the same theme in the *Trionfi*.

Another interesting use of the triumphal pageant is found in Thomas Dekker's *Seven Deadly Sins of London* (1606).[4] Dekker depicts each of the Seven Deadly Sins as a triumphant personification "Drawen in Severall Coaches"; the personifications, "Politike Bankeruptisme," "Lying," "Slothe," "Apishness," "Shaving," and "Crueltie," have of course no direct relation to the *Trionfi*, but their use underlines the facility with which devices borrowed from the iconology of the *Trionfi* could be used to represent non-Petrarchan subject matter.

The impact of the iconographic devices of the *Trionfi* on seventeenth-century literature is best seen in the court masque, and chief among these is Ben Jonson's magnificent *Masque of Queens* (1609), with sets designed by Inigo Jones. The masque opens with an antimasque, consisting of a dance of twelve "Hagges," intended no doubt to accentuate the beauty of the twelve queens who are to occupy the House of Fame at the conclusion of the masque.[5] After the twelve hideous creatures have performed their dance, we are introduced to the figure of *Fama bona:*

Here, the Throne wherein they sate, being *Machina versatilis*, sodaynely chang'd; and in the Place of it appeard *Fama bona*, as she is describ'd in Iconolog. di Cesare Ripa attir'd in white, wth white Wings, hauing a collar of Gold, about her neck, and a heart hanging at it ... In her right hand she bore a trumpet, in her left hand an oliue.[6]

Ripa, "the dean of these iconologists," as Panofsky terms him, had himself drawn heavily from the Renaissance representations of the *Trionfi* and was in turn also greatly responsible for continuing the tradition of such representations. *Fama bona* turns and speaks to Vertue to enlist her aid in presenting a triumph of Fame; that triumph contains all the details of the Petrarchan trionfo, derived from Cesare Ripa's *Iconologia*, from the triumphal pageant, and from the Renaissance representations of the *Trionfi*. *Fama bona* speaks:

In mine owne Chariots, let them crowned ride;
And mine owne Birds, & Beasts in geeres apply'd,
To draw them forth. Vnto the first *Carre*, tie
Farre sighted Eagles, to note Fames sharpe eye;

67

Vnto the second, Griffons, that designe
Swiftnesse, and strength, two other guifts of mine:
Vnto the last, Or Lions, that implie
The top of graces, *State*, and *Maiestie*.
And, let those *Hagges* be led, as captiues, bound
Before theyr wheeles, whilst I my trumpet sound.[7]

At this point the twelve queens enter, the last of whom is Queen Anna herself, and they proceed to the House of Fame. Some of the twelve—Camilla, Berenice, and Zenobia—are mentioned in the *Trionfi*, but it is unlikely that Jonson drew them from the poem, because he carefully noted all his sources in marginal comments and nowhere mentioned Petrarch. The twelve queens enter "three triumphant chariots," after which there is singing, dancing of galliards and corantos, and much "triumphing about the stage" before the participants return to the House of Fame.

Several other Jonsonian masques and entertainments are also based on Petrarchan themes. "Love Freed from Ignorance and Folly," for example, is a sort of triumph of Chastity which opens with the figure of Syphax "leading Love bound"; "Love Restored" has strong similarities to the "Trionfo d'Amore"; "Time Vindicated" is a variant of the "Trionfo del Tempo"; and "Love's Triumph through Callipolis" is a very obvious triumph of Love, though, like many of the other masques, it lacks chariots and the other paraphernalia of the Petrarchan triumph.

Jonson's fascination with the triumphal pageant extended into his lyric poetry as well: one of his most famous lyrics, written to "Charis" and included in a posthumous collection entitled *Underwoods* (1640), is a perfect triumph of Love or Chastity that seems to draw its details and organization from the Renaissance representations of Petrarch's "Trionfo d'Amore":

HER TRIUMPH

See the Chariot at hand here of Love,
　　Wherein my Lady rideth!
Each that drawes, is a Swan, or a Dove,
　　And well the Carre Love guideth.
As she goes, all hearts doe duty

Unto her beauty;
And enamour'd doe wish, so they might
  But enjoy such a sight,
That they still were to run by her side,
  Through Swords, through Seas, whether she would ride.
Doe but looke on her eyes, they do light
  All that Loves world compriseth!
Doe but looke on her Haire, it is bright
  As Loves starre when it riseth!
Doe but marke her forehead's smoother
  Then words that sooth her!
And from her arched browes such a grace
  Sheds it selfe through the face,
As alone there triumphs to the life
All the Gaine, all the Good of the Elements' strife.

Have you seene but a bright Lillie grow,
  Before rude hands have touch'd it?
Have you mark'd but the fall o' the Snow
  Before the Soyle hath smutch'd it?
Have you felt the wooll o' the Bever?
  Or Swan's Downe ever?
Or have smelt o' the bud o' the Brier?
  Or the Nard i' the fire?
Or have tasted the bag o' the Bee?
O so white! O so soft! O so sweet is she.[8]

Even those poets whose knowledge of Italian literature was extensive tended to draw triumphal imagery and triumphal scenes from the iconographers and from pageants and masques rather than from Petrarch proper. Milton, for example, was surely thoroughly familiar with Petrarch's Italian poetry, as we know from his great interest in the Petrarchan sonnet, which he wrote with ease in both Italian and English; still, when he spoke of triumphs or described them in his own poetry, he clearly thought of them as forms of processions, as "solemne pompes." It is in precisely this sense that he used the word in *L'Allegro*: "Where throngs of Knights and Barons bold, / In weeds of Peace high triumphs hold";[9] and again in *Paradise Lost*: ". . . he oft / Frequented thir Assemblies, whereso met, / Triumphs or Festivals."[10] Milton was also fully conscious of the popularity of the masque, and in presenting Sabrina riding in a triumphal chariot in Comus, he was relying heavily on the traditional central theme of the court masque—the triumph of Virtue over Vice—and the traditional devices and machinery of the masque rather than on Petrarch's *Trionfi*. Similarly, the magnificent Chariot of Paternal Deity in which Christ triumphs in Book VI of *Paradise Lost* is derived principally from Ezekiel (1:4–28), though that passage and the concluding triumphal procession of Christ must have derived at least in part from the complex and rich history of graphic representations of the *Trionfi*:

> Disburd'n'd Heav'n rejoic'd, and soon repair'd
> Her mural breach, returning whence it roll'd.
> Sole Victor from th' expulsion of his Foes
> *Messiah* his triumphal Chariot turn'd:
> To meet him all his Saints, who silent stood
> Eye-witnesses of the Almighty Acts,
> With Jubilee advanc'd; and as they went,
> Shaded with branching Palm, each order bright,
> Sung Triumph, and him sung Victorious King,
> Son, Heir, and Lord, to him Dominion giv'n,
> Worthiest to Reign: he celebrated rode
> Triumphant through mid Heav'n, into the Courts
> And Temple of his mighty Father Thron'd
> On high; who into Glory him receiv'd,
> Where now he sits at the right hand of bliss.[11]

It was not until the Romantic revival of interest in medieval literature that the *Trionfi* itself received attention once more from Italian as well as from English readers, and it is fitting that it should have provided the framework and inspiration for the last work of the most Italianate of all the English Romantic poets. Shelley's *Triumph of Life* (1821) was written in imitation of Petrarch's *Trionfi*, and Shelley apparently understood fully the mood of the original, as well as its rhetorical and stylistic devices.[12] His poem opens with a vision in which there appears a chariot bearing a personification of Life, "the just similitude / Of a triumphal pageant"; as in the Petrarchan "Trionfo d'Amore" and the scores of Renaissance illustrations of the poem, the chariot is surrounded by a captive multitude of famous men— Rousseau, Napoleon, Voltaire, Plato, Bacon, Caesar, other Roman emperors, and some of the church fathers—now all fallen victims to Life and her triumphant chariot. In the obscure final section, the narrator, Rousseau, tells of awakening from a sleep of death, and the poem closes with the poet asking the narrator to define Life. Shelley never lived to finish the poem, but even in its incomplete state it is the last successful attempt on the part of a major English poet to use the form and conventions of Petrarch's *Trionfi*.

Editorial Procedure

I have examined all five existing copies of Morley's *Tryumphes:* the originals of the two British Museum copies, the Bodleian copy, the Sion College Library copy, and a microfilm of the copy in the Henry E. Huntington Library (see Bibliographical History of Morley's *Tryumphes*). All five copies of the work are identical, and the choice of a copy text was therefore completely arbitrary; I have used the Huntington Library copy. To make the text legible, I have applied the following principles:

Accidentals. Sixteenth-century typographical conventions have been ignored: the modern usage of u/v and j/i has been followed; ligatures, catchwords, signatures, variations in kind and size of type, ornamental devices, and woodcuts have all been ignored. Contractions such as ẏ or ꝥ for *the*, *that*, and *it* have all been silently expanded, as have the ampersand and the tilde. Obvious printer's errors such as turned letters and the use of lower case in the initial letter of a first word of a line of verse have all been silently corrected.

Punctuation. With the exception of the dedicatory epistle, which is logically and adequately punctuated, Morley's punctuation is extremely sparse. I have therefore provided the rest of the translation with modern punctuation. However, Morley's syntax and sentences do not always yield to modern rules of punctuation, and in those cases where special difficulties arose I was guided by what I believed to be the sense of the passage rather than by arbitrary rules.

Introduction

Capitalization and Orthography. The capitalization of the copy text has been retained, even when it does not conform to modern practice. In the many cases where the copy text does not capitalize proper names or personifications, I have capitalized and recorded the fact. The spelling is also that of the copy text, including the sixteenth-century use of *c* for *t* in medial position. In the three cases where I have departed from this practice (*Pistoia, Vesta,* and *Acys* for *Piscoia, Vesca,* and *Atys*), the departure has been dictated by etymology or by the need for clarity. In all these cases I have recorded the changes under the heading "Changes in Capitalization and Orthography" at the end of the appropriate section of notes.

The archaic spelling of names has been retained on the assumption that in most cases they will be recognizable to readers of this edition. Where the form of a name is so unusual that it may present some difficulty to the reader (for example, *Gueynor* for *Guinivere*), I have retained Morley's spelling in the text and provided the modern spelling in the notes. In the few cases where an unusual spelling is the result of a printer's error (for example, *Lucides* for *Thucydides* and *Thenostoctes* for *Themistocles*), I have attempted to provide a spelling as close as possible to sixteenth-century usage.

Emendations. Obvious errors in grammar, consistency of pronouns, and the like have been corrected and recorded, but there are numerous cases where particular constructions are ungrammatical by modern standards but may well have been acceptable usage in the sixteenth century. In such cases I have let Morley's usage stand, and the reader is invited to judge for himself whether the construction is a genuine error or accepted usage by sixteenth-century standards.

Explanatory Notes. Another aim of the present edition is to illustrate as concretely as possible how a sixteenth-century translator worked. The art of translation was in large measure viewed as a patriotic endeavor, an attempt to bring to England the best that had been thought and written in foreign vernaculars. Thus Morley, referring to a French translation of the *Trionfi*, remarked that "I beynge an Englysshe man, myght do as well as the Frenche man, dyd translate this sayde worke into our maternall tounge." But Petrarch's *Trionfi* is a difficult poem by any standards. Its language is stilted and arch, its syntax tortuous and Latinate and, to a certain extent, precious; its self-conscious erudition would exasperate the most thorough and learned of scholars. It is no accident, then, that so few sixteenth-century translators would hazard themselves on its rocky crags. It is therefore to Morley's great credit that he took on so difficult a task, and no doubt his audience, while fully aware of the flaws of his translation, was thankful to have the *Trionfi* in a more or less readable version. Accuracy and fidelity to the original seemed to be of secondary importance, provided the translator transmitted the spirit of the original. Morley himself insisted that he had not "erred moche from the letter," but his translation is fraught with periphrases and expansions intended to round out a rhyme or cover his failure to grasp the meaning of the original, and he expanded 1,953 lines of the original to 2,750. I have therefore considered it useful to compare Morley's version with the original and to record all those instances in which he misunderstood the original or rendered it inaccurately. The following terms are used in the notes to describe Morley's treatment of the original:

Expansion: denotes that Morley understood the original and that he amplified its meaning.

Blurring: describes those instances in which a word, phrase, or nuance of the original eluded Morley, though he still grasped the overall sense of the passage.

Misreading: notes those instances which are outright misunderstandings of the Italian.

For: indicates Morley's practice of substituting phrases of his own invention when he did not understand Petrarch's Italian.

Added by Morley: This phrase is used extensively in the notes. A line number followed by the phrase, for example:

24. Added by Morley.

signifies that the entire line is Morley's addition. A note in this form:

159. that . . . by. Added by Morley.

indicates that the phrase was added by Morley and that the remainder of the line faithfully renders some portion of the original.

Where Morley's translation is so hazy or so inaccurate that the reader may be confused, I have provided either my own or Professor Wilkins's translation to assist him.

Names, places, and events which occur in the text have been explained briefly in the notes with a view to rendering Morley's text more comprehensible, but the notes are not intended to provide an exhaustive commentary on the poem. For an excellent commentary on the original poem, the reader is referred to Carlo Calcaterra's splendid edition of the *Trionfi*. All the passages from the *Trionfi* cited in my notes are drawn from this edition.

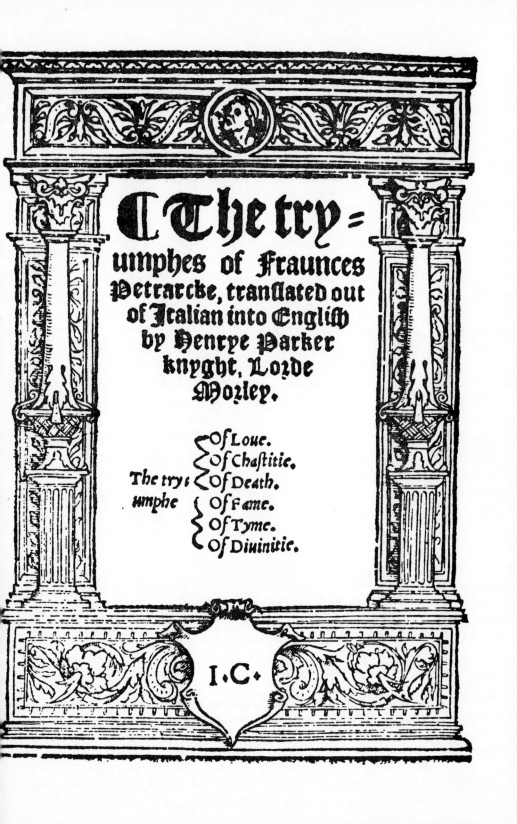

❡ The try=
umphes of Fraunces
Petrarcke, translated out
of Italian into English
by Henrye Parker
knyght, Lorde
Morley.

The try=
umphe
{
Of Loue.
Of Chastitie.
Of Death.
Of Fame.
Of Tyme.
Of Diuinitie.
}

I·C·

The title page of Lord Morley's *Tryumphes of Fraunces Petrarcke* on page 75 is courtesy of the Trustees of the British Museum. British Museum C.13.a.7(2)

[The Epistle]

Unto the mooste towarde yonge gentle Lorde Matravers, sonne and heyre apparaunt to the worthy and noble Earle of Arundel, your poore frende Henry Parker knyght, Lorde Morley, prayeth to God that the vertue whiche doth floryshe in you in this youre tender age, maye more and more increase in you, to the comfort of all that love you, unto the laste age.

The fables of Isope (mooste towarde younge Lorde) are not only had in commendation amonge the Philosophers, as with Plato, Aristotle, and diverse other of the moste excellent of them: but also the devines, when in theyr preachynges there cometh to theyr purpose any matter, to rehearse to the rude people, they alledge the allegorye sence of them, to the muche edificacion of the hearers. I saye therfore, that amonge other his wyttye fables (not to you noble gentleman unknowen) he telleth, how that the cocke scrapynge on a doungehill, found a precious stone, and when he sawe it, disdayninge, he spurned it from hym, sayinge, what have I to do with the, thou canste not serve me to no kynde of use, and so dispysynge it, left it where as it laye on the dongehyll styll. Even so there be a number of that sorte, that percase when they shall eyther heare redde, or them selfe reade this excellent tryumphes, of this famous clercke Petrarcha, shall lytle set by them, and peradventure caste it from them, desyrynge rather to have a tale prynted of Robyn Hoode, or some other dongehyll matter then of this, whiche I dare affirme, yea, and the Italians do the same, that the devine workes set aparte, there was never in any vulgar speche or language, so notable a worke, so clerckely done as this his worke. And albeit that he setteth forth these syxte wonderfull made triumphes all to the laude of hys Ladye Laura, by whome he made so many a swete sonnet, that never yet no poete nor gentleman could amend, nor make the lyke, yet who that doth understande them, shall se in them comprehended al morall vertue, all Phylosophye, all storyall matters, and briefely manye devyne sentences theologicall secretes declared. But alas who is he that will so reade them, that he wyl marke them, or what prynter wyll not saye, that he may winne more gayne in pryntynge of a merye jeste, then suche lyke excellente workes, suerlye (my good Lorde) very fewe or none, whyche I do lamente at my harte, consyderynge that aswell in French, as in the Italyan (in the whyche both tongues I have some lytle knowledge) there is no excellente worke in the latyn, but that strayght wayes they set it forth in the vulgar, moost commonly to their kynges and noble prynces of theyr region and Countreys: As one of late dayes that was grome of the chaumber with that renowmed and valyaunte Prynce of hyghe memorye, Fraunces the Frenche kynge, whose name I have forgotten, that dydde translate these tryumphes to that sayde kynge, whyche he toke so thankefully, that he gave to hym for hys paynes an hundred crounes, to hym and to his heyres of inheritaunce to enjoye to that value in lande for ever, and toke suche pleasure in it, that wheresoever he wente amonge hys precyous Jewelles, that booke was alwayes caryed with hym for his pastyme to loke upon, and as muche estemed by hym, as the rychest Diamonde he hadde: whiche sayde booke, when I sawe the coppye of it, I thoughte in my mynde, howe I beynge an Englyshe man, myght do aswell as the Frenche man, dyd translate this sayde worke into our maternall tounge, and after much debatyng with my selfe, dyd as your Lordshyppe doth se, translate the sayde booke to that moost worthy kynge our late soveraygne Lorde of perpetuall memorye kynge Henrye theyghte, who as he was a Prynce above all other mooste excellente, so toke he the worke verye thankefullye, merveylynge muche howe I coulde do it, and thynkynge verelye I hadde not doone it, wythoute helpe of some other, better knowynge the Italyan tounge then I: but when he knewe the verye treweth, that I hadde traunslated the worke my selfe, he was more pleased therewith then he was before, and so what his highnes dyd with it, is to me unknowen, one thynge is, that I dyd it in suche hast, that doubtles in many places (yf it were agayne in my handes) I thynke I coulde well amende it, albeit that I professe, I have not erred moche from the letter, but in the ryme, whiche is not possible for me to folow in the translation, nor touche the least poynt of the elegancy that this elegant Poete hath set forth in his owne maternall tongue. But as it is, if in the translation there be anye thynge to be amended, or any wyll deprave it, I shall, praye you (mooste noble younge Lorde) the very myrroure of al the younge noble gentelmen of this realme in vertue, in learnynge, and in all other feates appertayning to such a Lorde as you be, to defende it agaynst those that will more by envy then by knowledge deprave it, and then I do not feare but those that knowe and can speake the Italian, will beare with the simple translation, and commende the worke, as it is so muche commendable, that it can not be to dere bought, I desyre God noble yonge gentleman, to make the lorde Matravers an olde gentleman, and then thy worthy father the Earle of Arundell my most speciall good Lorde and frend, shall make an olde Earle and lyve *usque in senium et senectum.*

Dixi   Henry Morelye

The First Chapter of the
Tryumphe of Love

In the tyme of the Renewinge of my suspyres,
By the swete remembraunce of my lovely desyres
That was the begynnynge of soo longe a payne,
The fayre Phebus the Bull dyd attayne
And warmyd had the tone and tother horne
Wherby the colde wynter stormes were worne
And Tytans chylde with her frostye face
Ran from the heate to her aunciente place.
Love, grefe, and complaynt oute of reason
Had brought me in such a case that season
That myne eyes closed, and I fell to reste,
The very Remedye to such as be oppreste.
And there on the grene, as I reposed fast,
Sodenly me thought, as I myne eyes up cast,
I sawe afore me a marvelous great lighte
Wherin as well comprehend then, I myghte
Was doloure ynough wyth smale sporte and play.
And thus in my dreame musyng, as I laye
I sawe a great Duke victorious to beholde
Tryumphyng on a chayre, shynyng as golde,
Muche after the olde aunciente sage wyse
That the bolde Romayns used in there guyse
When to the Capytoll the vyctors were brought
With right riche Robes curiously were wrought.
I that such sightes was not wont to se
In this noyous worlde wherein I fynde me,
Voyde from the olde valure and yet more in pryde,
Sawe comming towardes me ther on every side
Dyverse men wyth straunge and queynte arraye
Not usyd amonge us at this present daye,
Which made me wonder what persons thei shuld be.
As one glad to learne, and some new thinges to se,
There sawe I a boye on a firye chayre on hyghte
Drawen with foure coursers all mylke whight

Wyth bowe in hande and arrowes sharpe and keene
Against whome no shylde nor helme so sheene
Myght in no wyse the mortale stroke wythstand
When he shote wyth his most dreadfull hande.
To this also (a straunge sight to se)
Two wynges upon his shoulders had he,
Wyth coloures more then I can wryte or tell
A thousande dyvers (this I noted well)
And all the rest were nakyd to the skynne.
Aboute the chayre where that this boye was in
Some laye there deade gapynge on the grounde;
Some with his dartes had taken meny a wound;
Some were prysoners and could not scape away,
But folowed styll the chayre nyght and day.
I that sawe this wonderfull straunge sight,
To know what it mente, dyd that I myght
Tyll at the last I dyd perceave and se
My selfe to be amonge that company.
So had love led me on that dawnce
That as it lyked her, so must I take the chawnce.
I then among that great number in that place,
Lokyng here and there in eche mannes face
Yf any of myne Acquayntaunce I coulde se,
But none was there except perchaunce that he
By age or death or payne was chaunged quyte
As that I never had hym knowen by syght
Wyth folowing that great kyng in that houre
That is the grounde and cause of all dolowre.
Thus all astonied as I loked here and there,
All sodenly afore me then dyd there appeare
A shadowe much more sadde for to regarde
Than all the reste that I had sene or harde.
This sayd shadowe called me by name
And sayd: "By love is gotten all this fame."
Whereat I marveyled and sayde to hym agayne:
"How knowest thou me, to learne I wold be faine,
For who thou arte I doo not knowe at all.
So wonderous derke is here this ayre and all

The Tryumphe of Love, I: 73–110

That I can nether perceave nor yet well se
What man thou art nor whence that thou should be."
To that anone this shadowe to me sayde:
"I am thy frende; thou nedest not be dismayde,
And borne in Toscane where thou was borne, perdye—
Thyne auncient frende, if that thou lyst to se."
His wordes, whiche that I knewe by dayes paste
By his speche, I knewe hym at the last
All though his face I coulde not then well se.
And thus in talkyng together went we,
And he beganne and thus to me dyd saye:
"It is right longe and thereto many a day
That I have loked the my frynde to se
Amonge us here in this our companye,
For thy face was to me a token playne
That ones thou shouldest know loves payne."
To whome I made aunswere and sayde:
"These wordes by me they cannot be denayde,
But the sorowe, the daunger and the dreade
That lovers have at the ende for theyr meade
So put me in feare that I left all asyde
Leste that my servyce should be cleane denyde."
Thus sayd I, and when he well perceyved
Myne entention and my wordes conceyved
Smylynge he sayde: "What flame of fyre
Hath love kyndled in thy hartys desyre?"
I understode then lytle what he ment,
For his wordes unto my heade then went
As fyrme and fast sure set anone
As they had bene prynted in a marbell stone.
And thus, for the newe game that I begane,
I prayde hym tell me of verie gentlenes than
What people these were that afore me went.
He aunswered bryfely to myne intente
That I should knowe what they should be
And be shortly one of theyr companye,
And that it was my destany and lotte
That love shoulde tye for me such a knotte

That I shoulde fyrst chaunge my heade to graye
Or that I coulde unclose that knot away.
"But to fulfyll thy yonge desyre," sayth he,
"I shall declare what kynde of men they be.
And fyrst of the capteynes of them all
His maner playne declare the I shall.
This is he that love the worlde doth name—
Bytter (as thou shalt well conceyve the same)—
And much the more when the tyme shall be
That thou shalt be amonge this companie,
A meke chylde in his lustye yonge age
And in elde one all full of rage.
Well knoweth he that thys hath provyd.
When thou by hym art heaved and shoved,
Thy selfe shall well see and understand
What a maister thou hast then in hande.
This god hath his fyrst byrth of ydelnes,
Noryshed with mankyndes foly and wantones
And of vayne thoughtes plesaunt and swete.
To a sage wyse man nothynge mete,
Callyd a god of the people most vayne,
All be it he geveth for theyr rewarde and payne
Some the death forthwyth out of hande,
Some a longe tyme in miserye to stand
To love (I say) them that loves not hym,
Fast tyed and fetred both cheke and chynne.
Nowe have I declared to the this goddes feste.
Nowe wyl I tell the in order of the reste.
Hym that thou seest that so lordely doth go
And leadeth wyth hym his love also,
It is the valeaunte Cesar, Julius.
Wyth hym is quene Cleopatra the beutiouse;
She tryumphes of hym, and that is good ryghte
That he that overcame the worlde by myght
Should hymselfe over commen be
By his love, even as thou mayest se.
The next unto hym is his sonne deare,
The great Augustus that never had peare,

That lovyde more justly then Cesar playne,
By request hys Lyvyahe dyd obtayne.
The thyrde is the dyspytefull tyraunte Nero
That furyously, as thou seest, doth go.
And yet a woman hym overcame
Wyth her regardes. Lo, she made hym tame!
Beholde the same is the good Marcus,
Worthy to have prayse for his lyfe vertuouse;
Full of phylosophy both the tounge and breste,
Yet for Fausteyn he standeth at arreste.
The tother two that stand hym by
That loke both twayne so fearefullye,
The tone is Denyse, the tother Alexander
That well was rewarded for his sclaunder.
The tother was he that soore complayned
Under Antander wyth teares unfayned
The death of Creusa and toke awaye
The love from hym (as the poete doth saye)
That toke from Evander his sone deare;
Among the rest thou mayest se hym here.
Hast thou harde ever reason heretofore
Of one that never would consent more
To hys stepmothers foull and shamefull desires,
But flye from her syght and her attyres?
But (wo, alas) that same chast honest mynde
Was his death, as thou mayst playnely fynde,
Because she chaunged hyr love unto hate.
Phedra she hyght that caused the debate,
And yet was it hyr owne Death also,
A sore punyshment unto both them two,
To the sens that deceyved Adryan.
Wherefore it is full often founde than
That one that blameth another (parde)
He hym selfe is more to blame then he,
And who so he be (wythouten any doubte)
That by fraude or crafte doth go aboute
Another that trusteth hym for to beguyle,
Yt is good reason that wyth that selfe wyle

He be servyd wyth that same sawse.
Lo, what it is a lover to be false!
This is he, the famouse worthy knyght
That betwyxt two systers standeth upryghte.
The tone by hym was cruelly slayne;
The tother his love in joye dyd remayne.
He that goeth with hym in the route
It is Hercules the stronge, fierce and stoute
That love caused to folowe hyr daunce;
The tother, whiche in lovynge had hard chaunce,
It is Achylles the Greke so bolde
That for Polexemes love dyed, as it is tolde.
There mayst thou see also Demophone
And Phylys, hys love, that sore dyd mone
Hys absence, wherby that she dyed.
Lo, those that stande upon the tother syde
Is Jason and Medea, that for his love
Deceaved hyr father his trueth to prove.
The more ungentle is Jason in dede
That gave hyr suche rewarde for hyr mede.
Hysyphyle foloweth, and she doth wayle also,
For the barbarouse love was taken hyr fro.
Next in ordre there commeth by and by
He that hath the name moost excellently
Of bewtye, and with hym commeth she
That oversone behelde his beutye,
Wherby ensued innumerable of harmes
Thoroughe out the world by Mars charmes.
Beholde, I praye the, among the companye
Enone complaynynge full heavely
For Parys that dyd hyr falsly betraye
And toke in hyr stede fayre Helen awaye.
Se also Menelaus the Grekysse kynge,
For his wyfe Helene in greate mournynge;
And Hermon the fayre Horestes for to call;
And Laodome, that standeth all apall,
Crye for hyr love, the good Protheossolaus;
And Argia the faythfull for Pollynisus.

The Tryumphe of Love, I: 225–250

Here, I pray the, the grevous lamentynges,
The syghes, the sorowes and the bewaylynges
Of the myserable lovers in this place
That are brought into so dolorous case
That there spyrytes they are about to rendre
Unto the false God that is so sclendre.
I can not nowe tell the all the names
That the false God of love thus tames,
Not onely men that borne be mortall,
But also the hyghe greate Goddes supernall
Are here in this greate and darke presse.
What shulde I any more nowe rehearse?
Se where Venus doth stande with Mars,
Whose heade and legges the yron doth enbrase;
And Pluto and Preserpyne on the other syde;
And Juno the jelyous (for all hyr pryde);
And Apollo with his gaye golden lockes,
That gave unto Venus scornes and mockes.
(Yet in Thessalia with this boyes fyrye darte
This great God was pearsed to the harte.)
And for conclusion, the Goddes and Goddesses al
Of whome Varro doth make rehearsall,
Beholde how afore loves chayre they goo,
Fast fettred and chayned from toppe to too,
And Jupiter hym selfe, the great myghty kynge,
Amonge the other, whiche is a marvelous thing.

The Second Chapter of
the Tryumphe of Love

All musynge wyth greate admiration,
As one astonnyed to see the fasshyon,
Nowe here, nowe there, I loked all aboute
To se the order of this greate huge route.
And as my harte from thought to thought past,
I sawe twayne together at a caste;
Hande in hand they went in the prease;
Reasonynge together they dyd not sease.
Theyr straunge habyts, and theyr araye,
And theyr language more straunge (I saye)
Was unto me so darke and obscure
That what they ment I knowe not (be ye sure)
Tyll my felowe by his interpretation
Of that whiche they talked made declaration.
And then when I knewe what they were,
Into theyr presence I drewe me nere
And perceaved that the one spirite was
Frende to the Romaynes that there dyd passe,
The tother contrary, a perpetuall foo.
I lefte hyr then and to the tother dyd goo
And sayde: "O, Masinissa, I the praye,
For Scypyons sake which thou dydst love alway,
And for Sophonysba that standeth the by,
That I am so bolde be thou not angrye
To demaunde the what thou doest here."
Masinissa aunswered with a sad chere:
"I do desyre to knowe what thou shulde be,
For it is (I tel the) a great wonder unto me
That thou doest spye my great affection
Whiche that I beare with suche dilection
To this my love and to my tother frende.
That desyre of me, and I wyll condescende
To all that thynge that thou wylt have me do."
I aunswered gently: "O hyghe prynce, not so!

My poore estate desyreth no suche mede.
A small lytle fyer farre of in dede
Bryngeth forth but a small lyght;
But thy royall fame, O noble kynght,
Is every where blowen and spredde.
This duke afore whome thou arte ledde,
(I praye the gently, kynge) expresse
Whether he doth lede you both in peace,
You and Sophonysba, for I suppose
That twayne suche lovers as together goese
In all the worlde were harde to fynde."
He aunswered and sayde: "Thy wordes are so kind
That although thou knowe hole the case
Of all my love howe grevous that it was,
Yet wyll I tell the, thy fancy to appease
And thy mynde to set at rest and ease;
That noble Duke that onlye had my harte
So true and sure and fast in every parte
That I in frendshyp with Lelius may compare,
Whersoever his worthy baner dyd fare,
There was I wyth that moste worthy knyght,
But not so fortunate as he deserved by ryght,
For full of goodnes and grace was he,
As well wyth soule as in the fayre bodye.
Nowe after the Romaynes by singler honoure
Had sprede theyr armes by myght and power
To the extreme partes of the occident,
Thither wyth this valeaunt Scipion I went.
There was I in love fyrst taken than
Wyth this Sophonisba, this swete woman,
And she with me in such a fervent guyse
That I affirme (and with so true advyse)
That never two lovers loved better,
Nor two true loving hartes nor sweter
Agreade in one—not yet never shall.
But the tyme of duryng (alas!) it was but small,
For sone vanished away our lovely chere
As I tell the, yf that thou wilt me here.

For albeit I toke her to my wyfe
And thought with her to have led my lyffe,
The bond was broken forthwith in twayne
By his holy wordes, that more myght certayne
Then all the worlde in such farvente case.
The knot he losed, and I my selfe gave place
And nowe wonder, for I in hym dyd see
So highe vertue in all kynde of degree
That, as I may say by good comparison,
He is all blynde that cannot see the sonne.
And albeit that justice was offence
To oure true love, yet his high prudence
And his deare frendshyppe dyd me compell
For to folowe his sage worthy councell.
In honour a very father was he,
And in love a chylde in yche degree;
A brother in yeres, which me constrayned
Wyth hevy harte, with sighes depe payned
Scipio to obeye, whereby my wyfe
Was constrayned for to lose her lyfe,
And that wyllingly rather than she
Into vyle servitude brought should be.
And I my selfe the mynister was—
To my great doloure—to execute this case.
So ardently she desired the death,
That I my selfe, as the trueth sayeth,
To her prayer dyd then condiscend,
To my great hevynes. This was the ende:
I sent her venyme for to drynke
Wyth such a sorowe (as thou mayest thynke,
Yf ever thou felte of loves woo and payne)
That it semeth my harte wolde brest in twayne.
She knoweth this, and so well knowe I;
Be thou the Judge, and thynk I do not lye.
Thus loste I my dere hope and luste
To kepe my fayth and not to be unjuste
Unto my Scipio. Nowe seke (yf thou may)
Yf thou canst se in all this great arraye,

The Tryumphe of Love, II: 111–148

Or ells perceave in all this lovers daunce,
So wonderfull and so straunge a chaunce."
Wyth these wordes that he declared to me,
Calling to minde (as I myght playnely se)
The hoote fyery love betwixt them twayne,
My harte even there so relentyde playne,
As doth the snowe agaynst the fervent sonne
When that his beames to sprede he hath begonne.
And this, as these twayne passed by,
I harde her say (and that right hastely):
"This felowe pleased me nothing at all.
I am determined (ye, and ever shall!)
To hate hym and all his nacion."
When that I harde her speake of this facion,
I sayd: "Sophonisba, I praye the, be in peace
For, bryfelye the truth to the to reherse,
Two times the Romaynes thy Cartage oppressed,
That as theyr subjectes to be they all confessed.
The thirde tyme they destroyde it cleane,
That nowe unneth thereof is nothyng sene."
Sophonisba answered to me agayne
With short wordes and in great disdaine:
"Yf Aufrike wept, Italie had no nede
For to make bost of theyr lucky spede.
Aske those that your hystoryes do wryte,
For they the trueth of both perties do endite."
Thus they went both together in fere
Among the great prease here and there,
Smiling and talkyng that I ne might
No more of them have after that a sight.
Then, as one that at adventure doth ride
To knowe the right way on every syde
Nowe standeth, nowe goeth, now hyeth a pase,
Even so my fancye at that time it was
Doubtefull and desyring to knowe by prove
Howe farvently these twayne dyd love,
Tyll at the last, as I cast myne eye
Upon the lyft hande, I sawe me by

One that had this straunge effecte—
To seme angry because he dyd abjecte
His wyffe, which he loved above all other,
By pytie to geve her to a nother
And rejoysed much so for to doo.
And all together as lovers they dyd goo,
Talkynge of this merveylouse case
And of Syrya, that countre where it was.
I drue me nere to these spirites thre
That were aboute, as farre as I can see,
To have gone from thense another way,
And to the first of them thus dyd I say:
"I pray you," sayde I, "a whyle for to abyde."
Anone the fyrste he dyd cast his heade asyde
When that he harde me speake Italyan,
And wyth a ryght angrye countenaunce than
He strode styll and streyght began to tell
That which I thought to be a great marvell:
"Thou desyrest, my frende, to knowe," sayeth he,
"What I am and what that I should be.
I am Seleucus, brifely to discus,
And this afore the is my sonne Antiocus,
Which had great warre with the Romaines nation;
But right agaynste fierce hath no dominion.
This woman that thou sest was fyrst my wyfe.
And after was his for to save hys lyfe.
It was then lefull for us so to doe.
Her name is Stratonica (she was called so),
And oure chaunce by love was thus devyded,
And under this facyon the matter was guyded.
My sonne was contented to release to my hande
His great kyngdome and all his large lande,
I unto hym my love and lady deare.
When that I sawe hym for to chaung his chere
And day by daye to drawe unto the death
So that unneth he myght not drawe his breath,
I marvayled muche what the cause shoulde be.
Secretely my wyfe for trueth loved he,

The Tryumphe of Love, II: 187–224

That not disclosinge his wofull payne
My dere sonne by love was well nere slayne
And had ben deade, but that the wyse phisician
Disclosed to me the very cause than
Of all his sycknes, whiche he kept close.
Surely this came of a vertuouse purpose
And of a wonderous fatherly pytie of me."
Sayinge these wordes, awaye went he
So that I coulde unneth bydde hym farewell.
And this was all that then he dyd me tell.
After that the shadowe thus was gone,
Syghynge and sadde, I made great mone
Because I myght not to hym disclose my hart.
But styll as I stode thus musynge aparte
I knowe that Zerzes, the great kynge of Perce
Whiche ledde an Army (as hystories reherce)
Of men innumerable, had never such a sort
As there was of lovers barrayne of comforte,
So that myne eyes coulde not well suffyse
To se theyr straunge fashyons and theyr guyse.
Varyable of tounges, and of so dyvers landes
That amonge a thousand one that there standes
I knewe not theyr person nor theyr name,
Nor yet in hystorye coulde descryve the same.
Parseus was one, and fayne I woulde desyre
Howe Andromeda dyd hyr selfe so attyre
That although she blacke were (pardie),
Borne in Ethiope, that whote countrie,
Yet her fayre eyne and her cryspe heare
This Parseus harte in love so dyd steare
That as his love the virgin dyd he take,
And never after dyd that mayde forsake.
There was also the folysh lover playne
That loved his owne pycter vayne,
That therby unwysely he was brought to death;
And after (as the hystorye playnly sayth)
He was converted by the divine power
Unto a fayre goodly pleasaunt flower,

Without for to brynge any frute at all.
And by hym emong these lovers thrall
Was she that was turned unto a stone
And now aloude doth aunswer every one
When she is called with voyce clere.
Next unto this Ecco that dyd appeare
Was Yphys, that had her selfe in hate,
Wyth other dyvers in a full pyteouse state—
Whiche were to longe theyr names for to reherse,
Eyther in prose, or elles in ryme or verse.
But yet of some I wyll declare and tell:
Of Alcione and Ceice that loved so well
That love them had so joyned for ever
That nothynge could make them to dissever—
Nowe clepyng, now kyssynge, as they dyd flye,
Serchynge the kyngedome of Esperye;
Now restynge together on a salte stone,
And by the Sea theyr nestes to make alone.
And I sawe also amonge that great route,
As here and there I loked me about,
The cruell doughter of kynge Nysus.
With flyght she fledde, which is marvelouse.
Atlanta was amonge them in the presse
With three gay golden apples doubtles
She was vanquyshed (yea, and overcome!)
By Hyppomone. Lo, this is all and some.
Glad he semed to have had the vyctory.
And amonge the other of this companye
I sawe Acys, and Galathea in his lappe;
And Poliphemon with greate noyse and clappe;
And Glauco shovynge amonge the sorte,
Crying for his love without comforte;
Canente and Pico, of Italy sometyme kynge,
Turne to a byrde, which was a mervelouse thing.
There sawe I also Egeria complayne
Because Syllayn was turned certayne
Into a greate harde rocke of stone
Whiche in the sea maketh many to mone.

The Tryumphe of Love, II: 263–274

Amonge the other that I have rehearsed
Was Canase, by hyr father oppressed.
In the tone hande a penne dyd she holde,
A sworde in the tother, with pale face and colde.
Pygmalion was there among the reste
With his wyfe alyf that he loved best.
And amonge these I harde a thousande synge
In Castallia where these Poetes brynge
These lovers with them—more then I reherse
In prose, in ryme, in metre, and in verse.
And at the last Cydippe dyd I see,
Scorned with an apple there was she.

The Thyrde Chapter of the Tryumphe of Love

So muche was my hearte a marveld of this syght,
That I stode styll as one that had no myght
To speake or looke but to holde hys peace
As desyreous to have some councell doubtles,
When that my frende gentylly to me sayde,
"Why doest thou muse? Why arte thou dismayde?
Shewe forth a better chere and porte
And se how that I am one of the sorte
That wyll I, nyll I, must folowe the rest."
"Brother," sayde I, "and thou knowest best
Myne entention, and the hote love I feale,
Whiche is so whote that it cannot keale,
So that suche busynes doth travayle my mynde
That what I wolde saye I leave behynde."
He aunswered and sayde: "I do heare it all,
And well understande by thy memoriall.
Thou wouldest knowe yet what these other be,
And I shall shewe thee yf thou wylte heare me.
Seest thou yondre great man of honoure?
That is Pompeus (so great of power!)
That hath with hym Cornelia the chaste,
Complaining of the vyle Tholome the unstedfast,
That betrayed so noble and worthy a man.
The tother is the great and myghtie Grecian
Alexander, the lorde of lordes all.
Egystus and Clytemistra, see where they stall,
And howe by them one may soone fynde
Love unconstant, waveryng, and blynde.
More faste love founde she that standeth by:
Ipermistra it is, that fayre swete ladye.
See also where Piramus doth goo,
And with hym Thisbe that he loved soo
That in the derke mette oft together;
Leander in the see and Ero at the fenester;

And hym that thou doest se so pensyfe and sadde
It is Ulixes that so chaste a wyfe hadde
That dyd longe abyde hys returne from Troy.
Nowe on Cyrces he hath all his joye.
And yonder man that thou doest adverte
That made all Ytaly sore for to smerte
It is Amilcars sonne in very deade
That made all the Romaynes to feare and dread.
And althoughe he made yche man to quake,
A vyle wench prysoner doth hym take.
And yonder woman with the short heare,
Loke howe she foloweth here and there
(All though she were quene of Ponto)
Her husbande whersoever he doth goo
As a servaunte and not as a wyfe.
She ledde wyth hym a full harde lyfe.
The tother thou seest is Porcia the true,
The chastiste wyfe that ever man knewe.
Because that yron men dyd her forbyde,
The fyre she swallowed tyll she were dede.
Beholde where is Julia that soore complayned
That she best loved her husband unfayned,
And yet he lovide hys second wyfe better.
There could to her be no payne greater.
Turne thyne eyes on the other syde,
And see the olde holy father begylde
And dysdayne not for to take the payne
To serve seven yeares to have Rachell agayne.
O lyvely love, that with labour doth encrease!
See the father of this Jacob neverthelesse,
And the graundefather of Sara take delyght.
Thus doth love wyth his power and myght.
After loke howe love cruell and envyll
Overcame Davide and made hym to kyll
His faythfull servaunt, which he repented sore.
In a derke place he dyd repentaunce therefore.
A lyke mysty cloude (pyte to thynke upon!)
So derkyd the great wysedome of Salomon

That well neare it quenched hys hygh fame.
Se also, I praye the, among the same
He that lovyde and hatyd in a whyle,
And it is he that Thamar dyd beguyle,
Wherefore she complayned to Absolone;
Of hyr mysfortune she made wondre mone.
And lytle afore hym (see, there he went!)
The stronge Sampson that sore dyd repent
For putting his heade in his loves lappe,
Tellyng her hys secretes. He hadde hard happe.
After beholde amonge swordes and speares
Judeth that hent hym by the heares
The proude Holiferne vanquished by love,
Whereby she savyde her citie from reprove.
There was no moo but she and her mayde
That dyd thys wonders acte at that abrayde.
Doest thou not see Sychen afore thine eyes
Emonge the circumcysed people howe he dyes,
Scorned in lyke maner as the tother was?
Thys was love that brought hym to that case.
Lo, where thou mayest see the greate Assuerus,
That for to heale hys malady amarouse
Left the tone and toke hym to a sweter.
There is no remedy agaynst love better
Then one nayle to knocke out with another.
A stronge example this is among the other.
But nowe wylt thou see in one tyrantes hart
Love and crueltie, which is a divers parte.
Beholde Herodes howe he doth complayne.
Thys myschevouse tyrante inhumayne
To late repentyd, soo doth dyvers mo.
The deade ones done, it cannot be undoo.
Maryamne hys love he calleth and clepeth,
And all in vayne, wherefore he wepeth.
And lo there one may beholde and see
Three fayre swete Dameselles where they be—
Procry and the good gentle Arthemesia,
And in there companye there standeth Deidamia.

The Tryumphe of Love, III: 111-148

These were not soo good, but the other be as yll
That foloweth this loves tryumphe styll:
Semiramis and Biblia and Mirra the gent,
That of theyr vyle love do soore repente.
I am not advysed theyr offences to name;
Therefore I leve it for very pure shame.
Nowe foloweth they that fyll bokes wyth lyes:
Launslote and Trystram, that for Ysode dyes;
And Quene Gueynor with other lovers moo,
But specially the fayre gentle Darmino,
That made for his love great complaynte
And she for hym wexed pale and faynte."
Thus spake my frende, and I which herkened well
All these hystories that he to me dyd tell
Stode astonied, as in dreade and feare
Of hurt to come that hastyth nere and nere,
Pale and wane as he that is so taken
Oute of his tombe newe rysen and awaken.
When that all sodenly by me there stode
The fayrest yonge mayden of face and mode
That ever I sawe, whyter then a dove,
Which unprovided toke me soore in love.
And although that I dyd pretende
By strenght agaynst her me to defende
And that I would resyst in the place
A man of armes in such a soden case,
Yet for hyr wordes and with her smyling chere
She bounde me fast and toke me prysoner.
And evyn then for trueth in that degree
My frende drue nere and, smyling, sayde to me,
In myn ere wysperyng: "Nowe speake thou may
What love is and all her nyce playe;
Nowe mayest thou knowe it as well as I;
Both we be spottyd wyth one maladye."
I than was one of this great arraye
That more dyd lament the trueth, I saye,
Of other mens love that prosperde well
Then of myne owne doloure, of which I tell.

And as he that repenteth all to late
Of hurte taken unwysely allgate,
So of my loves beautie dyd I make
Myne owne death, which wyllyngly I take
By love, by jelozy, by envye also.
Burnynge lyke fyre, thus dyd I love in woo.
The fyre was kyndled in that most fayrest face.
Even as a sycke man that an appetyte hase
And desyreth that to hym semeth swete
Yet to his helth it is nothynge mete,
Even so was I unto all other pleasure
Deaf and blynde out of all measure,
Folowynge hyr by so doubtfull wayes
That it to remember, those tymes and dayes,
I tremble and quake when therof I do thynke—
More then I can wryte with pen, paper, and ynke.
So that from the tyme that this befell,
Myne eyes for moysture semed a well;
My harte was pensyfe, my lodginge was in dede
Brokes, sprynges and ryvers; so dyd I lede
My lyfe in busshes, in grovets, and in woodes
Amonge the stones; I sought none other goodes,
And to this so many papers whyte
As in hyr prayse I payned to endyte,
When after I tore them into peces smal,
I was compelled agayne to wryte them all.
And all in loves cloystre what is done
(I know it well) it cannot be undone;
That there is feare, and there is hope also
Who wyll it rede, and take hede thereto,
In my forehead there maye ye se it playne—
All my sorowe, my douloure, and my payne.
And for all this, that wylde joly dame
That is the causer of all this same
Goeth afore me and careth not at all
Whether that I flete, I synke or fall.
So is she proude, in vertue set so hye,
That in hyr selfe she taketh glorye

To have me so fast hyr servaunt bounde,
That I knowe not howe to heale my wounde.
And to this (it is a marvelouse thynge)
The God of love, this great myghtye kynge,
It seemeth of hyr he is soore afearde
When that she lyst to loke hym in the bearde.
So that hope doth me so ofte forsake
That Love hym selfe no remedy can make.
For when he wyll any thynge with this mayde,
She doth not as other do that are afrayde,
But, as one that is free, she goeth in the race,
Not bounde, but at lybertie with hyr fayre face.
And no wondre, for she doth appeare
Emonge the starres as the Sonne cleare.
Hyr porte is synguler; hyr wordes are marvelous,
Hyr heare spyred as the golde moost beutiouse;
The eyen kyndled with a celestiall lyght
That well content to burne is my delyght.
Who can compare with hyr angelyke demure?
It passeth my connyng (ye maye be sure)
As muche as the Sea passeth a lytle broke,
For who on good maners doth prye and looke,
A newe thynge it is, and not afore seene,
Nor after shall not (so dulse and sheene),
So that all tounges hyr beutye to expresse
Are and shalbe muete doubtelesse.
With suche a one am I taken, and with hyr tyde,
And she free from all love on every syde.
O wycked starre that my destanye doth leade!
Howe is it that I have no better speade?
Day and nyght upon hyr I do call,
But she nothyng bouse to pytie at all,
Nor scant will tary to heare what I saye.
Alas! For pytye well mourne I maye.
A harde lawe it is thus to love be kynde,
The waye not ryght, but crooked for to fynde.
But yet to folowe it why shulde I saye naye
When that not onely men doth goe that waye,

But the Goddes also that be celestiall
Are not free from this payne at all?
He that is a lover ful well knowes this—
How that the hart from the bodye departed is;
How nowe he is in warre, and forthwith in peace;
Howe when his love doth shewe ungentlenes,
He wyll not be aknowen, but his malady hyde,
Thoughe that it prycke hym both backe and syde.
This evell feele I, and yet more thereto.
When with my love I have to do,
The bloude for feare renneth to my harte
And streyght abroade in my vaynes doth starte.
I knowe also howe hydde under the floure
The serpent lyeth the lover to devoure;
How always the lover lyeth in dread and doute,
In great suspecte for to be put oute
By another, and so no rest I take,
Neyther when I slepe, nor when I wake.
I knowe also howe to seke the place
Where my love is ay wont to passe.
And yet I stand in feare hyr to fynde,
Althoughe hyr selfe is prynted in my mynde.
I knowe also my selfe howe to beguyle
With lovynge and mornynge a great whyle,
Folowynge the damesell (it is even so)
That wyll burne me folowyng—yet after I go!
I knowe, moreover, how love cryes and calles
And wyll not be shytte out with dores nor walles,
But puttes by reason and wyll not go awaye
Tyll he pearce the harte and all. I saye
I knowe also how sone a gentle harte
Is tyed with a small lace and cannot start
When the sences have the better hande
And reason put by and wyll not withstande.
I knowe, to, this: how that love doth shote;
How he flyes and strykes without gevyng boote;
How he threateth and robbeth with forse and might,
And thus wronges his servantes against al right.

The Tryumphe of Love, III: 263–278

And I am not ignoraunt how unstable is his whele—
The hope doubtfull alwayes for to fele,
The doloure sure, his promyse untrue,
Ay desyrous to chaunge for thynges newe,
And how to this in the bones doth rest
The hyd fyre that lyeth so opprest
In the lovers vaynes, and that with such a wound
That at the last it bryngeth hym to the ground.
In conclusion, I know love so to be
Inconstaunt, waveryng and fearefull (trust me),
Havyng in it a lytle small swetenes
Mengled with extreme payne and bytternes.
When he woulde speake, cannot though he would;
Sodeyne scilence when his tale should be tolde;
A shorte laughynge with complaynt styll and longe;
Gall tempred with hony—this is the lovers songe!

The Fourth Chapter of
the Tryumphe of Love

After that my fortune thus hade me broughte
And love soo sore in my hart wroughte
That cut were al my weake sely vaynes,
My lybertie gone, and I in wofull paynes,
I that afore was wylde as any harte
Was made then tame for my parte,
As well as all the other that were there,
And well knew theyr travayle and theyr fere
And wyth what wyte, crafte, and chaunce
I and they were brought to loves daunce.
And then, as that I loked all aboute
If I myght spye among that hudge route
Any person of cleare and high name
That by wryting have eternall fame,
I sawe hym that Erudyce dyd call
Apon Pluto, the great god infernall,
And folowed her (as these hystories tell)
Downe unto the depe dongeon of hell,
And dying dyd his love clepe and call.
I sawe also evyn among them all
Alceo, Nacreon and the wyse Pyndarus,
That in love were all thre studiouse.
Vyrgyll was there, I say, in lyke case,
Wyth other excellent poetes in that place.
The tone was Ovyde, the tother Catullo.
Propercius also and eke Tibullo,
That of love wrote many a verse and songe.
And with this excellent Poetes amonge
Was a Grecian that with her swete style
Of love full many a songe dyd fyle.
Ay lokyng thus about me here and there
I sawe in a grene fielde with sadde chere
People that of love reasonyng went,
Dant with Beatryce fayre and gent.

The Tryumphe of Love, IV: 35–72

Lo, on the tother syde I might also se
Cino of Pistoia, wyth hym (trust me)
Guydo of Rezzo, and in that place
Two other Guydos in lyke manner and case.
The tone of them was borne in Boleyne;
The tother was a very ryght Cicelien;
Senicio and Francisco (so gentle of condicion)
And Arnolde and Daniell in lyke facion,
A great maker and dyvyser of love,
And dyd great honour to his Citie above.
There was Peter also the Clerke famouse,
And Rambaldo with his stile curiouse
That wrote for his Beatryce in Mont Ferrato;
The olde Peter and with hym Geraldo;
Filileto that in Marsill bare the name
And the prayse from Geneway by the same;
Geffray Rudell that sought his death (Alasse!)
Upon the water as he hym selfe dyd passe.
There was also Wubon at that houre,
That in wryting to his Peramoure
Passyd many other in his dayes.
Among these other that of love sayes
Was Amerego, Barnardo, Hugo, and Anselme,
That in stede of speare, shilde, and helme
Was theyr tounge and theyr fayre speach
The love of theyr Ladyes to besech.
I turned myne eyes from that companye
And streight wyse I dyd there espye
The good Thomaso, that gate great prayse
In Boleyne that citie in hys dayse.
O fleyng swetenes! O paynefull wery lyfe!
What chaunce hath taken wyth woo and strife
These my deare fryndes away from me?
Why am I not styll in theyr company?
Well may I perceave howe feble and frayle
Is mans lyfe all full of travayle.
Well may I say it is none other thing
But as a dreame or a shadowe passyng,

Or as a fable that when it is tolde
The wynde and whether doth it holde.
Unneth was a lytle past the rule
Of the commen lernars in scole
When fyrste I dyd Socrates workes se
And Lelius howe fayre they dyd agree.
Wyth these men I entende styll to goo
Which I have named hether unto,
As those whose laude no man can well rehearse,
Neyther in ryme, in prose, nor yet in verse.
Wyth these two and dyverse other in my dayes
Have I searched many dyvers wayes,
And from these noo man can me devyde,
But for alwayes I wyll wyth them abyde
Untyll the houre come that I shall dye.
For wyth these two gotten yet have I
The gloriouse Laurell wherewith my heade
As a garlande all aboute is spredde.
In memory of her of which I wryte,
Verses of prayses as I can endyte,
But of her which I so much commend
For all my servyce that I do pretend,
I cannot get neyther boughe nor lefe
But payne, heavines, doloure, and grefe.
And or I wryte the cause why she doth so,
I wyll wryte of the pensyfe woo
That these unwyse lovers have to love.
The thyng is so farre my wytte above
That for great Omer or for wyse Orpheus
It were well mete they shoulde it dyscusse
Then in folowing of my golden penne.
I wyll declare howe I and all these men,
Folowed this god by Dykes and by Dales,
With peynes and busines and with many tales.
This chylde unto his kyngdome came
Where Venus hys mother was resydent than,
But so overwhart thyder was the wayes
By busshes and woodes and other brayes,

That not one amonge all wyste where he was,
Nor howe it was wyth hym, nor in what case.
There lyeth beyonde Egeo, that grete see,
A delectable yle to beholde and se
Because the sonne softly doth it warme.
The byrdes there full swetely charme.
In the myddes of this yle now expressed
Is there a mountayne, fayre ydressed
With fayre flowres and fayre cleare water
That it taketh awaye all sadde matter
From the hartes of suche as be there.
This is the lande to Venus moost dere,
Wherein the olde auncient men
Made to this Venus a temple then,
And yet of vertue it is so barrayne, I saye,
That as it was, so it is at this daye.
In that selfe same place tryumpheth this Lorde
Of us and other that he doth bynde in corde
Of all nations, from Tyle unto Inde.
Innumerable of all men one maye fynde
This Prynce, in token of his great victory
That he hath obteyned of lovers so gloriouslye,
Caryeth with hym of poore lovers the spoyle
To gyve to hys wanton mother in that soyle.
Fyrst of all the lovers thoughtes in his lappe
He hath with hym fast closed in a trappe.
Vanytie embraseth hym and with hym doth go.
Fugytyve pleasure doth folowe hym also;
In wynter Roses he caryeth about,
In Somer yse, this great God so stoute;
Doutefull hope before, and behynde
Shorte Joye, waverynge and blynde.
Penaunce and sorow doth folowe the rest.
As in Rome and in Troy, when it was opprest,
Thus with a noyse and a huge shoute
Redounded the valleye there all aboute
With a consent of byrdes fayre and swete.
And the ryvers that ranne by the strete

Were of couloure (breifly to endyte)
Greene, blewe, redde, yalowe, and whyte.
And ever the Ryvars rynnyng in that place
When that the tyme of greate heate was;
Apon the freshe, fayre greene flowres
To comforte the herbers and the bowres;
Shadowes softe to kepe the sonne away;
The wether temperate by nyght and daye;
The Sonne nether to hoote nor to colde;
Plenty of deynties eate who woulde
And pleasures dyvers to make a symple wytte
Have an olde feble harte for to use it.
It was about the Equinoctiall lyne than
When the fayre bryght Phebus began
To chase the longe wynter nyghtes awaye
And Prougne laughes early afore daye.
In that tyme and in that selfe howre
This great God of so hyghe powre
Woulde tryumphe then and there worshipped be.
O our unstable fortune for to se!
We ne coulde but as this God us leade.
Hym to worshyppe, se howe we speade.
What death, what sorow, woo, and payne
Hath the lover, his purpose to attayne!
Nowe for to declare this matter by and by:
This Goddes chayre, where that he sat on hye,
There was about it errour and dreames
And glosynge ymages of all nations and realmes;
False opynion was entrynge the gate
And slypper hope stode by theyr ate;
Wery rest, and rest with wo and payne,
The more hygher he clam, the lesse he dyd obtayn.
Damnable lucre was not wantynge there,
Nor profitable hurte alwayes in fere;
Cleare dishonoure, and glory obscure and darke;
False lealtie lefte not there to warke,
Nor beguyldynge fayth, nor furious busynes,
Nor slowe reason lacked not in the presse.

A pryson open, entre who woulde;
When he was in gotten, oute he ne coulde.
Within trouble, confusion, and mysery;
A sure sorowe, a myrth uncertaynly.
Lyppary nor Ischa nor Volcan boyls not so
Stronglie (and Mongebell put therto)
As boyled the place where the castell was.
And, briefly, whosoever thyther dyd pas
Is there bounde in hote and in colde,
In darkenesse everlastynge in that holde;
Holden and tyed and kept by forse,
Crying for mercy tyll that he be horse.
In this castell syghynge for Sorga and Arno
Was I prysoner many a longe daye so
That by my wytte I coulde no meanes fynde
Oute for to gette (there I was so blynde).
One remedye at the leaste there I founde:
Whyles that I was in love thus bounde,
My wytte on hyghe thynges was evermore set
To knowe what love is whiche was so great
That I therby coulde well discerne
What was to be done in suche harme.
And thus, havynge great compassion
Of suche that were in loves pryson,
My harte relented, even as doth the snowe
Agaynst the hoote Sonne (ye may me trowe),
Merveylynge to se so many noble men
To be in so darke a pryson there and then.
None otherwyse but as one that doth se
A pycture well made in conformyte
Goeth the foote forwarde it for to espye
And yet loketh backwarde with his eye,
So at that tyme I loked all aboute
To consydre this greate companye and route.

The ende of the Tryumphe of Love.

The Excellent Tryumphe of Chastitie

When that I sawe evyn afore my face
In one tyme and in one Selfe place
The hyghe god that reigneth above
And men mortall subdewede also by love,
By theyr example and by there great fall
Some profyte to my selfe then dyd I call
And some comeforte it was also to me
Even as other were I for to be.
When Phebus, a god, was taken in that lure
And the yonge Leander (a man pure),
Both twayne strycken wyth loves darte,
And Juno and Dydo lasyd with that parte
(Not that Dydo that men doth wryte,
That for Eneas wyth death was dyte,
But that noble Lady true and juste
For Sychen her joye and hartes luste),
I ought not to morne, thoughe that unware
I were taken in loves craftie snare,
Being but a very yonge man of age
For to be vanquished wyth such a rage.
And yf that my Lady that I love best
Wyll not with love in no wyse be opprest,
But be mine enemy in such a thyng,
I have no cause of great mournyng,
For as muche as I do call to mynde
What hurt by that, that she should fynde,
I knowe also that by her reason
She doth so guyde her in eache season
That love by her is so abatyd
That it doth seme this god is hatyd.
Which when that love dyd playnely se,
He was so chafed (trust ye well me)
That the lyghtnyng that falles from the skye
And beryth downe all even by and by,
Nor the lyon soo woode in his rage
So assayde not that tyme for to assuage

The Tryumphe of Chastitie, 37–74

Wyth all his argumentes that he coulde make
This Lady I reason of prysoner to take;
Nor she agayne (I say) for her parte,
When that she well and wisely dyd advert
What Cupyde was aboute wyth her to do,
The whurling wind flieth not so faste so
As she agaynst hym wyth vertue went
To let this great god of his intent.
What should I say? Etna, that hyll
That boyleth and burneth evermore still,
Maketh not a more terrible soune
When that Enchelado would shake it downe,
Nor Sylla nor Carrybdys when angry they be
Then love assayde (you may trust me)
To wyne my Lady in suche wyse.
When that he sawe hyr love dyspyse,
Eche man there drue hymselfe aparte
(The great horrible stryfe for to advert)
Up to a place that were mervelously hye
To loke to what ende this should applye.
Thys god that the vanquer (as is tolde)
Of mortall men both of yonge and olde,
Toke in his ryght hand Arrowe sharpe and kene
And in the tother a bowe bryght and shene
And drewe it up, this Lady to feare,
In great hast and anger up to his eare.
And this dyd he in such great violence
That a Leoparde that maketh pretence
The fugytyfe hart for to cache and take
Coulde not more hasty haste make
Then love dyd wyth his fyery face
This fayre Lady with craft to compase.
I that sawe the maner and the guyse
Was soore moved in double wyse:
Pyte ferde me lest that I shoulde se
So swete a Creature vanquished for to be;
Desyre agayne would have me gladde
That I my purpose myght then have hadde.

But vertue, that with the good is ever,
Shewed at that tyme that he dyd never
Forsake hym that hym doth truste.
This fayre Lady, my hartes luste,
When she dyd se the stroke at hande,
Was never mayster that doth withstand
In the shyppe on the parlouse Rocke to fall
Then she that then and forth with all
Dyd awaye from loves stroke glyde
Wyth such a honestie one every parte and syde,
Which then apperyd in her swete face
That loves fyery darte had there no place.
I that stode styll with wonderouse sadde entent
To se wherunto this matter went,
Hopyng the vyctorie to me should fall
And that I shulde be hyrse hole and all.
As one that hath or he would speake
Wrytten in hys heade and harte eke
What he wolde say, even so do I
Thynke to say even by and by,
"My lord, yf that you wynne the fyelde,
Bynde me with her, for I doo yelde,
And let me never from her depart
Whyles that the lyfe is in my harte.
And yf that unworthy that I be
To be with this Lady in company,
All though for ever in love I dure,
Here styll wyth you do tye me sure."
Whyles that I mynded thus for to saye,
She loked on me (that moste swete may)
Wyth such a grave and a wyse sadde chere
That for to speake it I dreade and feare.
For I not onely that have smale wytte,
But that man also for to declare it
That had the moste excellent wytte and reason
Should have marveyled at that tyme and season,
For this loves golden and fyery shafte
Even by it selfe there it fell aparte,

Seyng the honestie (as I have here tolde)
In my loves breste that then was colde.
So that Camilla, that fayre ladye gent,
That with the lyfte brest to battell went,
Nor Cesar in Tessalia agaynst Pompeus
Was nothyng to speake of so Valerouse
As she was agaynst love there and than
That every stronge shielde breake it can.
Armed was she with all her route
With vertues compassed all about.
O what a gloryouse bande there was
That agaynst love with hyr dyd passe!
Twayne and twayne and hande in hande
This noble army together dyd stande.
Honestie and Shamefastnesse they went before,
A great gyfte of God for evermore
That made this Lady for to shewe and shyne,
Not lyke no mortall, but lyke devyne.
Wyt and Sobernes folowed the trace,
Well set in hyr harte without arrace,
And Perseveraunce came with the reste,
Whiche kept her honour not to be opprest.
Fayre Entreatynge was not behynde,
Nor Clemesse, nor Curtesy that is so kynde.
Purytie of Heart and Feare of Shame
Was there in presence Love to tame;
Olde Wyse Thoughtes in a yonge tender age
And Gratiouse Concorde all fury to asswage,
And Beuty lacked not, with a Chast Clene Thoughte.
All these agaynst love my Lady broughte
With the favoure of Heaven that halpe therto,
And the blessed holy saynctes ayde also
That unneth my syght coulde well susteyne
To se suche a company in that playne.
There sawe I this felowshyp take the spoyle,
A thousande palmes in that great soyle,
Awaye from the handes of them that were
Lovers in that companye there and there.

The sodeyne throwe that fierse Hannibal
Had of Scipion, the captayne generall
Of the Romaynes, when he had obteyned
So many victories so many mayned;
Nor the great Colyas was not more abashed
When with the stone his heade was dashed
By David yonge and tendre of age;
Nor Cirus more astonied in that rage
When that the wydow the vengeaunce did make
For the death of her son, and for hyr loves sake,
As was love, whiche stode in the place
Muche lyke after the fashion and case
As he that thynkes hym selfe safe and sounde
And with a pange doth fall to the grounde.
Even so there dyd love poorely stande,
Unto hys eyes puttynge up his hande
As he that both with angre and feare
Even with a moment appeared there,
And he so chaufed with his adventure
That the ragyouse Sea (ye may be well sure)
Nor Mongebello, nor yet Enchelydo
Never more chaufed then he dyd tho.
Thus passed this great company gloryouse
That I dyd se tryumphynge thus,
But theyr excellency for to declare
My connynge and my wytte is all to bare.
I therfore wyll tourne to my fayre Ladye
And to the rest of hyr chast company.
She had, this excellent dame victoriouse,
A whyte vesture, gaye and gloryouse,
The shielde in hande of pure Jasper cleane
That evyll sawe Medusa that Quene
With a pyller in the myddes fynely set.
A chayne with a Dyamount therto was fret,
And a Thopasion, a preciouse stone
Used sometyme and nowe cleane gone.
I sawe hyr there even afore myne eyes
So bynde love in suche a wonderouse wyse

That it semed vengeaunce (I say ynowe)
To make hym stoupe, to make hym for to bowe.
And I therefore dyd nothynge then repent
What my love dyd; I was therwith content.
What more shulde I nowe saye or wryte?
It passeth my connyng, it passeth my myght,
The sacred and holy virgins to tell.
Caliope and Clio (I knowe it well)
With the rest of the muses nyne
Shulde lacke eloquence that to defyne.
But parte of them of moost hygh honeste
I wyll declare what persons they shulde be:
Lucrecia on the ryght hande there she stode,
And swete Penelope so mylde of mode;
These twayne had broken in pecis small
Loves bowe, his dartes, arrowes and all
And pulled his wynges quyte from hys backe.
Thus this greate God dyd go to wracke.
Virginea with hir fierce father was there
With swearde in hande and armed clere,
That chaunged the state of Rome towne
And raysed up libertie that was put downe.
And after that one myght beholde and se
Of the Germaynes maydens a huge company,
That for to save them from vyllany
Were all contented with good wyll to dye.
Judith the Ebrewe, the wyse and the stronge,
With the Grekes Lady she was amonge,
That leped into the great perylious See
To kepe hyr body from all vyllanye.
With these swete sorte I sawe divers moo
That in this tryumphe forth dyd goo,
Tryumphynge of Love that tryumphed before.
Yet amonge other there sawe I more
The meke vyrgyn of Vesta (there she was)
That proved hyr chastitie by suche a case
She bare fayre water in a large Seve,
Wherby she voyded all and yll repreve.

Hersilia also passed with that route,
Wyth all hir Sabyns that stode there aboute,
And emong these other fayre Ladyes free
I sawe hyr of muche hyghe state and degree
That for hyr husbande was content to dye—
And not for Eneas, so affyrme I.
(Let the vulgar people then holde theyr peace!)
It is that Dydo that I do here rehearse,
That honest love broughte unto an ende,
And not vayne wanton love that dyd her offende.
At the last I dyd se one of that lande
Where as the large ryver of Arno doth stande,
Closed hyr selfe up in a secrete place
To kepe hyr vyrgynitie, but (woo, alas, alas!)
Hyr fayre thought by force it was lette.
There emonge other I sawe her sette.
This excellent tryumphe whereof I wryte
Went with great glory even forth ryght
To Baia, the seasone all softe and fayre,
To the place sometyme that Sibilla dyd repayre
Callyd Cumana by her surname,
And from thens passyng by the same
Streyght to Linterna that castell they went.
In that smale citie, where it is bent,
Dwellyd that vallyaunt Romayne than
That was surnamed Scipion the Affrican.
There the tone salutyd gently the tother.
And evermore among the one and the other,
Not she that was fayrest but chastyst and beste
Was most honored among all the rest.
It pleased then this Romayne for to goo.
Among the other there in ordre also
Unto the temple that Sulpicia made,
Where all the hole flame that love hade
They quenched it out, and from thense all went
Unto that fayre temple wyth good entent
Of honorable Chastitie (so is the ryght name)
Because there appertayneth unto the same

The Tryumphe of Chastitie, 265–278

To kyndle good wyll in a gentle harte,
Specially to noblenes that thereto doth advert.
In that holy temple there offered this Lady
The gloriouse spoyle of her high victorye,
And leves of the Laurell tre there dyd she spred
Of hyr freshe garlande aboute her fayre hed.
There the younge lover, the Toscan, left asyde
The wounde that was both large and wyde
That Love had geven hym, and all because
To fle the suspect to folowe Loves lawes.
Where as was with hym dyverse other mo:
The gentle and faythfull true Ypolito,
And Josephe the Ebrue, honest and juste,
That vanquisshed love and all his foule luste.

The Tryumphe of the excellente Poete Fraunces Petrarcha, of fearful death mooste elegantlye wrytten, ye that reade it, remember it

This most noble and mooste gloryouse Ladye,
That nowe is a spirite and in the earth doth lye
And somtyme was the hygh pyller of valour,
Turned from hyr warre with laude and honour,
Gladde to have overcomen an enemy so great
That with his wyt turneth all men under feet.
With none other armour she dyd this deade,
But with a chast hart at the tyme of nede;
With a swete face and with a clene thoughte
And with an honest speche this hath she wrought.
It was a newe wondre for to beholde and se
Love to be overcome in suche wyse and degre,
Hys bowe broken, his arrowes cast asyde
That slayne had so many men of pryde
And taken prysoners infinite of men.
This noble Lady with hyr company then
Turned (as sayde is) from that hygh victory,
All together going under a fayre canapye.
There was but fewe (no mervayl at all);
Vertuous glory is rath and ever shall.
But those that were present in that place
Eche one by them selves (it is a playne case)
Semed well worthy of laude to reherse
Of Poete or Oratour in prose or verse.
Hyr vyctoriouse standerde was this:
In a greene felde a whyte armyne is
With a chayne of golde about his necke;
A fayre Topazion therto dyd it decke.
Nothynge after mortall mens rate
Was nether theyr speche nor yet theyr gate,

But all devyne for to beholde and se.
Happy are those that have suche destanye!
They semed all fayre bryght starres,
The Sonne in the myddes that not debarres
The lyght away, but geveth them lyght,
Havynge on theyr fayre heades on hyght
Rose garlandes and vyolets fresh and gay;
And as a lovynge gentle hart alwaye
Getteth honour for his vertuouse lyfe,
So past this company without debate or stryfe.
When that all sodenly there dyd appeare
A sadde blacke baner that approched nere,
And a woman wrapped all in blacke
With suche a fury and with suche a wracke
That unneth I cannot the truth tell.
In the tyme of the great myghty gyauntes fell
Were any so lothesome for to beholde and see.
Unto this Lady so gastly moved she
And sayde: "O swete and excellent mayde,
That goest here moost perfytely arayde
With youth and beautye and doste not se
The terme that I shall present arrest the!
I am the same importune cruell best
Callyd Death fearefull that doth arrest
All creatures wyth my greate force and myght
Or the daye ende, makyng it the nyght.
It is I that hath quite and cleane wastyd
The great Grekes nation and also hastyd
The noble Troyans unto theyr declyne,
And last of all hath made to ende and fyne
The Romaynes glory wyth this blade kene
That prycketh and cutteth all away cleane
And infinite of other barbarouse nations,
Using evermore these wayes and facions.
When that they loke not for me at all,
Wyth sodeyne stroke I make them downe to fall.
A thousand thoughtes of men frayle and vayne
I have broken (this is true and certayne),

And nowe to you when lyfe semeth best
Here am I comen your body to arrest.
Or any harde fortune to you chaunce to fall,
I wyll you take and ende, not one but all."
This excellent Lady, having no peare
In al the worlde, wyth sad and wise chere
Aunswered unto Death there present agayne:
"In these chast companyes (this is true and playne),
Thou hast no reason, nor yet noo power,
And lesse of all other in me at this houre;
Onely the spoyle that thou shalt have
It is my chast body unto the grave.
That well knoweth one as well as I
That taketh well my death most heavely;
Hys lyfe on my health all doth depende,
But unto the this is thy small ende.
It shalbe to me no displeasure at all
To departe the frayle world. Lo, this is all."
This cruell beast with hyr wyse reason
Was no lesse marveld at that tyme and season
Than one that doth a thynge in soden haste,
And when the dede is so done and paste
Doth blame hym selfe of that that he hath done.
Even so dyd this terrible monster soone
And when she had her selfe paused a whyle
With a more softe speache and gentle style:
"Thou," sayes she, "that present here doest guyde
This fayre chast bande on every syde,
That nast not yet my fearefull stroke assayde,
By my councell be not so sore afrayde,
For that I wyll nowe do is for the best—
To make the fle (O mayde) from age opprest,
Whiche hath alwayes longynge therunto,
Muche grief and dolour with payne and longe wo.
And to this nowe present, disposed I am,
Thou fayre creature and swete woman,
To do the suche honor present in this place
That thy spirite shall from the body passe

The Tryumphe of Death, I: 107–145

Without feare, dolour, or grief at all.
Be of good comfort, O mayde, I have sayde all."
This Angelyke creature when she had harde
What Death had sayde, agayne aunswerd:
"As it pleaseth Christ our Lorde almyghtye,
That ruleth and tempereth all thynges eternally.
Do thou unto me as thou doest to all men."
Thus this fayre Lady aunswered there and then.
And lo even there present all sodenly
Full of dead bodyes that great place dyd lye
In such a number that them for to rehearse
It cannot be countyd in prose nor yet in verse.
Of Cateya, of Marow, of Spayne and Inde—
Innumerable deade of all mankynde.
There were those that men happy dyd call—
Kynges, Emperours and Bysshoppes all.
Now be they poore, as poore as beggers be.
Where is there ryches and honour, trowe ye?
Theyr scepters, theyr crownes with theyr preciouse stones?
Theyr myters of purple dected for the noones?
Gone is all theyr glory and theyr freshe luste.
A foole is he that to such thinges doth truste,
But those that wyll nedes hope therunto
At length shall se the matter to be so,
Them selves utterly scornyd and beguyled
When all theyr fancys shalbe quyte exiled.
O blynde fooles, even worse then madde!
For all the pleasures and joyse ye have hadde,
To your olde mother ye muste nedes passe,
And your names forgotten and turned to was.
What profyte hath it then bene unto you
Wyth swerde and blode strong nacions to subdue,
To mucke up treasure and your soules to defyle?
It had bene better to have lyved a whyle
Porely in thys world with browne bread and water.
But nowe wyll I returne agayne to my matter.
I say, than, whan the extreme houre was come
Of thys fayre Lady (this is all and some)
And that she must the doubtfull passe assay

120

That puttes all the worlde in dreade and fraye,
There came to se her of women many one
To knowe and se or that the lyfe were gone
What payne the fayre Creature dyd abyde,
Both fryndes and Neybors divers on eche syde.
And, lo, as they her great beautie dyd beholde,
Death dissolved the fayre here of golde.
And so the fayrest flower that ever was
She dyd roote up (Alas, I say, Alas!)
Not for no hate that she to her then hadde,
But in heaven for to make her spirite gladde.
O howe many complayntes and bewaylinges,
Syghes and teares and other lamentinges
Were there than among the women all
When that those fayre bryght eyes celestiall
For which many a swete songe I made,
Many a sonete, many a freshe balade
Were closed and shot up! Alas, O wo is me!
This fayre Creature, what trowe ye then did she?
Syt styll and glade in quiete and pease
And gether the fructe of her vertuousnesse.
Go thy wayes, O deare godes, well content
In peace and quiet with all thy vertues excellent.
But litle it avayled agaynst deathes myght.
Then if she have agaynst such a one ryght,
What shall it be, trowe ye, of the reste?
O humayne hope with al mysery opprest!
In a fewe nyghtes so swete a mayde
Goone and past in so short a brayde!
So many teares for her death sprede!
Thou that seste it or heryst it redde
Thinke what it is the worlde for to truste
When such a creature is turned unto dust.
It was, for truth, the sixe day of Apryll
That Love to love hyr dyd me compell,
And even that same selfe houre and daye
Death dyd take my love and joye awaye
And nowe, as fortune is wont for to chaunge,
Hath broken the knot and eke the raunge

The Tryumphe of Death, I: 185–222

With suche sorowe unto my wofull harte
That I am afrayde (I saye, as for my parte)
To tell it ether in verse or in ryme,
It was to me so sorowfull a tyme.
"Vertue," sayde they that were present there,
"Excellent beutye and moost womanly chere
Nowe is deade and gone. What shall we be
When she is past the death, as we do se?
Where shall hyr peere or lyke be seene agayne?
So great perfection in one for to remayne!
So swete a speache, so Angelyke a voyce!
This above all other was the choyce."
And the spyryt when it shulde depart,
As they myght se and perfytly adverte,
With all other vertues gathered in one,
Where as it went the ayre moost bryghtly shone;
None evyll adversary was so hardy there
Afore hyr presence to stande or appeare
With foule semblaunt to put hyr in dread
Tyll death his assaute had done in dede.
But after that when all the feare was past
And by disperation they sure at the last
Eche one dyd beholde that moost swete face
How preciouse it was, how full of grace,
Not dyssolved with no vyolent payne,
But passynge awaye with an easy vayne,
Even as a swete lyght that commeth to decay,
Lytle and lytle consumynge awaye.
When that the byrth lycoure is past and gone,
The flame extincte, then lyght is there none.
Not pale she laye, but whyter then the snow
That the wynde agaynst the hyl doth blowe.
As he that wery is, and woulde have rest,
So she laye when death had hyr oppreste.
And as one that slepeth softe and quietlye,
So myght they all then and there espye
Dreadful death (that fooles have in disgrace)
Fayre and beautifull in that swetest face.

The Seconde Chapter of
the Tryumphe of Death

The nyghte folowynge that this horrible chaunce
Fell to my hartes joye and pleasaunce,
That made in maner the sone lese his lyght
And from the erth toke also all delyght
And the fayre flowre in heaven on hygh set,
My guyde gone, and I with sorowe fret
And blynde lefte from al joye and pleasure,
The swete, softe season pleasaunt (be ye sure)
With the colde that spredde was in the ayre,
Afore Aurora moste delicate and fayre
Taketh awaye with her holsome streames
All untrue and fayned false dreames,
Even at that tyme to me dyd appeare,
Semblaunt to that season, a mayde fayre and cleare,
Crowned with ryche orient pearles whyte.
And, for to encrease the more my delyght,
Hyr fayre hande stretche forth then dyd she
And, softely syghyng, gently spake to me:
"Doest thou not knowe me," sayth she me tell,
"Hyr that sometyme thou dyddest love so well,
Of whome thy harte was all set on fyre
And made the forsake all foule and vyle desyre?"
Thus sayinge, with a sadde sobre countenaunce
She sat her downe, my joye and my pleasaunce,
And made me syt by hyr even there.
Apon a bancke me thought we twayne were
Whiche was shadowed with the Lawrell tree;
A greate beche therby well myght I see,
And I so set muche lyke in suche a case.
As he that speaketh and wepeth a great pace,
Soo dyd I aunswer unto this Lady deare:
"O thou fayre creature without to have a peare,
Howe shoulde it be that I the shoulde forgette
Sythyns that ever my hart on the was set?

The Tryumphe of Death, II: 35–72

Arte thou alyve or deade? I longe to knowe."
"I am alyve," sayes she, "thou mayst me trowe,
And thou arte deade (and soo styll shalbe)
Tyll that the last houre that taketh the
From the earth. Now marke wel what I saye:
The tyme is shorte, and oure wyll alwaye
Is longe, and therefore I the rede
What thou wylt saye that it be sayde with spede,
Lest that the daye that commeth at the hande
Make thou shalt not here no longer stande."
Then sayde I: "O Lady swete and pereles,
That hast proved (I se it doubtles)
That lyfe and death are both certayne,
Tel me yf death be so great a payne."
She aunswered forthwith and to me sayde:
"Mens blynde opinion makes it to be frayde.
But for to tell the what it is in deade:
Death is dissolvynge of all doubte and dread
And cleane delyvers us from a pryson darke,
Specially to hym that gently doth warke.
But unto hym that hath done amys
And all on covetousnesse his harte set is,
It is a payne and doloure infinite.
But I that from that am free and quyte
For this death whiche I dyd assaye,
For whiche thou hast mourned to this daye,
Woulde make the mery and all thy soores heale
If halfe the joye thou haddest that I do feale."
Thus spake she, and hyr celestyall eyes
Devoutly she lyfte up unto the skyes
And those rodye lyppes more swete then rose
She helde them styll tyll I dyd purpose:
"Silla, Nero, Cayus, and Maryus
(With these tyrauntes put Maxentius)
Syckenes in the brest and in the flanckes
Payne of burnyng, fevers and cranckes
Makes the death more bytter then gall."
She aunswered me then forthwith all:

124

"I cannot," sayes she, "for truth denye
But that the payne moost certaynlye
That goeth afore that the death doth come
Is wonder grevouse, this is all and some.
But that which grevith most of all
Is the feare of losse of the lyfe eternall.
But the spirite that comfortes hym in good
And with his harte doth dread his rodde,
Unto hym I say what is the death
But even a syght and a short stopping breath?
This by my selfe dyd I well knowe and se.
At the laste houre when death dyd take me.
The body was sycke, but the soule was well.
When that I harde one by me there tell,
'O howe wreched and miserable is he
That compteth the dayes of the infenyte
That Laura is in and thinketh every day
A thousand dayes, I dare ryght wel say,
Her excelente person to se and to beholde
And never after se, his comfort should;
Sekes for her the water and the lande
And never for her in quyete doth stande,
But always folowinge one maner of style,
Howe that he may in every tyme and whyle
On her to thynke, on her with penne to wryte,
On her to speake, on her for to endyte.'
This heryng, casting myne eyes asyde,
Hyr amonge the other there I espyde
That often moved me, the for to love,
And kyndled in thy hart farre above
The love I bare always unto the.
I knowe her well, that it was very she
That much comfortyd me or I dyed
With her wise wordes on every syde.
And playnely to the when that I was
In my best tyme, and in that honest case
In youth but tendre, and unto the moost dere,
Whiche made many and dyvers here and there

The Tryumphe of Death, II: 111–148

To speake both and ofte of the and me,
The lyfe wherein thou sawest me for to be
Was but bytter (I sweare nowe on my fayth)
To the respecte of my most pleasaunt death,
Whiche to men mortall is very rare.
So that when my lyfe awaye dyd fare,
Even at that poynt I was moost mery and glad,
Savynge that of the great pytie I hadde
To departe this worlde (trust thou me)—
As one in exyle his owne countre to se."
Then sayde I to hyr even there agayne:
"On the fayth, Madame, whiche you are certayne
That I ought you without for to chaunge,
Tell me nowe, and be not to me straunge,
For you knowe all (seynge that gloryous syght
Above oure knowledge, the eternall light)
Had you ever pitie in your harte
Of my greate sorowes and paynes smarte,
Not leavynge aparte your hygh chast wayes,
Whiche that you used with me alwayes?
Nowe shewynge to me a swete dysdayne,
Nowe a swete angre to double my payne;
Nowe shewynge a peax wrytten in your eyes
That hylde me so tyed and in suche wyse
That doubtfull I was in what case I stoode.
Many yeares thus I in love abode."
Scant had I these wordes to hyr sayde
When that I sawe even at a brayde
That swete smylyng and fayre countenaunce
That somtyme was my joye and plesaunce,
My comforte, my lust, and my rejoysinge,
In this wise to me moste graciouse speking:
"From the my hart was never devyded,
Nor never shall, but that I provided
Dyvers tymes with my wyse regard.
I tempered thy love (that well neer thou had marde)
Because there was as than none other way
Oure fervent love with honesty for to stay.

Therefore in lyke case as thou sest a mother
Correcte her deare chylde for no nother
But all to brynge it to good frame,
Even so dyd I then use the same,
And sayde to my selfe full many a season:
'This man not lovys but burnes out of reason,
Wherefore it behoveth me for to provyde
In this hard daungerouse case on every syde.
And surely full evyll provydeth he
That loketh outwarde and doth not se
What is inwarde in such a perylious case.'
This in my pitefull harte toke then place,
And thys to the as a brydell was than
As thou seest a horse reuled by a man.
Wherefore somtime I shewed me wonders glade,
Somtyme agayne to be as sober and sadde.
And yet I loved as hoote and true as you,
Allwayes saving the chosen honest dowe,
Which soo my will than and ever opprest
That reason reulde my desyre at the lest.
And when that agayne I dyd beholde and se
Thy sorowe to grevouse and paynefull for to be,
Swetely and gently on the myne eyes I sett,
Thy helth and welfayre agayne for to gett.
Thys was ever my wise honest wayes
That I honestly used with the in those dayes.
And when I sawe the teres droppyng avayle
Downe thy pale chekes lyke unto the hayle,
Then I dyd pray and softly then I sayde:
'Here it is necessarye I geve anone an ayde.'
And when that thou were forthwith agayne
Into to much hope my love for to attayne,
Anone unto my selfe even thus sayde I:
'Here of necessitie must be had a remedye;
A harde and strayt byt I muste nowe put to.'
Thus with dyvers colours many mo,
Wyth hoote, with grene, with golde, with white
I kepte the always styll in honest plyte.

Thou knowest this well and hast it tolde,
And in many a swete sonet it enrolde."
When she had sayde these wordes to me playne,
With tremblyng voyce I sayd to her agayne:
"Your wordes to me should be passyng swete,
For the greate love and most fervant hete
That I have ever borne, my joy, to you,
If I belevyde them faythfully to be true."
"O unfaythfull man," then answered she,
"Why shoulde I say these wordes unto the
If that my wordes were not true and juste?
Nowe then I tell the (disclose my hart I muste!);
If in this world lyving to my sight
I toke in the juste pleasure and delight,
I kept it secret, where thou (I say agayne)
Thy love to all men dydest make it playne.
There was no dyfference in our love at all,
But that my true love was joyned all
In moost honest wyse so for to be.
But nowe one thynge I wyll demaunde of the:
When that thy swete balettes I dyd synge
Dyddest thou then doubte of me in any thynge?
I thynke playnly nay, and therfore thus:
Though for a tyme I was contrarius
By lovynge straunge and semyng so to be,
A thousande tymes (thou mayst trust me)
With my thoughte alwayes so I farde
Thou haddest of me an inwarde swete regarde,
And more thy mynde at that tyme to appease
I wyl tell the that thynge that shal the please.
It greveth me sore that I was not borne
By thy fayre citie. I saye to the therforne,
Althoughe my countre full pleasaunt be,
I woulde my nest had ben nere to the,
Lest that percase thy mynde shulde chaunge
And love some other amonge so great a raunge."
To these wordes no worde then I sayd.
The thyrde celestial speare had so arrayde

And lyfte in love so sore my lovynge thought
That aunswer hyr at that tyme coulde I nought.
Then she to me with a benigne love and chere:
"I have in this world by the great honour here,
And shal have alwaye. Marke wel what I shal say:
The nyght is past, now commeth the bryght daye.
Yf that to me thou wylt more saye, swete hart,
Be short, I byd the, for I must hence departe."
"O," sayde I, "myne owne swete Lady dere,
For al the sorowe and payne I have had here
In lovinge you, these wordes so fayre and swete
Doth recompence my love and makes all mete;
But from you thus for to be seperate playne
Is unto me a deadly mortall payne.
But one thynge nowe to me you must declare,
Or that ye from my wofull presence fare:
Shall I lyve longe (tell me) after you
Or shortly (as I woulde, O Lady) you ensue?"
She aunswered gently as farre as she coulde tell
Longe after hyr on earth here should I dwell.

The ende of the Tryumphe of Death.

The Excellent Tryumphe of Fame

After that Deathe had triumphed in that face
Which often of me had tryumphed in lyke case
And that the sonne of our world was dead and past,
This ougly and dispytefull beaste at the last,
Pale and horrible and proude for to se,
With hyr blacke baner awaye goeth she
When that she had extincte out quyte
Of perfyt beutye the very clere lyght.
Then, as I dyd loke about on every part,
Commyng towardes me there I dyd advert
Hyr that mans lyfe for ever doth save
And pulleth hym out alyve from his grave.
This gloryous fayre Lady muche lyke was she
Unto that bryght starre that goeth (trust me)
In the orient or the cleare day appeare.
Even in lyke maner was this Ladyes chere,
So that there is no mayster in no Scole
Can take upon them to descrybe that Sole
That I go aboute with symple wordes to tell.
So muche great in glory this Lady dyd excell
That all the element about her dyd shyne,
Not as a mortall, but lyke a thyng devyne.
Graven in theyr foreheades were the names
Of the honorable people whose hyghe fames
By valure and vertue can never dye.
Folowynge this noble Fame there sawe I
Many of those of whyche I tofore have rehersed
That by love (as sayd is) were sore oppressed.
On her ryght hand there fyrst in my syght
Was Cesar and Scipion, that honorable knyghte,
But which of them twayne next to Fame was
I do not remember, but there they both dyd pas.
The tone in vertue, the tother in love
Was taken, though he semed somewhat above.
And then forthwith was shewed unto me
After these twayne captaynes that so excellent be

The Tryumphe of Fame, I: 37–74

Men of hyghe valure armed full bryght
As unto the Capitall they went full ryghte
By that selfe waye that Sacra called was,
Or by Via Lata whereunto they dyd passe.
They came in suche an honest ordre (as I saye)
And had wrytten and graved (this is no nay)
Theyr excellent names in theyr foreheads on hie.
And even as I behelde them thus attentyfely,
Their maner, their port, their chere, and everithing,
To these twayne most hyest in ordre folowyng
Ensued the tone his nevew to hym dere,
The tother his sonne that never yet had pere.
And those that thou seest with the swerd in the hand
The twayn fathers and the sonnes that by them stand,
Agaynst these enemies that Italy dyd invade,
Armed in bryght stele they no dreade hadde.
Two there folowed fyrst, and twayne after past.
But he that in ordre was semyng to be laste
In dede of the thre was worthyest of fame.
And after these of excellent and renoumed name,
Even as the Ruby most oriently doth shyne,
Went he with his hand and with his councel fyne.
It was Claudius, that with his wyse foresyght
As a swyft byrde that taketh his flyght
So dyd he go to the fielde at Metaurus
And pulled up the wede, this knyght gloryouse.
He had eyes and tymes convenient for to spy
And wynges as a byrde to execute it by and by.
There folowed then after in that worthy race
The great old captayne that let not to byd bace
Unto the fierce captayne Hannibal. And therunto
Adjoyned unto hym was a nother Fabio;
Twayne named Catones with these also went,
And two noble Paulus, wyse to all intent;
Two Brutus and also twayne Marcellus,
And one renowmed worthy captayne Regulus
That more truly loved Rome then (I saye) that he
Loved his owne selfe excedyng in degree.

There was there also Curio and Fabricius,
That with theyr wise povertie marvelouse
Were more prayse worthy then Myde was
Or Crassus with all the great golde that he has,
For golde made them vertue to expell
And povertye these twayne in glory to excell.
There folowed these twayne even syde by syde
Cincinato, to whom the Romaynes cryed
For helpe in theyr extreme daunger and nede;
He was equall to the tother twayne in dede.
Camillus ensued, the noble valyaunt knyght,
That had liver dye for the maintenaunce of right
Then otherwise to do but as a vertuouse man.
The favour of heaven brought hym to Rome than
(Where envy had banyshed hym from the towne)
Home to his countrye, this knight of high renoun.
There was also the vallyaunt and fresh Torquatus,
That slewe his owne welbeloved son Chevalerus.
Rather then he would knyghtly ordre breake,
He would be childles. Thus the olde stories speake.
Both the twayne Decius were also in the place,
That theyr cruell enemies cleane for to deface
Vowed themselfes, alas, and that willingly.
O cruell vowe, themselfes forthwith to dye!
No lesse dyd he the vallyaunt hardy Curio,
That entred unto the great large hole so
That horrybly was opened in Rome, that riall towne.
Wyllyngly hymselfe therein he entred downe;
Mummio, Levio went also in ordre there,
And the good noble Attilio with a manly chere;
Titus Flaminius that the Grekes dyd subdue
Most with gentle pytie there dyd he ensue.
There was also there in the presse he that made
A great large circle in Syria with hys rode
And with his hardy and ferse loke and countenaunce
To his wyll and intent (so was this Romaines chaunce)
He the great and pussaunt kyng so constrayned
That all his hole request thereby he obteyned.

And by hym in good ordre there was also he
That kept, as he was armed most valliauntly,
The hyll from his cruell enymies all
And after in that same place hymselfe had a fall.
And with this company was that most valiaunt man
That kept the brydge from all Toscan,
And next in ordre unto this hardy knyght
Stode that ferse warrear that in great dispyte
Burnte hys ryght hand because he fayled
To sley the king his enemie which he then assayled
Even in the mides of all his noble men.
Thys was a merveylouse hardy dede there and then!
And I sawe also there in the huge prese
He that fyrst vanquished on the great Seese
The Carthagines and scatred all abroade
By Cycell and Sardinia by evyll chanse al the rode;
I sawe among the others him with the grave sight
Called Appius, that with his forse and myght
Kept the men vulgar people in great dread and awe,
So strayt and hard he bound pore men to a lawe.
And after, as all about I dyd cast myne eye,
I dyd that person among other rest espye
That with his swete facyons usyd hym soo
That next the fyrst in fame he myght goo,
But that the ende turnyd unto blame.
Wherefore I may ryght well affirme the same,
That often it is sene a long prolonged lyfe
Turneth good renowne into payne and stryfe,
And certenly he was no lesse in fame and myght
But as Bacus and great Alcides by ryght,
Or as to Thebus the good Impammunda was.
Among the other nobly he dyd there pas.
And after this great and worthy myghty man
I sawe folowing among the other than
Hym that in his yonge flowryng age
Had great lawde and prayse for his vassalage;
And even as much as thys ferse champion
Was terrible and cruell in his naturall regyon,

He that folowed hym was as merciable;
I know noo Duke to be more commendable.
There went in ordre after by and by
He that wyth hys wysedome sapiently.
The noble Volumines he was there in the prese;
Hys lawde is praysed and shall never sease.
Cosso was there, Philon, and Rutilio
And the hardy captayne Lucio Dentato
With Marco Sergio and Sceva the bolde.
In armys as lyghtnyng one myght them behold,
Their harnes broken, their shelde in twenty places
Persyde thorowe with swordes, dartes, and mases.
The last of them that there was in dede
With no lytle fame the rest dyd succede.
And after these noble men afore rehearsed
Dyd folowe ferse Marius, which reversyd
Jugurta of Numedy the myghty kyng
And the Cymbers, that with them dyd brynge
The Almaynes in fury and in rage.
Thys Marius dyd their great myght asswage.
There went by the Marius by and by
Fulvius Flaccus, that with witty polecy
Destroyed those that at Rome dyd rebell;
But he that folowed dyd farre passyng exell:
It was Fulvio (so was his very name),
Well worthy among other to folowe Fame.
There was also one Romayne named Graccus,
That had among that people much matter contrariouse,
To his ruyne at the last in Rome towne.
There was he, thys knyght of high renowne,
And he also that much fortunate semyde
(Though by me he cannot so be demyde)
Was there, and after hym there came
The two worthy Marcelles in ordre than
That kept all close in theyr hartes (I say)
Theyr secretes. They went aboute alway.
These two had great prayse in Numyddia,
In Macedon also, and in the Yle of Creta,

And in lyke maner in the Realme of Spayne.
Three vallyaunt famouse knyghtes for certayne!
And I sawe also even at that tyde
The good Vaspacion, and by his famouse syde
His eldest sonne, but not his cruell brother—
He was not worthy to be amonge the other.
And so folowed after in good ordre than
Narva the auncient and gentle Trajan,
Helio and Adrian and the mercifull Antonius
With fayre succession unto Macronius,
That were no more covetouse of croune imperial
Then desirous for to lyve in vertuous naturall.
And whiles that I thus loked all aboute,
I sawe fyve kynges amonges that rowte;
The syxte an evyll happe dyd hym take,
As one that foloweth vice and vertue doth forsake.

The Seconde Chapiter of Fame

Full of greate and infynyte marvayle,
I stode beholding these noble Romaynes well
Whiche of al other hadde never no peere;
And as I revolved their famous actes cleare
Which I have sene in bookes wrytten and tolde,
More was there of them dyvers and manyfolde
Then I have here in this place set in by name.
Therfore I nowe for this tyme passe the same
To loke upon straungers vertuous and excellent.
The fyrst was Hannybal that in ordre went;
The next was he that syngyng made his men
To have the vyctory, and there folowed then
Achylles the Greke, that in his havynge dayes
Gate by his prowes a great laude and prayse.
Twayne noble worthy Troyans were there also,
And twayne hardy Persiens in ordre ther did go;
Philip of Macedon, and his sonne Alexander,
That dyd bryng downe the Persiens great power
Unto subjection, (as in olde bookes we fynde)
And conquered therunto al the regyon of Inde;
After noble Fame they passed in that place.
And another named Alexander folowed a pace,
Not farre from the tother that went before.
But O, fortune, howe doest thou evermore
Dyvyde those that in the put theyr truste
From true honoure! Thou arte so unjuste!
There ensued in ordre there by and by
The gloryouse captayne valyaunt and worthy
Of Thebes, that ryall Citie of hygh renowne.
There was also he that had the famous crowne,
And twayne Achilles, and the wyse Ulixes,
And the hardy valiaunt Greke Dyomedes;
Nestor the sage that lyved so many yeares—
There was the olde kynge amonge his peeres;
Agamenon the great and the kynge Menelaus,
That both their two wyves to to ungracious

Muche hurt unto the hole worlde dyd they.
Folowed hardy Leonydes, that purposed (I saye)
To his men a harde dyner, but hardyest of all
Was the supper whereto he dyd them call.
With a fewe men he dyd a mervelouse dede.
Amonge the other there this captayne yede.
There was also the fayre knyght Alcibiades
That dyd straunge and great wonders in Athenes
With his fayre eloquent speche and fayre face;
Amonge the rest he was there in that place.
Melciedes was next that made all Grece free;
His sonne folowed the example of pytye,
That alyve and dead his father dyd ensue.
And among the other in prease there I knewe
Themistocles and the valyaunt Theseus;
Arystides and the good faythfull Fabricius,
Whiche theyr unkynde countrey (I do saye)
Woulde not suffre theyr bodyes to lye in claye.
Alas, this was a foule and an unkynde dede,
So to reward them for theyr well doynge mede!
The good Phocion folowed, whom I did regard
For his good dedes; they gave hym lyke rewarde.
And as I turned here and there my syght,
I sawe Pyrrus, that noble warlyke knyght,
And the good gentle kynge Masinises,
That semed angry because that doubtles
Amonge the Romaynes that he was not set.
With hym I knewe Iero of Syracuse the greate
And cruell Amylcar devyded from these twayne.
It was he that yssued from the fyre and rayne,
A manyfest token that nether helme nor shielde
Agaynst false fortune can never wynne the fyelde.
There was Sciphas much after that rate and sorte,
And Brennius, for all his great pryde and porte,
That was cast downe by Apollos temple syde;
After the other in ordre there he hyde.
In dyvers straunge garmentes and araye
Went this tryumphe onwarde on theyr waye,

And I that chaunced to cast my loke asyde,
I sawe a great huge number go and ryde,
Amonge them one that would Gods temple make,
And he fyrst began it for his love and sake.
This was the fyrst (I saye) in all that rowte.
But he that fynyshed that worke out of doubte,
That holy buyldyng of whiche that I do meane,
Was not inwarde so vertuouse nor so cleane
As the fyrst good kynge wheron I do saye.
Nowe he that folowed him in that greate arraye
Was he that spake to God face to face.
There was few or none that ever had such grace.
And after hym in lyke order by and by
Came he that stayde the Sonne so wonderly
Tyll he his enemies had taken and slayne.
O gentle trust most sure and certayne,
In servynge God as dyd this noble knyght,
With symple worde to stay the heavenly lyght!
I sawe after hym where that there went
Our olde father, whiche for good entent
God badde he shoulde his lande forsake;
And he for that shoulde possesse and take
The place that was helthfull to all mankynde.
Electe of God, there dyd he that countre fynde.
Folowed after this father his sonne moost dere
And his welbeloved nevew also he was there,
Whiche had the yoke in havynge wyves two.
There was with hym the chast Joseph also,
That from his father went full many a daye,
Thus here and there castynge myne eyes alwaye
I sawe the juste and good kynge Ezechias
And Sampson that so stronge and myghtye was;
And not farre distaunt from hym there went he
That made the great wonderfull shyppe of Noe;
And he also that the great hygh towre began,
Charged with synne and with errour than.
The good valyaunt Judas that noble knyght,
He there folowed after in ordre ryght,

That would not his holy godly lawe forsake.
Alas, he for Justice the death dyd take!
My desyre with seyng all these noble men
Was well nere fully satisfyed there and then
When that sodenly I dyd there espye
Of worthy ladyes a more gorgeous company
That pleased my syght as much or more
As all the syght that I had sene before.
There sawe I goyng together in a bande
Antiope and Orithia well armyd stand,
And fayre swete Ipolita sory and sadde
Because that no comforth of her sonne she had;
And Manylipe that vanquished Hercules
And her Suster also was there in prese;
The tone Hercules toke unto hys wyfe,
The tother with Theseus led her lyfe.
There folowed the hardy wydowe that dyd se
Hyr dere sone slayne most constantly,
And revenged hys death upon kyng Cyrus.
It was a noble hardy acte and valerouse.
She abatyd therby so his gloriouse fame
That wel nere it blotted his dedes and eke his name.
There was also she her selfe that lost her joye
By great mysfortune comming unto Troye.
And among other that bolde Lady of Italye
That domagid bi armes the Trojans marvelously;
And even by her went that hardy Lady
That halfe her fayre here bounde up curiously
And let the tother for to hange besyde
Tyll she abatyd the Babilonicall pryde;
Cleopatra, that was burnte with loves fyre,
There she was with all her hote desire.
And among the thickest of the prese
Was Xenobia, which was doutelesse
Wondre fayre and swete for to beholde;
Soo much of hardines her high harte dyd holde
That with her helme of stele on her hedde
She put in daunger, in feare, and eke in dreade

139

The high mightye Emperoure of Rome towne
Tyll fortune unkynde dyd thrawe her downe
That at the last she was made (I saye)
Unto the Romaynes a great huge pray.
And albeit that I do here forgete
Both men and women that wer highe and great,
Yet the chast Judeth wyll I call to mynde,
That slewe dronken Holyferne in love blynde
And dronken as he lay routing in his bedde.
Wyth hys owne sworde she smote of his hedd.
But, alas, why do I present her forget
That noble gentelman among the rest to sett
Which pride brought from his trone doune opprest
To lyve seven yeares as a brutyshe beste?
Or why do I not remember in this place
Zorastro, that the fyrst inventor was
Of arte magyke (of Errour the ground)?
Or why art not thys twayne here founde
That passyd Euphrates and put Italye to sorow?
Or Metridates, that both even and morowe
To the Romaynes was ennemie perpetuall
And wynter and somer fled over all?
Great thynges in fewe wordes I do tell.
Where is kyng Arthur, that dyd excell?
And the thre Cesares surnamed Augustus?
One was of Aufryke a Prynce gloriouse;
The tother he was of the Regyone of Spayne,
And the thyrde of the country of Lorrayne.
But setting this nobles for a whyle a syde,
The good Godfrey after Fame faste hyde,
Surnamed Bulleyne, that toke with his hand
Jherusalem the Cytie and eke the holy lande,
Nowe (alas, I say) a place neclecte of us!
Wherfore ryght well I may saye thus:
"Go ye, proude and wreched Christen men,
And consume the tone the tother then,
And care not (for shame!) among you at all,
Though dogges possesse the sepulcre royall.

Alas, why do you suffer it, for pitie!"
But after these, as farre as I coulde se,
Fewe or none was that deserved fame,
Saving that behynde there went by name
One Sarracene that dyd much payne and wo
To Christen men (it is even playnely soo)
And Saladyne after dyd folowe a great pase;
And one Duke of Lancaster after there was,
That with sheilde, and swerde, and bowe, and launce
Was a sharpe scourge unto the realme of Fraunce.
And thus marveylyng as I lokte all aboute,
As one that was desyrouse amongest the route
To se more of these valliaunt men,
At the last I dyd behold there and then
Twayne worthy men that lately (alas!) dyd dye.
There they went in that honorable companye:
The good kyng Robert of Cecyll he was there,
That with his wyse syght sawe fare and nere
And my good Columnes went in that arraye,
Vallyaunt and free and constant alway.

The Thirde Chapiter of Fame

I coulde not in noo wyse away put my syght
From these greate honorable men of myght
When as me thoughte one to me dyd saye,
"Loke on the lefte hande; there see thou may
The dyvyne Plato that goeth, I say, full nye
Unto the marke of fame even by and by.
Next unto Plato Aristotle there he is;
Pytagoras foloweth, that mekely calde Iwys
Phylosophy; he dyd geve it that name.
Socrates and Xenophontes folowed the same,
And that fyery olde auncient man
To whome the musys were so frandely than
That dyscryved Argo, Micena, and Troye,
Howe that for Helene they lost all their joye;
And he dyd wryte of Laertes sonne also,
And of Achilles that was the Troyanes woo.
He was the fyrst paynter, it is so tolde,
Of the auncient and venerable actes olde.
There went with hym in that place hand in hand
The Mantuan poete (I do well understand),
Stryvyng which of them should goo before.
And there folowed after in hast more and more
He that, as he passyde in that noble passe,
It semed the flowres dyd spryng on the grasse;
It is he, the most eloquent Marcus Tullius,
The selfe same eyes and the tunge gloriouse
Unto all the Latynes; there was he,
And after hym there came Demostyne,
That semyd to be not very well content
Because he was not accompted most excellent
To goo hymselfe next unto worthy Fame.
He toke it to be to hym great wrong and shame;
He semyd to be a lyghtnyng all one fyre,
But next unto hym (all full of grete desyre)
Went Eschynes, which myght perceave and se
Howe unmete he was unto Demostyne.

I cannot saye in ordre, nether wryte nor tell
Of one and other that dyd there exell,
Nor howe I dyd them se nor when,
Nor who went foremost nor hynmost then,
For it were so to do to great a wondre.
They went not fare, these clarkes, a sondre,
But so thycke that both eye and mynd
In lokyng on them theyr names I could not find.
But well I knowe that Solon he was there,
That planted soo good holsome frute to bere,
And yet to lytle effect at length it was.
With hym the syx wyse sage Grekes dyd pas
Which Grece doth boste of for theyr wyt.
In one bande together they were knyt;
And I dyd with these also well beholde
Varro, which all our nacione had enrolde
As theyr Duke. The thyrde in place was he
Of all the Romaynes in that high degree.
The more that I lokte upon hym there,
The more his face semed fayre and clere.
Crispo Salustius went with him hande in hande,
And Tytus Livius by hym dyd there stande,
Scant contented, but lokyng very sadde
Because the fyrst honoure there he ne had.
And as I loked fast on this Tytus Livius,
Came by me the excellent naturall Plinius,
Quick in wrytyng but quycker to the death;
To muche boldenes dyd stoppe, alas, his breath.
I sawe after hym the great clarcke Plotinus,
That, wenyng by hys lyfe solytariouse
To have prevented his harde chaunce and destenye,
Yet fell he therin (for truth, this is no lye);
His sage foresyght dyd profyt hym nothyng
When necessitie therto dyd hym brynge.
There was in lykewyse among the rest also
Crasso, Antonio, and sage Hortensio,
Sergius Galba, and the disdayning Licinius,
Whiche were to muche proude and to to curiouse

For with theyr tunges untrue and unjuste
They sclaundered Cicero; they were the lesse to trust!
There folowed after Thucides in that pres,
That ordeyned with wisedome the howres doutles,
And wrote of the battels and wher they were done;
And Herodotus with his style holesome
And he beganne the crafty sciense of Geometre,
The triangle and the rounde Orball in degre
And of the quadrant fyrme and fast also,
The Sophisticall Porphirus next hym dyd go
And falsely dysputed agaynst our religion;
And he of Coo that with his disputacion
Made muche matter in his Amphorisomis;
Apollo and Esculapius with hym is,
Howbeit they were so auncyent and olde
That scant I could decerne what they would.
There was one in that prease of Pargamo;
His science is now past (it is verye so),
But in his tyme it was muche set by;
Anaxarco, without dread, most hardye;
And Xenocrates more fyrme then a stone,
So that there coulde no evyll temptation
Move hym to any thinge that was vyle
Or by unclennes his chast body defyle.
There folowed hym self there Archemenides;
With sadde regarde he stode in that pres;
And the pensyfe Democryte next in ordre there;
Blynde of both his eyes, he had no pere.
There was Hyppia also of great auncient age,
That durst affyrme that he was so wyse and sage
That he knewe and understode all thynge;
Archisilao ensued, not much unlyke such rekening,
That he accompted by hys scyence playne
All thynge to be doubtfull and certayne.
I saw Heraclito with wordes covert and close,
And Diogenes folowyng his sensual purpose
That lytle shamed his desyre to ensue.
Amonge the other this straunge clerke I knewe.

And he that shewed a gladde mery chere
When al his landes were lost and other gere.
There was also Dicearco the Curyouse,
Quintilian, Sceneke, and Plutarke the famouse;
And after these excellent and connynge men
I sawe a great number together then
Disputinge of dyvers sundry cases,
Not to knowe but to fynde secret places,
One contrarye unto the tother alwayes
That it semed there clateryng was lyke jayes
With a romblynge as the shyppes that be
In a ragynge tempest upon the large see.
Even as Lyons and serpentes hurle together,
Withoute profyte, nowe hyther, nowe thyther
Was there disputation. And after these than
Wyttye Carneades, that well lerned man,
That coulde with speach a case so fyle
That were it true or false hys subtyll style
It was harde his craft to knowe and discerne.
He lyved longe without all syknes and harme
Tyll false envy agaynst hym dyd soo aryse
That he coulde not, although he were wyse,
Resyst the fury of them that hym hatyd
Nor the veneme that agaynst hym was debatyd.
There was also the bablynge Epicurus,
That agaynst Syros was greatlye contrariouse,
That affirmed oure soules never to dye.
This Epycure cleene contrary dyd denye,
And sayd that our soules were very mortall
And perysshe as best soules do with the body all,
Wherby he deserved to have reprove and blame
And scant worthy for to folowe Fame.
I sawe dyvers other folowinge thys secte:
Lyppo and Metrodorus and Aristippus the electe,
For theyr excellent conninge that they then hade
Praysed greatly, though theyr saynges were bad.
There was also that Phylozopher that in very dede
Spune the subtle and wonderouse crafty threde;

The Tryumphe of Fame, III: 151–162

Hys wyt was so excellent and his learning so fine
That he semed to have a knowledge devyne.
Zenone, the Father of the Stoykes secte,
Above the rest he was best electe;
Well declared he as he dyd there stande
By the palme and closyng of his hande
Howe the truth was in eche season and case,
For he so declared it with his wyse face,
The vayne argumentes from the true even so,
That many after hym dyd ensue and go.
Here I do leve to speake more of the rest,
And nowe wyll tell of that thyng which is best.

The ende of the Tryumphe of Fame.

The Excellent and Moste Dyvyne
Tryumphe of Tyme

Frome hys golden harboroughe and restyng place,
The fayre Aurora going afore his face,
Yssewed out the sonne so clear and fyrmely set
With radient and bryght beames burnished and bet,
That thou woldest have said even with a thought:
"Thys faire swete planet was gotten up a loft."
Thus up rysen in lyke maner and guyse
As do these sage men sober sadde and wyse,
He loked all about and to hymselfe he sayde:
"What doest thou nowe? I se well at this brayde
Yf to thyne one selfe thou take no better hede,
All thy great glory wylbe gone in dede.
Take thou then, I advyse the, good and wise cure;
For yf that it be very certeyne and sure
That worthy men by fame dyeng do not dye,
Thys universall and fyrme course eternally
Of the large heven most sure and certayne
Shalbe accompted at the last but vayne.
And yf fame mortall forever do encrease,
That a litle short houre shuld cause to sease,
I se my great excellence shall soone declyne;
And howe can I have a worse ende and fyne
Than to have no more in the hevenly skye
Than man in earth that dying cannot dye
That thynke my selfe equall by speciall grace
Above all other to have the highest place?
In the great wyde and large see Occeane
Foure horses of myne are there and than
That with great studye I nourishe and dresse
In theyr rennyng course of infinite switenesse,
And yet for all theyr great wonderfull hoste
Cannot a mortall man that is dead and past
Put in forgetting neyther his laude nor fame.
It muste neades greve and anger me that same,

Not onely I my selfe, the chefe in my degree,
But the thyrde or seconde wold therat greved be.
I must than hast my selfe with a great zele
Agaynst these men for the wrong that I fele
In doublyng my course to there double harme,
For I do envy there fame that is so farme
That after a thousand and a thousand yeares
Theyr high renowme and theyr glory cleres
Much more after theyr death then in theyr lyfe,
Which playne is unto me a perpetuall stryfe,
That am nowe no higher nor in no better rate
Than I was or the earth was in his firste state,
Goyng in compasse with my beames bryght
By thys great round bole which is infinite."
When this fayre beautifull sonne had thus sayde,
Dysdaynyng furthwith and even at a brayde,
She toke her course far more swyfter, I say,
Then Faukon that from a high flyeth to the praye.
Her wonders swiftnes I can nether tel nor write,
For it is not possible for me it to endyte,
Nor, I say, with my thought to expresse it in dede.
So that to remember it I am in feare and dreade.
Then, I saye, when that wyttely I mynded this,
I compted oure lyfe to be a vyle thynge as it is,
And none other nor no better but a terrible vanite
To put oure hartes on that which sone doth fle
So fast away that even with a thought,
Wenyng to holde hym, we holde hym noughte.
He whosoever doth loke unto his state,
Let hym sone provyde for hym selfe algate
Whyles he hath his fre wyl in his propre myghte,
In thynges that be stable to set his delyght.
For when I sawe the tyme goo so fast
After his guyde that maketh post hast
(I wyll not saye it, for tell it I ne can)
For I sawe even at one verye poynte than
The yse and the rose one after the other—
Nowe colde, nowe hote even with the tother—

That for to tell it is a marvelous case.
Nowe after the tone the tother hyeth a pase.
He that with a wyse judgement this markes
Shall se by true experience all these warkes,
Which lytle I noted in my yonge lusty age,
And that maketh me nowe with my selfe to rage.
For then, I confesse, all my hoole delyght
Was in folowyng my folysh appetyte;
But now afore my feble eyes is a glasse
Wherin I spye my greate faulte that was,
Styll goynge downeward to my last ende and fyne,
Remembryng therto howe fast it doth declyne.
I was a chylde even this same present daye,
And nowe an olde man prest to passe away
So that (for a very truth to tell it I shall)
Lesse then a sely daye is oure lyfe mortall,
Cloudy and colde, and ful of woo and payne,
That semeth to be fayre, and yet is but vayne.
This is the unstable hope of all our kynde.
Why are we then so proude? Why are we so blynd,
When no man knoweth hys lyfe nor his death?
And this note onely, as the sage man sayeth,
Doth not touche me but all that be alyve.
The fast course of the Sonne doth away dryve,
That plainly and manifestly the truth note I shal.
The ruyne of the worlde is knowen to us all.
Then, ye yonge men that be in your fresh lust,
Measure the tyme longe and put therto your trust
Folyshly, I say playnly! Why cal ye not to mynd
Afore consydered hurte lesse hurteth by kynde?
Onles I blowe these wordes to you in vayne,
But I do tel you (note it for truth and certayne)
Ye that do not mynde, nor well remember this:
With a slepy lytargy your brayne combred is,
For the howres flye a pace, so doth the dayes.
The monethes and the yeares folowe alwayes
Together in a breif shorte distaunce and tyme.
So that yf ye well and wysely note this ryme,

We must all mortall men to another countre pas,
And all our great glory shalbe turned to was.
Goo ye not then agayne the truth, I do saye,
But amende your evyll lyves whyles that ye may.
Do not abyde tyll dreadfull death you take,
As the most part of the unwytty doth, I undertake.
O that ye wyll not this well understande!
Of fooles there is doubtles an infinite bande.
Sythens then I do knowe and playnly se
This great planet howe fast it doth fle,
Which tyme when I myght, by folye I have not taken,
But with muche great losse this tyme forsaken.
I sawe amonge these unwyse foles all
A nation that by theyr science lytle cared at all,
Nor feared not oft tyme the course rabidouse.
These, I saye, removed and people most gloriouse
Whiche hystorians hath taken in theyr garde,
And poetes also that wrote howe that they farde.
Of this it semed then the sonne had envye,
Whiche by them selfe so mounted to hyghe glorye,
Passyng awaye from the madde vulgar quyte
By the honorable vertuous wayes noble and right.
He hasted then this Sonne a wonders spedy pas
With moche more forse then ever there was,
And to his swyft horses he doubled the meate,
Passynge by the great beare, this planet great,
So that the quene of whome I have sayde
Would have departed from the sonne at the brayde.
I have hard saye (I wote not well of whome)
That even as a wede wasteth our glory is goone,
And that all our fame is but blynde and derke
And a perpetual forgetfulnes al our labor and werk;
And he sayd further that all the longe yeares
And the processe also of the lusters and speares
And of worldes infinite hereafter for to come
Shall vanysh awaye our fame al and some—
Doubtles of as many (it is playne even so)
As are betwyxt these places Peneo and Hebro,

Or as far a sunder as that ryver of Zanto
Is distaunt by measure from the valey of Thebro—
And that oure glory is to be sayde by ryght
Even as we se the ayer fayre and bryght
Made darke and hydde with a mysty cloude.
And, breifly, this alwayes note wel we should:
A hasty longe rynnyng awaye of the tyme
Is a poyson to fame to cause it to declyne.
Our Tryumphs shal passe, our pompes shal decay;
Our lordshyppes, our kyngdomes shall all awaye,
And al thynge also that we accompt mortall
Tyme at the length shal clene deface it al.
And to this those that are but meanly good
(They affirme and say playne that who so understode)
Not onely our bodyes sone away doth passe,
But all our wyttes and eloquence in lyke case.
Thus not goyng but flying the world doth go,
Nor resysteth, nor tarieth not (it is playne so)
Tyl he have brought al false worldly luste
To no better thynge but to bare ashes and duste.
Why than hath humayne glory so much hy pryde?
When that it is very playne sene on every syde
(Although the vulgar doth not this thinge marke)
We shuld wel by ryght experience know this wark
That these foles do bable they wote not what
If that the case were, our short lyfe declyned not
So sone nor so swyftly unto the last ende.
Al the hye fame whereto that men pretende
Even as the smoke doth vanyshe awaye;
So at the last al thynges do plane decay.
This hearing, me think it standes with good reason
Not for to deny the truth at no season,
But to agre to that thynge we do wel know.
Even by comparison as the sonne melteth the snow,
So doth the tyme put awaye and shall
Not a thousande famouse, but at the last them all—
Though that the moost part thynke it be not so.
O therfore, I saye, howe blynde are they therto

The Tryumphe of Tyme, 187–204

That thynke it muche better for to die in age
Then lyinge in the cradle to go that passage!
To how many men had it ben far passing better,
Yea, and I affyrme it a thousand tymes more sweter,
To have dyed beyng yonge then to have died old?
Many excellent clarckes doth it by reason holde
That muche more fortunate the unborne chylder be
Then chyldren that be borne such payne to se,
But the great number hath alway greatest error.
If it were so certayne and therunto so sure
That after a longe lyfe shuld come a longe fame,
Who be they, I pray you, that wyll folow the same?
The covetous time turneth al thinge up so doune,
And our great fame that doth so hyghly soune
It is no nother to be named but a second death,
Nor stay is there none, as the true truth sayth.
Thus tryumpheth tyme and hasteth so a pace,
That all our glory and fame it doth deface.

The ende of the Tryumphe of tyme.

The Excellent and Moste Devyne
Tryumphe of Dyvynitie

Sythyns that under the heaven nothing I se
Stable and fyrme but all mere vanitie,
I remembred my selfe and to my selfe dyd say:
"In whome doest thou trust, tell me, I the pray."
Softly I am answered: "Unto that Lord I trust,
That of his promise is to faythfull and just
That who so in hym hath a true perfect fayth
Shall never be dysceyved, so his wordes sayth,
For well I se the false worlde dyd me but scorne,
And I knowe what I am and what I was beforne.
And I se the tyme not for to go but to flye,
And I know not in dread of whome to be sorye,
But of my selfe that have deserved blame
That have not or nowe remembred the same.
The faulte is in me, that longe (I say) or this
Shuld have considered my great foly, Iwys,
And so opened myne eyes and not fallen to slothe,
To have perceyved and knowen the trouthe
In differing my lyfe unto the last combrous age,
Which by course of tyme continually do asswage.
But slowe was never the devyne grace
To call me to goodnes and vertue apase.
In it I put my trust that yet in me shall be
High operacion from all evell to flye."
Thus with my selfe disputing to and froo
I thought even very thus: "Yf that it be soo,
These thinges that in this wise turne about the ski
And guide and governe it in ordre so mervelousli,
After so much turnyng and revolving to and froo,
What ende shall I have, I would fayne knowe soo?"
And as that I was solitarie in this meditatione
It semed to me I sawe a wonderfull facion,
A newe fayre worlde stable and eterne
And this olde world that semeth so ferme—

The Tryumphe of Divinitie, 35–72

The sonne and the stares and the heaven rounde
And the great se also with the earth and ground—
To vanyshe clene awaye and in theyr rome and place
A newe merier world made by Godes grace.
What great (trowe ye, then) admiracion had I
When I sawe the sonne, firmament, and the skye
Stand fyrme on one fote sure, stable, and faste
That with his swyft course runnyng at the laste
Changed all thinges mortall and then restrained,
His thre partes brought to one part unfayned
And then no distinction, no difference of them at al,
But the herbe and grasse and flowers with all
All bareyne and bare before and behynde,
Which variacion doth naturally bekynde
Much bitter sorowe to our nature frayle,
All at ones together then and there to fayle.
Then the thought passeth as the sonne the glasse
And much more, for nothing the powre hase
It for to holde or elles for to refrayne:
O what grace shall that be for man to attayne
To se in that place the everlasting God
And none evell at all which of the Tyme woode
Onely commeth and goeth here and there,
To be out of doubte of all dread and feare.
The sonne than shall have no more his place,
Neyther in the hornyd Bull, nor in lyke case
In the Fyshe, in which two variable sygnes
Varieth the yerbes, the season, and the tymes.
Nowe we do sowe and after we do reape;
Nowe creasynge, nowe discresing, so is our heape,
But happye and blessed be those spirites certenly
That be found in that holy state eternally,
Sure and very certayne in honor to encrease,
Without terme or tyme, never to sease.
O, howe happye is he that fyndeth that way
To passe this Rabidus and dul passage, I say,
That is called in this unstable world a lyfe,
And is so troublouse and so ful of stryfe.

Blynd and wretched, I say, are the mortal
That hoopeth in thynges that sone doth fall,
Which tyme taketh away with a thought
And turneth al our fancis and foly to nought.
Surely they are both unwise, deffe, and frayle,
Poore of judgment and of Counsayle—
Yea, and worse then sike in dead and wretched therto—
That doth not as our deutie is—regard Hym so
That with His becke may trouble and appease
The elementes al as it doth Hym please,
Whome to honour we are not bound onlye
But the Aungels that sit in the heaven hye
Are contented of the thousand partes as one
With the sight of his godhead in his gloriouse trone
And so stand stedfast with a fervent Intention.
Are not our myndes then worthy of reprehencion,
To loke on that which in the very ende
Commeth to no profite, thereunto to pretende?
For that which we so fast gather together
With much paine in mani years hether and thether
With great and troubles cumbrance of mynd
To day and to morowe at the last we fynde
As the shadowe doth passe away and glyde;
Even at the poynt so shall all our pryde.
Then remember ye well, I truly counsell, this:
That after Goddes great dreadfull judgment "is"
"Was" and "shalbe" shall have no more time and place,
But one eternitie together in one selfe space.
Nor further there shalbe none objecte at all
To hurte by our sight our weake memoriall,
Which is the occacion and the very cause
Many an unprudent person in vanitie to pause
That the lyfe present semeth but a playe,
Thinking they are to morowe as to day.
But then all otherwyse shalbe no division at all,
But litle and litle the hole universall
Shalbe together and wynter and somer paste,
And tyme quiete gone and no lenger laste.

Nor these yeares that we do nowe presently name
Shall have no more the domynion of fame,
But ones theyr famouse that shall never dissever,
But in eternitie to endure famouse forever.
O happie are those soules that are in that way,
Of which so much I nowe speake of and say,
Injoy glory and rest styll to Endure
That are, and shalbe perpetually, so sure.
And amonge the other that so gracious be,
Most blessed of all other playnly is she
That cruell death kylled or she came to age.
There shalbe seene in that angelyke vysage
The honest wordes, the thought cleane and chast
That nature had set in her in olde tymes past.
And for because that every thought and thynge
Is playne and manyfest to the eternall kynge
When the blessed elect soules turned be
Unto the moost happy state of theyr fyrst degre,
With the poyntinge of the fynger even then
Shalbe sayde how, where, and also when.
Lo, this is he whiche that love deteyned
And longe and many a day lamented and complained,
And yet was most fortunate for to se the cheare
Above al other joyes in the world of his lady dere.
And she also (of whome that wepyng I synge)
Shall of her selfe have greate marvelyng
To beholde and fele in every wyse and degre
Her selfe above all other in Joy and felicitie.
When this shalbe God wote I cannot tell,
But she that is nygh of the great Goddes councel
This hygh prevy secrete in parte doth know,
And, for to declare and tel that I trowe,
It is (as I do ymagin) very nygh at hande.
And when that commeth, men shal understande
How evyl they theyr wanton tyme have spent
In gettyng worldly goodes, landes, and rent,
Wenyng for ever them to holde and possesse.
And yet for the final conclusion, it is doubtles

They shal se them selves in very dede
Mockt and scorned to trust unto suche mede.
No secrete nor hyd thing shalbe then and there,
But all secretes unshote, open, playne, and cleare
All our conscience, whether it be bright or darke;
Before al the world shall appeare our werke.
And then the myghtie and gloriouse king celestiall
That in His fearefull Judgment is not percial
(As reason is, and as it ought to be)
His wise Judgment therto shall agre.
And when that sentence is both gone and past,
Eche man his viage with great dread and hast,
As the wylde beastes that hast them fast to flye
Afore the barkyng doges for feare they in be,
Even in lyke wyse scattered here and there
Shalbe these proude men with all there gay gere
And playnely perceave that to there hurt it was
All such lucre when these thinges come to pas.
But those that by grace have brydled such delight
In refraining their vayne and covetouse appetite
And measured false fortune with an honest use
Be mery together without fraude and abuse.
Those be sure and certayne for to be
With the saintes in perpetuall joy and felicitie.
These fyve Tryumphes that I have here rehearsed
And under a straunge colour them expressed
Have nowe by Godes sufferaunce an ende,
With this the sixt whereto I dyd pretend.
Then ye that rede thys thynke this state eterne
And thinke that the Tyme that doth discerne
This unstable world turnyng to and froo
And fearefull gastly Death (it is playne so)
All shall vanyshe doubtles forever away.
Beleve me, this is sure after the last day.
And those that have worthely by vertuouse fame
Spent well there tyme lyving without blame,
And by vertue made both Death and Tyme to fere
Whyles that they lyved in this frayle world here,

In theyr most freshe and lustye young courage
They shall aryse tryumphantly about that age
With beautie immortall and high fame eterne,
Never after that tyme for to feele no harme.
But then afore all other that there shall be
In that endles glory we shal beholde and se
My fayre swete lady, of whome so much I write,
More beauteous then the sonne in his hyest light.
There is a litle ryver, Gebenna men it call,
Where first in love I chaunced for to fall.
There love dyd make me so longe a cruel warre
That yet I dread to thynke upon that starre.
Happy is that stone that covereth that swet face
Wherin there resteth so much beautie and grace.
If that then I were happy in thys lyfe it to se
Here on this vyle earth so perfect in degree,
After that this swete gratiouse Lady hath taken
That same fayre dispoyle that semyth now forsaken,
What shal it be (I praye you to tel me this)
Then to beholde hyr eternall blysse?

The ende of the Tryumphes of Fraunces Petrarcke.

Vyrgyll in his Epigrames
of Cupide and Dronkenesse

Nec vini nec tu veneris capieris Amore

That wonderous wytty Virgil that so wel cold endight
The wayes to wyne to vertue righte harde for to attayne
In his sentensiouse verses declareth with reason right
Howe that both wyne and women doth put a man to payne.
He sayth in passyng measure with eyther of these twayne
It is a thyng abhominable. Nowe here what he doth tell.
Although my ryme be rude to touche so high a vayne,
Yf that ye marke this doctrine, doubtles ye shall do well.

Thus sayeth our famouse poete: Love not to much wyne,
Nor yet on wanton Venus set not to much thy mynde.
For lyke as wanton Cupide thy strength doth quyte declyne,
So doth thys wyne thy force and all thy senses bynde,
Maketh a man to stacker and stumble as the blynde
That he forgetes hym selfe his enemie to repell,
Altereth and defaseth mans nature and his kynde.
Yf that ye marke this doctrine, doubtles ye shall do well.

Venus is ful of pleasure. Who can to this say nay?
But if it fall to rage, then reason goeth asyde;
Then turneth it to werynes and to a grevouse playe,
Most paynefull to hymselfe when he is most in pryde,
Unneth his secrete pastymes the foole he doth not hyde,
No more then doth the dronkerd that all on wyne doth smell.
They are not much unlyke when reason hath them tryed.
If that ye note this doctrine, doubtles ye shall do well.

Who that with wine is whitled no counsell will he kepe.
As well his frende as foo shall knowe all his entent.
Who so with Lady Venus in brased armes doth slepe
Doth now and then disclose that thing he doth repent.
And this is not the worse that on this twayne is ment;
These bryng in warre and wo, the one the other to quell,

159

Somtime but for a tryfle tyll lyfe and all be spent.
If that ye note this doctryne, doubteles ye shall do well.

Parys by Venus councell brought Helene unto Troy.
Though that the pryce was swet, the ende was passyng sower,
For many a worthy warryor therby dyd lese theyr Joye,
And Troy turned unto Asshes both castel wall and towre.
This wanton wylfull dalyeng raysyd so great a shoure
That of that happe that happened the worlde doth speake and tel.
Loo howe Venus can flatter when she thinketh to devoure!
If that ye note this doctrine, doubtles ye shall do well.

Then yf that wyne and Venus have ones the upper hande
And on the one or both the mynde set in a rage,
All honestie is excluded and wytt tyed in a band,
And vertue fayre and dread fast locked in a cage.
Although he be a lorde, yet serves he as a page,
Two perlouse noughty vices worse then a fend of hell.
Where that these monsters rule right hard for to aswage.
If that ye note this doctryne, doubtles ye shall do well.

Wyll ye then be wise and learne to rule these twayne?
Do as oure Virgill counseles and ye shall lyve in reste.
Tye up both wyne and Venus fast fetered with a chayne,
Lest that with theyr rewardes the mynde be not opprest.
Let wyne but quenche thy thurst (so is that lycour best);
Let Venus serve to multiply our nature that doth excel.
But and ye passe these bondes, then is the goodnes ceast.
If that ye note this doctryne, doubtles ye shall do wel.

Measure is more worth then golde or precious stone,
And in forsakynge measure a good thynge turnes to vyce.
To to muche at length hath caused many a one
For to descende as fast as they dyd up aryse.
Then thus for to conclude: I count hym perfyt wyse
That rules hym selfe in measure and to to doth repell.
So use both wyne and wemen that ye be not to nyse.
If that ye note this doctryne, doubtles ye shall do well.

Finis.

Bibliographical History
of Morley's *Tryumphes*

Morley's translation of Petrarch's *Trionfi* is one of the rarest books in the English language, as well as a literary curiosity of a very special kind. The translation appeared in only one edition, and there are no extant manuscripts of the work; its licensing and printing cannot be traced because it appeared before the incorporation of the Stationers's Company in 1557. There exist only five copies of the work: two at the British Museum, one at the Bodleian Library, one at the Sion College Library in London, and one at the Henry E. Huntington Library in San Marino, California. For some reason, the Sion College Library copy eluded the compilers of the *Short Title Catalogue* (who assigned the number 19,811 to the *Tryumphes*); it was also missed by David Ramage in his survey of rare books in libraries in the British Isles.[1]

Of the two copies of Morley's *Tryumphes* at the British Museum, the first, C.13.a.7(2), is bound together with another sixteenth-century translation from Petrarch, Thomas Twynne's *Physicke Against Fortune* (1579), a rendering of *De remediis utriusque fortune*. The Bodleian Library copy and the Sion College Library copy are also bound together with Twynne's translation, a circumstance perhaps indicating that sixteenth-century booksellers attempted to satisfy the demand for translations from Petrarch by providing two translations under one cover.

The other British Museum copy, G.10713, was originally housed at the British Museum, but was sold to the Grenville Library in 1832 at a sale of museum duplicates, and was subsequently listed in the catalog of the Grenville collection.[2] In 1847, after the death of a Lord Grenville, the entire Grenville collection was bequeathed to the British Museum, and the copy was returned to its original home.

The Bodleian Library copy of the *Tryumphes*, 4°.P.57(2).JUR, bound together with Twynne's *Physicke Against Fortune*, has a more complicated history. Neither the *Tryum-phes* nor the *Physicke* was mentioned in any Bodleian Library catalog until that of 1843, which mentioned only the *Physicke* (though an interleaved copy of that catalog has a manuscript entry for the *Tryumphes*). It is likely that the volume was acquired at some time between the appearance of the 1738 Bodleian Library catalog, in which neither the *Tryumphes* nor the *Physicke* appeared, and the 1843 catalog. A current librarian's examination of the handlist of books included under the rubric "JUR" suggests that the book was probably added to the Bodleian Library late in the eighteenth century.[3]

The present Henry E. Huntington Library copy of the *Tryumphes* belonged originally to Richard Heber, the early nineteenth-century bibliomane who scoured Europe for rare editions and eventually amassed a library of some 150,000 books. He died in 1833, and in the following year his entire collection was put up for sale and described in a catalog compiled by J. Payne Collier.[4] Collier noted that "a duplicate since discovered in the British Museum was sold by Sotheby, July, 1832, and bought by Thorpe for Mr. Grenville." He added that Heber's copy was "black letter, beautiful copy, in morocco with joints." At some unspecified time after 1834 the volume was purchased for the Britwell Court Collection; it remained there until March 15, 1923, when it was purchased for the Henry E. Huntington Library.[5]

For inexplicable reasons, the Sion College Library copy of the *Tryumphes* was overlooked by eighteenth-century bibliographers such as Thomas Hearne and Joseph Ritson, by the nineteenth-century bibliographers Collier, Hazlitt, and Lowndes, and by all the modern bibliographers.[6] The volume, according to the account of a Sion College librarian,[7] was acquired in 1711 as part of a collection made by one Thomas James, a London printer who was the grandson of the earlier Thomas James, the Bodleian's first librarian. James bequeathed about three thousand English books to "public uses," and his widow decided that Sion College would be a suitable recipient. The volume was entered in William Reading's printed catalog of the Sion College Library (1724),[8] but it appeared under "Henry Parker," not under "Petrarch" or "Morley" and was probably missed for that reason. The original binding, including Twynne's *Physicke Against Fortune*, was in poor condition and the two volumes were recently rebound separately.

Though Morley's translation of Petrarch's *Trionfi* is an extremely rare book, it has enjoyed a limited reputation among scholars and antiquarians since the eighteenth century, and perhaps even as early as the sixteenth century, if William Fowler's complaint about the poor quality of unnamed French and English translations is in actuality a veiled reference to Morley's *Tryumphes*.

Thomas Warton was one of the first to include Morley in a history of English literature, describing him as one of those members of the Tudor nobility who were "fond of making verses."[9] Following Bale, Warton described Morley as a writer of comedies and tragedies, and he seems to have known Morley's "Commentary on the Penitential Psalms," as well as the translations, which he had seen at the "royal repository" (as he called the forerunner of the British Museum). Oddly, Warton made no mention of either the *Tryumphes* or Morley's translation of Boccaccio's *De claris mulieribus*.

In the following century Morley's *Tryumphes* caught the attention of all the major bibliographers and antiquarians. The antiquarian Joseph Ritson, also following Bale, included Morley in his catalog of English poets from the twelfth to the sixteenth centuries, noted that he was a writer of "comedys and tragedys," but made no mention of the translations from Petrarch and Boccaccio.[10]

Some years later, in 1820, J. Payne Collier made Morley and the *Tryumphes* the subject of the second of ten "conversations" on rare and unique works in his *The Poetical Decameron*.[11] One of the speakers in the "conversation" notes that Morley lived and worked in the court of Henry VIII, but warns that his verses are not of the same quality as those of his contemporaries Wyatt and Surrey. After reminding the reader that Morley's translation of the *Trionfi* is not a very faithful one, Collier closes the conversation with the remark that the *Tryumphes* should be looked upon as "filling a place anterior to the date when they [Wyatt and Surrey] became celebrated."

In 1887 the Roxburghe Club published an unannotated edition of the *Tryumphes* with a scanty preface providing the barest details about Morley and his translation. The editing of the work had originally been assigned to Stafford Henry, Earl of Iddesleigh, by the vice-president of the Roxburghe Club. But Lord Iddesleigh died before the edition was finished, and its completion was assigned to Mr. J. E. T. Loveday, who used as his copy text an inaccurate transcript prepared by J. Payne Collier. Collier's transcript was collated with the two British Museum copies of the *Tryumphes*, and though Loveday presumably knew of the existence of the (then) Britwell copy and the Bodleian copy, he did not consult them. The Roxburghe Club edition contains an index of names which occur in the text, with modern spellings for those names which are not easily recognizable to modern readers, but neither Lord Iddesleigh nor Mr. Loveday attempted to provide historical and literary background for the translation, nor did they compare Morley's translation with the original.

Since 1887, no complete edition of Morley's *Tryumphes* has appeared, though Eleanor Prescott Hammond did include Morley's dedicatory epistle to Lord Maltravers and the entire first chapter of the "Tryumphe of Love" in her *English Verse between Chaucer and Surrey* (London, 1927).

General Bibliography

Commentaries, Editions, and Translations of Petrarch

Alunno, Francesco, ed. "Le Osservationi di M. Francesco Alunno sopra il Petrarca" in *Le Rime del Petrarca Novamente Ristampate.* Venice, 1550.

Appel, Karl, ed. *Die Triumphe Francesco Petrarca im Kritischen Texte Herausgeben.* Halle: Verlag von Max Niemayer, 1901.

Bishop, Morris, trans. *Letters from Petrarch.* Bloomington: Indiana University Press, 1966.

—— trans. *Love Rimes of Petrarch.* Ithaca: Dragon Press, 1932.

Boyd, Henry, trans. *The Triumphs of Francesco Petrarch, Florentine Poet Laureate.* London, 1802.

Calcaterra, Carlo, ed. *Francesco Petrarca: Trionfi.* Turin: Unione Tipografico–Editrice Torinese, 1927.

Castelvetro, Lodovico, ed. *Le Rime del Petrarca brevemente sposte.* Basel, 1582.

Chiorboli, Ezio, ed. *Le Rime Sparse e i Trionfi.* Bari: Laterza, 1930.

Costo, Tomaso, ed. *Il Petrarca Nuovamente Ridotto alla vera Lettione.* Venice, 1592.

Daniello, Bernardino, ed. *Sonetti, Canzoni e Triomphi di M. Francesco Petrarca, con la Spositione di Bernardino Daniello da Lucca.* Venice, 1549.

Dolce, Lodovico, ed. *Il Petrarca corretto da M. Lodovico Dolce.* Venice, 1547.

Fausto, Sebastiano, ed. *Il Petrarcha col commento di M. Sebastiano Fausto da Longiano.* Venice, 1532.

Forge, Georges de la, trans. *Les triumphes messire francoys petrarcque.* Paris, 1538.

Fowler, William. *The Works of William Fowler,* ed. Henry W. Meikle. 3 vols. Edinburgh and London: The Scottish Text Society, 1914–1940.

Gesualdo, Giovanni Andrea, ed. *Il Petrarcha con la Spositione di Giovanni Andrea Gesualdo.* Venice, 1541.

Henry, Stafford, Lord Iddesleigh, and J. E. T. Loveday, eds. *Henry Parker, Lord Morley: The Tryumphes of Fraunces Petrarcke.* London, 1887.

Hozes, Hernando, trans. *Los Triumphos de Francisco Petrarcha.* Medina del Campo, 1554.

Hume, Anna, trans. *The Triumphs of Love: Chastitie: Death.* London, 1644.

Illicino, Bernardo, ed. *Triumphi del Petrarcha.* Venice, 1488.

—— *Triumphi del Petrarcha.* Venice, 1490.

Leopardi, Giacomo, ed. *Rime di Francesco Petrarca.* Milan, 1826.

Maldeghem, Philippe de, trans. *Sonnets, Chansons et Triomphes de M. F. Petrarque.* Paris, 1597.

Muratori, Lodovico Antonio, ed. *Le Rime di Francesco Petrarca e le Osservazioni d'Antonio Muratori.* Modena, 1711.

Neri, Ferdinando, *et al.,* eds. *Rime, Trionfi e Poesie Latine.* Milan: R. Ricciardi, 1951.

—— *Rime e Trionfi di Francesco Petrarca.* Turin: Unione Tipografico–Editrice Torinese, 1963.

Obregon, Antonio de, trans. *Francisco Petrarca con los seys triunfos de toscano sacados en castellano.* Logrono, 1516.

Opède, Jean Meynier d', trans. *Les Triumphes Petrarques.* Paris, 1538.

Perna, Peter, trans. *Sechs Triumph Francisci Petrarche.* Basel, 1578.

Philieul, Vasquin, trans. *Toutes les Euvres vulgaires de Francoys Petrarque.* Paris, 1555.

Poggio, Jacopo. *Sopra el triumpho di Petrarca.* Florence, 1485.

General Bibliography

Rawski, Conrad H., ed. and trans. *Four Dialogues for Scholars.* Cleveland: Press of Western Reserve University, 1967.

Sonnets, Triumphs . . . of Petrarch. Bohn Illustrated Library. London, 1879.

Tassoni, Alessandro. *Considerazioni Sopra le Rime del Petrarca.* Modena, 1609.

Velutello, Alessandro, ed. *Il Petrarca con l'Espositione d'Alessandro Velutello.* Venice, 1550.

Wilkins, Ernest Hatch, trans. *Petrarch at Vaucluse: Letters in Verse and Prose.* Chicago: University of Chicago Press, 1958.

—— trans. *The Triumphs of Petrarch.* Chicago: University of Chicago Press, 1963.

Other Works Cited and Consulted

Allen, H. E. *Writings Ascribed to Richard Rolle, Hermit of Hampole.* New York: D. C. Heath and Co., 1927.

Appel, Karl. *Zur Entwickelung Italienischen Dichtungen Petrarcas.* Halle, 1891.

Aptekar, Jane. *Icons of Justice: Iconography and Thematic Imagery in Book V of "The Faerie Queene."* New York: Columbia University Press, 1969.

Ariosto, Lodovico. *Orlando Furioso,* trans. William Stewart Rose and ed. Stewart A. Baker and A. Bartlett Giamatti. New York: Bobbs-Merrill Co., 1969.

Ascham, Roger. "The Scolemaster" in *Roger Ascham: English Works,* ed. William Aldis Wright. Cambridge: Cambridge University Press, 1904.

—— *The Schoolmaster,* ed. Lawrence V. Ryan. Ithaca: Cornell University Press, 1967.

Azzolina, Liborio. "I 'Trionfi' del Petrarca," *Giornale Dantesco,* XIII (1905), 37–43.

Bacon, Francis. *The Works of Sir Francis Bacon,* ed. J. Spedding, R. L. Ellis, and D. D. Heath. 15 vols. London: Longmans, 1887–1902.

Bale, John. *Scriptorum Illustrium Maioris Brytannie . . . Catalogus.* Basel, 1557–1559.

Baker, Carlos. *Shelley's Major Poetry: The Fabric of a Vision.* Princeton: Princeton University Press, 1948.

Barrett, John. *An Alvearie, or Quadruple Dictionarie.* London, 1580.

Bernardo, Aldo S. *Petrarch, Scipio, and the "Africa": The Birth of Humanism's Dream.* Baltimore: Johns Hopkins Press, 1962.

Bertoni, Giulio. *Per la fortuna dei "Trionfi" del Petrarca in Francia.* Modena: Libreria Editrice Internazionale, 1904.

"Bibliographical Notes: Sion College Library," anon. review, *Times Literary Supplement,* 27 January 1940.

Biblioteca Grenvilliana, ed. John Thomas Payne and Henry Foss. 2 vols. London, 1842.

Biblioteca Heberiana, ed. J. Payne Collier. Part IV, Day 9. London, 1834.

Billanovich, Giuseppe. *Il Petrarca letterato.* Rome: Edizioni di storia e letteratura, 1947.

Bishop, Morris. *Petrarch and His World.* Bloomington: Indiana University Press, 1963.

Bishop, William Warner. *A Checklist of American Copies of the Short Title Catalog.* New York: Greenwood Press, 1968.

Boas, Frederick S. *An Introduction to Tudor Drama.* Oxford: Clarendon Press, 1933.

Boccaccio, Giovanni. "Vita di Dante" in *Il Commento alla "Divina Commedia" e gli altri scritti intorno a Dante,* ed. Domenico Guerri. Bari: G. Laterza e Figli, 1918.

Bosco, Umberto. *Francesco Petrarca.* Bari: Laterza, 1968.

Bradley, A. C. "Notes on Shelley's 'Triumph of Life,'" *Modern Language Review,* IX (1914), 441–456.

Brusendorff, Aage. *The Chaucer Tradition.* London: Oxford University Press, 1925.

Burckhardt, Jacob. *The Civilisation of the Renaissance in Italy*. London: Phaidon Press, 1951.

Calcaterra, Carlo. *Nella Selva di Petrarca*. Bologna: Cappelli, 1942.

—— "Il Petrarca e il petrarchismo" in *Questioni e Correnti di Storia Letteraria*, ed. Umberto Bosco. Milan: C. Marzorati, 1963.

—— "La prima ispirazione dei 'Trionfi,'" *Giornale Storico*, CXVIII (1941), 1–47.

Carnicelli, D. D. "Bernardo Illicino and the Renaissance Commentaries on Petrarch's *Trionfi*," *Romance Philology*, XXIII, Number 1 (August, 1969), 57–64.

Chaucer, Geoffrey. *The Works of Geoffrey Chaucer*, ed. F. N. Robinson. Boston: Houghton Mifflin Co., 1957.

Chew, Samuel C. *The Pilgrimage of Life*. New Haven: Yale University Press, 1962.

Christie-Miller, Sydney Richardson. *Catalogue of a Further Selection of Extremely Rare and Valuable Works in Early English Poetry and Other Literature from the Renowned Library Formerly at Britwell Court*. London, 1923.

Clark, J. M. *The Dance of Death in the Middle Ages and the Renaissance*. Glasgow: Jackson, Son and Co., 1950.

Clemen, Wolfgang. *Chaucer's Early Poetry*, trans. C. C. M. Sym. New York: Barnes and Noble, 1963.

Clements, Robert John. *Picta Poesis: Literary and Humanistic Theory in Renaissance Emblem Books*. Rome: Edizioni di storia e letteratura, 1960.

Collier, J. Payne. *A Bibliographical and Critical Account of the Rarest Books in the English Language*. 6 vols. New York, 1866.

—— *The Poetical Decameron*. 2 vols. Edinburgh, 1820.

Cooper, Thomas. *Thesaurus Linguae Romanae et Brittanicae*. London, 1565.

Curtius, E. R. *European Literature and the Latin Middle Ages*, trans. W. R. Trask. New York: Pantheon Books, 1953.

Davies of Hereford, John. *Works in Verse and Prose*, ed. A. B. Grosart. 2 vols. Blackburn, 1869–1876.

Dekker, Thomas. *The Non-Dramatic Works of Thomas Dekker*, ed. A. B. Grosart. 5 vols. London, 1884–1886.

Deyermond, A. D. *The Petrarchan Sources of "La Celestina."* London: Oxford University Press, 1961.

Dürer, Albrecht. *Drawings by Albrecht Dürer*, ed. F. P. Lippman. Berlin, 1883.

Dyer, Edward. *The Writings in Verse and Prose of Sir Edward Dyer*, ed. A. B. Grosart. 4 vols. Blackburn, 1870–1876.

Elizabeth I of England. *The Poems of Queen Elizabeth I*, ed. Leicester Bradner. Providence: Brown University Press, 1964.

Essling, Victor Massena, Prince d', and Eugene Müntz. *Pétrarque, ses études d' art, son influence sur les artistes, ses portraits, et ceux de Laure*. Paris: Gazette des beaux-arts, 1902.

Fairchild, Arthur Henry Rolph. *Shakespeare and the Arts of Design*. Columbia, Mo.: University of Missouri Press, 1937.

Fairholt, Frederick William, ed. *Lord Mayors' Pageants*. London, 1843–1844.

Farinelli, Arturo. "Petrarca e le arti figurative" in *Michelangelo, Dante, e altri brevi saggi*. Turin: Bocca, 1918.

Fletcher, Giles, and Phineas Fletcher. *Giles and Phineas Fletcher: Poetical Works*, ed. Frederick S. Boas. 2 vols. Cambridge: Cambridge University Press, 1908–1909.

Florio, John. *Queen Anna's New World of Words*. London, 1611.

—— *A Worlde of Wordes*. London, 1598.

General Bibliography

Forster, L. W. *The Icy Fire: Five Studies in European Petrarchism*. Cambridge: Cambridge University Press, 1969.

Fowler, Alastair. *Triumphal Forms: Structural Patterns in Elizabethan Poetry*. Cambridge: Cambridge University Press, 1971.

Fowler, Mary. *Catalog of the Petrarch Collection Bequeathed by Willard Fiske to Cornell University*. London: Oxford University Press, 1916.

Foxwell, A. K. *A Study of Sir Thomas Wyatt's Poems*. London: University of London Press, 1911.

Gilbert, Allan H., ed. *Literary Criticism: Plato to Dryden*. Detroit: Wayne State University Press, 1962.

—— *The Symbolic Persons in the Masques of Ben Jonson*. Durham: Duke University Press, 1948.

Giovio, Paolo. *A Shorte Treatise upon the Turkes Chronicles*. London, 1546.

Golenistcheff-Koutouzoff, Elie. "La première traduction des 'Triomphes' de Pétrarque en France" in *Mélanges de Philologie, d'Histoire et de Litterature Offerts à Henri Hauvette*. Paris: Les Presses Françaises, 1934.

Guerry, Liliane. *Le Thème du "Triomphe de la Mort" dans la Peinture Italienne*. Paris: G.–P. Maissonneuve & Cie., 1950.

Guiney, Louise Imogen, ed. *Recusant Poets*. New York: Sheed and Ward, 1939.

Hagstrum, Jean. *The Sister Arts*. Chicago: University of Chicago Press, 1958.

Hammond, Eleanor Prescott, ed. *English Verse between Chaucer and Surrey*. Durham: Duke University Press, 1927.

Hangen, Eva Katherine. *A Concordance to the Complete Poetical Works of Sir Thomas Wyatt*. Chicago: University of Chicago Press, 1941.

Harvey, Gabriel. *Marginalia*, ed. G. C. Moore Smith. Stratford-on-Avon: Shakespeare Head Press, 1913.

Hawes, Stephen. *The Pastime of Pleasure*, ed. W. E. Mead. Oxford: Early English Text Society, 1928.

Hazlitt, William Carew. *Handbook to the Popular, Poetical, and Dramatic Literature of Great Britain from the Invention of Printing to the Restoration*. London, 1867.

Hebel, J. W., and H. H. Hudson, eds. *Poetry of the English Renaissance, 1509–1660*. New York: Appleton-Century-Crofts, 1957.

Hietsch, Otto. *Die Petrarcaübersetzungen Sir Thomas Wyatts: eine sprachvergleichende Studie*. Vienna: W. Braumüller, 1960.

Hind, Arthur M. *Early Italian Engraving: A Critical Catalogue, with Reproductions of All Prints Described*. London: B. Quaritch, 1938.

Historical Manuscripts Commission. "Report on the MSS of Lord de l'Isle and Dudley Preserved at Penshurst Place," I (1925), 240, 259, 278ff.

Hughey, Ruth, ed. *The Arundel Harington Manuscript of Tudor Poetry*. 2 vols. Columbus: Ohio State University Press, 1960.

Jones-Davies, Marie Thérèse. *Un peintre de la vie londonienne: Thomas Dekker*. Paris: Didier, 1958.

Jonson, Ben. *Ben Jonson*, ed. C. H. Herford and Percy and Evelyn Simpson. 11 vols. Oxford: Clarendon Press, 1925–1952.

—— *The Complete Masques of Ben Jonson*, ed. Stephen Orgel. New Haven: Yale University Press, 1969.

Kelso, Ruth. *The Doctrine of the English Gentleman in the Sixteenth Century*. Urbana: University of Illinois Press, 1929.

Kernodle, George. *From Art to Theatre*. Chicago: University of Chicago Press, 1944.

Kerrick, Thomas. *Catalogue of the Prints which have been engraved after Martin Heemskerck.* Cambridge, 1829.

Lee, R. W. "*Ut Pictura Poesis:* The Humanist Theory of Painting," *Art Bulletin*, XXII (1940), 97–269.

Lever, J. W. *The Elizabethan Love Sonnet.* London: Methuen and Co., 1966.

Lewis, C. S. *The Allegory of Love.* New York: Oxford University Press, 1958.

Lowndes, William Thomas, ed. *Bibliographers's Manual of English Literature.* 6 vols. London, 1864.

Lydgate, John. *Fall of Princes*, ed. Henry Bergen. 4 vols. Washington, D.C.: Carnegie Institute of Washington, 1923–1927.

——— *The Minor Poems*, ed. Henry Noble MacCracken. 2 vols. Oxford: Early English Text Society, 1911–1924.

Mackie, J. D. *The Earlier Tudors.* Oxford: Clarendon Press, 1952.

Mâle, Emile. *L' art réligieux de la fin du moyen age en france.* Paris: A. Colin, 1908.

Marillier, H. C. *The Tapestries at Hampton Court Palace.* London: Her Majesty's Stationery Office, 1962.

Marschall, W. "Das Troja-Gemälde in Shakespeare's 'Lucrece,'" *Anglia*, LIV (1930), 83–96.

Mason, H. A. *Humanism and Poetry in the Early Tudor Period.* London: Routledge and Kegan Paul, 1959.

Matthiessen, F. O. *Translation, an Elizabethan Art.* Cambridge, Mass.: Harvard University Press, 1931.

Meiss, Millard. *Painting in Florence and Siena after the Black Death.* Princeton: Princeton University Press, 1951.

——— "The Problem of Francesco Traini," *Art Bulletin*, XV (1933), no. 2.

Melodia, Giovanni. *Studio sui "Trionfi."* Palermo, 1898.

Milton, John. *Complete Poems and Major Prose*, ed. Merritt Y. Hughes. New York: Odyssey Press, 1957.

Mommsen, T. E. *Medieval and Renaissance Studies*, ed. Eugene F. Rice, Jr. Ithaca: Cornell University Press, 1959.

——— "Petrarch and the Decoration of the Sala Virorum Illustrium in Padua," *Art Bulletin*, XXXIV (1952), 95–116.

More, Thomas. *The English Works of Sir Thomas More*, ed. W. E. Campbell and A. W. Reed. New York: Eyre, 1931.

Mumford, Ivy. "Petrarchism in Early Tudor England," *Italian Studies*, XIX (1964), 56–63.

Nashe, Thomas. *The Works of Thomas Nashe*, ed. R. B. McKerrow. 5 vols. London: Sidgwick, 1904–1910.

Nelson, William. *John Skelton, Laureate.* New York: Columbia University Press, 1939.

——— *The Poetry of Edmund Spenser.* New York: Columbia University Press, 1963.

Nichols, John, ed. *The Progresses, Processions, and Magnificent Festivities of King James the First.* 4 vols. London, 1828.

——— *The Progresses and Public Accessions of Queen Elizabeth.* 3 vols. London, 1823.

Nolhac, Pierre de. *Pétrarque et l'humanisme.* 2 vols. Paris: Champion, 1907.

Orgel, Stephen. *The Jonsonian Masque.* Cambridge, Mass.: Harvard University Press, 1965.

Osgood, Charles G., trans. *Boccaccio on Poetry.* Princeton: Princeton University Press, 1930.

Ovid, Publius Naso. *Fasti*, ed. and trans. James George Frazer. Loeb Classical Library. New York: G. P. Putnam's Sons, 1931.

169

General Bibliography

Ovid, Publius Naso. *Heroides and Amores*, ed. and trans. Grant Showerman. Loeb Classical Library. Cambridge, Mass.: Harvard University Press, 1947.
——— *Metamorphoses*, ed. and trans. F. J. Miller, 2 vols. Loeb Classical Library. Cambridge, Mass.: Harvard University Press, 1951.
Panofsky, Erwin. *Albrecht Dürer*. 2 vols. Princeton: Princeton University Press, 1948.
——— *Renaissance and Renascences in Western Art*. Stockholm: Almqvist and Wiksell, 1960.
——— *Studies in Iconology: Humanist Themes in the Art of the Renaissance*. New York: Harper and Row, 1962.
Parker, Henry, Lord Morley. *The Exposition and Declaration of the Psalme Deus ultionum Dominus, made by Syr Henry Parker, Knight*. London, 1539.
——— *Forty-Six Lives of Boccaccio*, ed. Herbert G. Wright. Oxford: Early English Text Society, 1943.
Peck, Harry Thurston, ed. *Harper's Dictionary of Classical Literature and Antiquities*. New York: Harper and Brothers, 1897.
Pollard, A. W., and G. R. Redgrave. *A Short-Title Catalogue of Books Printed in England, Scotland, & Ireland and of English Books Printed Abroad*. London: Bibliographical Society, 1926.
Praz, Mario. *Studies in Seventeenth-Century Imagery*. 2 vols. London: Warburg Institute, 1939–1947.
Proto, Enrico. "Sulla composizione dei 'Trionfi,'" *Studii di Letteratura Italiana*, III (1901), 1–96.
Puttenham, George. *The Arte of English Poesie*, ed. G. D. Willcock and A. Walker. Cambridge: Cambridge University Press, 1936.
Ramage, David. *A Finding List of English Books in Libraries in the British Isles*. Durham, Eng.: Council of the Durham Colleges, 1958.
Reading, William. *Bibliothecae cleri Londinensis in Collegio Sionensi Catalogus*. London, 1724.
Reed, A. W. *Early Tudor Drama*. London: Methuen and Co., 1926.
Rees, D. G. "Petrarch's 'Trionfo della Morte' in English," *Italian Studies*, VII (1952), 82–96.
Reid, George William. *Works of the Italian Engravers of the Fifteenth Century*. London, 1884.
Reiman, D. H. *Shelley's "The Triumph of Life": A Critical Study*. Urbana: University of Illinois Press, 1965.
Ripa, Cesare. *Iconologia*. Rome, 1613.
Ritson, Joseph. *Bibliographia Poetica, A Catalog of Engleish Poets of the 12, 13, 14, 15 and 16th Centurys*. London, 1802.
Salernitano, Masuccio. *Il Novellino*, ed. Alfredo Mauro. Bari: G. Laterza e Figli, 1940.
——— *The Novellino*, trans. W. G. Waters. 2 vols. London, 1895.
Sapegno, Natalino. *Il Trecento*. Milan: Vallardi, 1934.
Satterthwaite, Alfred W. *Spenser, Ronsard, and DuBellay*. Princeton: Princeton University Press, 1960.
Saunders, J. W. *The Profession of English Letters*. London: Routledge and Kegan Paul, 1964.
Schirmer, Walter Franz. *John Lydgate: A Study in the Culture of the Fifteenth Century*, trans. Ann E. Keep. Berkeley: University of California Press, 1961.
Schneider, René. "Le Thème des Triomphes dans les entrées solennelles en France à la Renaissance," *Gazette des beaux-arts*, IX (1913), 85–106.

Schubring, P. *Cassoni*. Leipzig: Hiersemann, 1915.

Severs, J. Burke. *The Literary Relations of Chaucer's Clerk's Tale*. New Haven: Yale University Press, 1942.

Seznec, Jean. *The Survival of the Pagan Gods*, trans. Barbara F. Sessions. New York: Harper, 1953.

Shakespeare, William. *The Complete Plays and Poems of William Shakespeare*, ed. W. A. Neilson and C. J. Hill. Cambridge, Mass.: Houghton Mifflin Co., 1942.

Sheavyn, Phoebe. *The Literary Profession in the Elizabethan Age* Manchester: Manchester University Press, 1909.

Shelley, Percy Bysshe. *The Complete Works*, ed. Roger Ingpen and Walter E. Peck. 10 vols. London: Gordian Press, 1965.

Shorr, Dorothy G. "Some Notes on the Iconography of Petrarch's *Triumph of Fame*," *Art Bulletin*, XX (1938), 101–105.

Sidney, Philip. *The Countess of Pembroke's Arcadia*, vols. I and II in *The Complete Works of Sir Philip Sidney*, ed. A. Feuillerat. 4 vols. Cambridge: Cambridge University Press, 1917–1926.

Skelton, John. *The Poetical Works of John Skelton*, ed. Alexander Dyce. 2 vols. London, 1843.

Southall, Raymond. *The Courtly Maker; An Essay on the Poetry of Wyatt and His Contemporaries*. New York: Barnes and Noble, 1964.

Spenser, Edmund. *Complaints*, ed. W. L. Renwick. London: Scholartis Press, 1928.

—— *The Faerie Queene*, ed. J. C. Smith. 2 vols. Oxford: Clarendon Press, 1909.

—— *The Works of Edmund Spenser: A Variorum Edition*, ed. F. M. Padelford, C. G. Osgood, Edwin A. Greenlaw, *et al.* 10 vols. Baltimore: Johns Hopkins Press, 1932–1949.

Surrey, Henry Howard, Earl of. *Poems*, ed. Emrys Jones. Oxford: Clarendon Press, 1964.

—— *The Works of Henry Howard, Earl of Surrey, and Wyatt the Elder*, ed. G. F. Knott. 2 vols. London, 1816.

Tatham, Edward H. R. *Francesco Petrarca*. 2 vols. London: Sheldon Press, 1925.

Tervarent, Guy de. *Attributs et symboles dans l' art profane, 1450–1600*. Geneva: E. Droz, 1958–1959.

Thomas, William. *Principall Rules of the Italian Grammar*. London, 1567.

Thomson, Patricia. *Sir Thomas Wyatt and His Background*. London: Routledge and Kegan Paul, 1965.

—— "Wyatt and the Petrarchan Commentators," *Review of English Studies*, X (August 1959), 215–233.

Thomson, W. G. *A History of Tapestry from the Earliest Times until the Present Day*. New York: G. P. Putnam's Sons, 1931.

Tottel's Miscellany, ed. Hyder Edward Rollins. 2 vols. Cambridge, Mass.: Harvard University Press, 1930.

Tripet, Arnaud. *Pétrarque ou la connaissance de soi*. Geneva: Librairie Droz, 1967.

Venezky, Alice. *Pageantry on the Shakespearian Stage*. New York: Twayne Publishers, 1951.

Venturi, Adolfo. "Il Petrarca e le arti rappresentative," *Fanfulla della Domenica*, XXV (1903), 52.

—— "Les Triomphes de Pétrarque dans l'art representatif," *Revue de l'art ancien et moderne*, XX (1906), 81–209.

Venturi, Lionello. "La critica d'arte e F. Petrarca," *L'Arte*, XXV (1922), 238–244.

General Bibliography

Vianey, Joseph. *Le Pétrarquisme en France au XVIe Siècle.* Montpellier: Coulet et Fils, 1909.

Virgil (Publius Vergilius Maro). *Opera Virgiliana cum decem commentis . . . ab Servio, Donato, Mancinello.* Leiden, 1529.

Waetzoldt, Wilhelm. *Dürer and His Times.* New York: Phaidon Publishers, 1950.

Waldron, F. W. *Literary Museum.* London, 1792.

Warton, Thomas. *A History of English Poetry from the Twelfth to the Close of the Sixteenth Century,* ed. W. C. Hazlitt. 4 vols. London, 1871.

Weisbach, Werner. *Trionfi.* Berlin: G. Grote, 1919.

Weiss, Roberto. *Humanism in England During the Fifteenth Century.* Oxford: Blackwell, 1957.

—— *Un inedito petrarchescho: la redazione sconosciuta di un capitolo del " Trionfo della Fama."* Rome: Edizioni di storia e letteratura, 1950.

Welsford, Enid. *The Court Masque.* Cambridge: Cambridge University Press, 1927.

White, T. H., ed. *The Bestiary: A Book of Beasts.* New York: G. P. Putnam's Sons, 1954.

Wilkins, Ernest Hatch. *Editions of the " Canzoniere" and the " Trionfi" in American Libraries.* Rome: Edizioni di storia e letteratura, 1960.

—— *The "Epistolae Metricae" of Petrarch: A Manual.* Rome: Edizioni di storia e letteratura, 1956.

—— *A History of Italian Literature.* Cambridge, Mass.: Harvard University Press, 1954.

—— *The Invention of the Sonnet and Other Studies in Italian Literature.* Rome: Edizioni di storia e letteratura, 1959.

—— *The Life of Petrarch.* Chicago: University of Chicago Press, 1961.

—— *The Making of the "Canzoniere" and Other Petrarchan Studies.* Rome: Edizioni di storia e letteratura, 1951.

—— *Petrarch's Correspondence.* Padua: Editrice Antenore, 1960.

—— *Petrarch's Eight Years in Milan.* Cambridge, Mass.: Medieval Academy of America, 1958.

—— *Petrarch's Later Years.* Cambridge, Mass.: Medieval Academy of America, 1959.

—— *Studies in the Life and Works of Petrarch.* Cambridge, Mass.: Medieval Academy of America, 1955.

Wind, Edgar. *Pagan Mysteries of the Renaissance.* London: Faber and Faber, 1958.

Withington, Robert, ed. *English Pageantry: An Historical Outline.* 2 vols. Cambridge, Mass.: Harvard University Press, 1918–1920.

Wright, Louis B. *Middle Class Culture in Elizabethan England.* Chapel Hill: University of North Carolina Press, 1935.

Wyatt, Thomas. *The Poems of Sir Thomas Wiat,* ed. A. K. Foxwell. London: University of London Press, 1913.

Yates, Frances A. "The Emblematic Conceit in Giordano Bruno's 'De Gli Eroici Furori' and the Elizabethan Sonnet Sequences," *Journal of the Warburg and Courtauld Institute,* VI (1943), 101–121.

Young, Frances. *Mary Sidney, Countess of Pembroke.* London: Nutt, 1912.

Notes

Abbreviations Used

BM   British Museum
Ca. Tr.   Carlo Calcaterra, ed., *Francesco Petrarca: Trionfi* (Turin: Unione Tipografico–Editrice Torinese, 1927)
FSLB   Henry Parker, Lord Morley, *Forty-Six Lives of Boccaccio*, ed. Herbert G. Wright (Oxford: Early English Text Society, 1943)
Wi. Tr.   Ernest Hatch Wilkins, trans., *The Triumphs of Petrarch* (Chicago: University of Chicago Press, 1963)

Introduction

The Life of Lord Morley

1. *FSLB*, pp. ix–xlvii. The facts for my account of Lord Morley's life are culled from this source, except where otherwise indicated.

2. The date of Morley's birth may be fixed by the statement in his epitaph that "Vixit annos 80, obijt anno domini 1556." See *FSLB*, pp. xlvi–xlvii, for the complete epitaph.

3. Alice and Henry Lovel were the children of William Lovel (d. 1475). Alice married Admiral Sir Edward Howard after the death of Sir William Parker in 1510 and she died in 1518. Morley's wife, Joan St. John, was also related to royalty through her grandmother, Margaret Beauchamp, who was the grandmother of Henry VII. Joan St. John died in 1552, aged sixty-six, four years before Morley's death. She bore him two daughters and one son. (See the *Dictionary of National Biography*, s.v. "Parker, Henry.")

4. *Ibid.*

5. Especially in BM MS. Add. 12060, fols. 19ᵛ–22ʳ, which are quoted extensively in *FSLB*, pp. xii, xlii–xlvii.

6. *Athenae Oxonienses*, ed. P. Bliss (London, 1813–1820), vol. I, col. 115.

7. These are preserved in BM MS. Cotton Vitellius B. XX.

8. See frontispiece. The original of the drawing is in the British Museum, but it is reproduced in *Drawings by Albrecht Dürer*, ed. F. P. Lippman (Berlin, 1883). On the lower half of the drawing are the words "heinrich morley aws engelland 1523" and on the right of the inscription is the Dürer monogram. See Erwin Panofsky's appraisal of the drawing in his *Albrecht Dürer*, 2 vols. (Princeton: Princeton University Press, 1948), I, 240.

9. Wilhelm Waetzoldt, *Dürer and His Times* (New York: Phaidon Publishers, 1950), p. 125.

10. BM MS. Harleian 6561, a collection of "Pistellis and Gospelles for the .lij Sondayes in the yere." Its probable date is 1532.

11. *FSLB*, p. xxiv.

12. The title page of the book bears the date 1534, but it was actually printed in 1539, as is indicated by the date 1539 in the colophon.

13. BM MS. Add. 12060.

14. BM MS. Vitellius F. V., fol 63ʳ, cited in *FSLB*, p. xlvii.

Morley as Writer and Scholar

1. This is even rarer than Morley's translation of the *Trionfi*. There are only three extant copies of it, one at the Bodleian Library, one at the British Museum, and one at the Archiepiscopal Library at Lambeth.

2. See Sir Sidney Lee's article on Henry Parker, Lord Morley, in the *Dictionary of National Biography*.

3. *FSLB*, p. lxxxi.

4. *The Exposition and Declaration* (London, 1539), sigs. Aii–Aiv.

5. Cited in *Tottel's Miscellany*, ed. Hyder Edward Rollins, 2 vols. (Cambridge, Mass.: Harvard University Press, 1928–1929), II, 245, which also includes (I, 113–115) an English version of a Latin epitaph written for Maltravers by Walter Haddon and translated by an unknown hand.

6. Eleanor Prescott Hammond's argument in *English Verse between Chaucer and Surrey* (Durham: Duke University Press, 1927), p. 383, that the translation was executed in the last decade of Morley's life therefore seems untenable.

7. The Latin text of the verses is included in my notes to Morley's "Vyrgyll in his Epigrames of Cupide and Dronkenesse" and is taken from the edition printed in Lyons in 1529. In this edition the "De venere" is accompanied by a commentary by the Flemish humanist Ascenius.

8. In *Literary Museum* (London, 1792). Morley's translation is incomplete, covering only 46 of the 104 biographies in Boccaccio's original. See *FSLB* for a complete account of Morley's translation and for a critical and annotated text.

9. See Hammond, *English Verse*, p. 386, for a list of the nineteenth-century anthologies which reprinted the two poems. One of these short poems, "Never was I lesse alone," has become something of an anthology piece, an example of the work of the "courtly makers" in the court of Henry VIII.

10. Laud. Misc. 684.

11. Formerly Phillipps MS. 10314, now in the possession of the Duke of Devonshire.

12. BM MS. Royal 17.D.XI. See *FSLB*, pp. lii–lxiii, for a discussion of the approximate dates of these manuscripts.

13. BM MS. Royal 17.D.II.

14. Bodleian Laud. Misc. 684.

15. BM MS. Royal 18.A.LXII.

16. BM MS. Arundel 8.

17. BM MS. Royal 18.A.LXII.

18. *Ibid.*, fol. 2ᵛ. For a complete edition of Masuccio's original, see *Il Novellino*, ed.

Alfredo Mauro (Bari: G. Laterza Figli, 1940). For a modern English translation of the forty-ninth novella, see *The Novellino*, trans. W. G. Waters, 2 vols. (London, 1895), II, 319–327.

19. BM MS. Arundel 8. For a translation of this work by one of Morley's contemporaries, see *A Shorte Treatise upon the Turkes Chronicles*, trans. Peter Ashton (London, 1546).

20. BM MS. Royal 18.A.LX.

21. BM MS. Royal 17.A.XXX.

22. BM MS. Royal 17.C.XVI.

23. BM MS. Royal 17.C.XII.

24. BM MS. Royal 17.A.XLVI.

25. BM MS. Royal 18.A.XV.

26. BM MS. Royal 2.D.XXVIII.

27. BM MS. Add. 12060.

28. *Ibid.*, fols. 19^v–20^r.

29. BM MS. Harleian 6561.

30. *FSLB*, pp. lii–liv.

31. Herbert G. Wright noted (*FSLB*, pp. lv–lvi) that he was unable to trace it either in Great Britain or in the United States. The designation for the manuscript was Phillipps 9375, and not (as is reported in the list of Morley's manuscripts in the *Dictionary of National Biography's* article on Morley) Phillipps MS.i.313.

32. BM MS. Royal 17.D.XIII.

33. *Ibid.*, fols 16^v–17^r.

34. *Scriptorum illustrium maioris Brytannie . . . Catalogus* (Basel, 1557–1559), II, 103.

35. *Ibid.*, I, 655.

36. See Frederick S. Boas, *An Introduction to Tudor Drama* (Oxford: Clarendon Press, 1933), and A. W. Reed, *Early Tudor Drama* (London: Methuen and Co., 1926), for a discussion of these playwrights and of other contemporaries such as John Redford, Sir David Lindsay, and Nicholas Udall.

37. Boas, *An Introduction to Tudor Drama*, p. 2.

38. *FSLB*, pp. 2–3.

Petrarch's *Trionfi*

1. The best recent biographies of Petrarch in English are Ernest Hatch Wilkins, *Life of Petrarch* (Chicago: University of Chicago Press, 1961), and Morris Bishop, *Petrarch and His World* (Bloomington: Indiana University Press, 1963). The ensuing discussion of the chronology of the *Trionfi* owes much to Wilkins's essay "On the Chronology of the Triumphs" in his *Studies in the Life and Works of Petrarch* (Cambridge, Mass.: Medieval Academy of America, 1955).

2. A fragment beginning with the line "Quanti già ne l'età matura ed acra" was discarded by Petrarch; it may have been intended originally as a second capitolo of the "Triumph of Chastity" or as the first capitolo of the "Triumph of Death."

3. There are also seventy-seven prose letters not included in any of his own collections; fifty-nine of these were collected in the nineteenth century under the title,

Epistolae variae. Excellent discussions of the Latin works can be found in A. D. Deyermond, *The Petrarchan Sources of "La Celestina"* (London: Oxford University Press, 1961), in Aldo S. Bernardo, *Petrarch, Scipio, and the Africa: The Birth of Humanism's Dream* (Baltimore: Johns Hopkins Press, 1962), and in Natalino Sapegno, *Il Trecento* (Milan: Vallardi, 1934). There is no complete modern edition of the Latin works, but the *Familiares*, the *Africa*, and the *Rerum memorandarum libri* are available in the Edizione Nazionale, which will eventually publish all of them.

4. "A General Survey of Renaissance Petrarchism," in Wilkins's *Studies in the Life and Works of Petrarch*, p. 281.

5. The translation is discussed by Ernest Hatch Wilkins in *The Making of the Canzoniere and Other Petrarchan Studies* (Rome: Edizioni di storia e letteratura, 1951), pp. 305ff.

6. Aage Brusendorff, *The Chaucer Tradition* (London: Oxford University Press, 1925), p. 161, argued that Chaucer relied on the "Triumph of Time," ll. 127ff, for his description of the rock of ice in the *Hous of Fame*, III, 110ff, but the proposal is rejected by Wolfgang Clemen, *Chaucer's Early Poetry*, trans. C. C. M. Sym (New York: Barnes and Noble, 1963), pp. 103–105.

7. *De obedienta ac fide uxoria mythologia*, which Petrarch translated into Latin from *Decameron*, X, 10. For the dispute as to whether Chaucer used Petrarch's translation, Boccaccio's original, or a French intermediary, see J. Burke Severs, *The Literary Relations of Chaucer's Clerk's Tale* (New Haven: Yale University Press, 1942).

8. *The Works of Geoffrey Chaucer*, ed. F. N. Robinson (Boston: Houghton Mifflin Co., 1957), p. 101.

9. *Fall of Princes*, ed. Henry Bergen, 4 vols. (Washington: Carnegie Institute of Washington, 1923–1927), pp. 8, 436, 476, 824, 918, 1,016. See also Roberto Weiss, *Humanism in England during the Fifteenth Century* (Oxford: Blackwell, 1957), p. 64 and chaps. iii and iv; Walter Franz Schirmer, *John Lydgate*, trans. Ann E. Keep (Berkeley: University of California Press, 1961), p. 217.

10. Eleanor Prescott Hammond, *English Verse*, p. 440.

11. *Ibid.*, p. 189.

12. *The Poetical Works of John Skelton*, ed. Alexander Dyce, 2 vols. (London, 1843), II, 170ff.

13. *FSLB*, p. 2.

Renaissance Editions and Translations of the *Trionfi*

1. This first edition of Petrarch's Italian poems, described in the Pierpont Morgan Library Catalog as "the rarest of all Italian first editions," bore no commentaries. For the location of copies of Petrarch's Italian poems in American libraries, see Ernest Hatch Wilkins, *Editions of the Canzoniere and the Trionfi in American Libraries* (Rome: Edizioni di storia e letteratura, 1960), as well as a work indispensable to all Petrarchan studies, Mary Fowler's *Catalog of the Petrarch Collection Bequeathed by Willard Fiske to Cornell University* (London: Oxford University Press, 1916).

2. See Wilkins, "The Quattrocento Editions of the 'Canzoniere' and the 'Trionfi'" in *The Making*. Wilkins had access to twenty-three of these twenty-five editions when preparing his study; he grouped them into four classes (labeled A, B, C, and D), each

of which he found to be independent of the other. Only Class D, which includes the annotated edition of 1475-1476 and its thirteen descendants, need concern us here. All editions of this class, including the 1488 edition and the 1490 edition, which I have examined for the ensuing section, are in two companion folio volumes, one for the *Trionfi* and one for the *Canzoniere*. In almost every case, the date of printing of the *Trionfi* is earlier than that of the *Canzoniere*, providing (perhaps) additional proof that the early editions catered primarily to a taste for the *Trionfi*, though it must be admitted that the 1488 and 1490 editions and all the subsequent editions of the *Canzoniere* were complete editions. See Wilkins, "The Separate Quattrocento Editions of the 'Trionfi'" in *The Making*.

3. All references to Bernardo's commentary are taken from the 1488 and the 1490 editions of the *Trionfi*, which I have examined at the Pierpont Morgan Library. These are identical editions, with the exception of the illustrations, which appeared as watercolors in the 1488 edition and as woodcuts in the 1490 edition.

4. *Sopra el triumpho di Petrarca* (Florence, 1485).

5. *Il Petrarcha con la Spositione di Giovanni Andrea Gesualdo* (Venice, 1541).

6. *Sonetti, Canzoni e Triomphi di M. Francesco Petrarca, con la Spositione di Bernardino Daniello da Lucca* (Venice, 1549).

7. "Le Osservationi di M. Francesco Alunno da Ferrara sopra il Petrarca" in *Le Rime del Petrarca Novamente Ristampate* (Venice, 1550).

8. *Il Petrarca con l'Espositione d'Alessandro Velutello* (Venice, 1550).

9. *Rime di Francesco Petrarca* (Milan, 1826).

10. See Pierre de Nolhac, *Pétrarque et l'humanisme*, 2 vols. (Paris: Champion, 1907), I, 66, 82, II, 47, for a fuller account of Pierre Bersuire. See also Jean Seznec, *The Survival of the Pagan Gods*, trans. Barbara F. Sessions (New York: Harper, 1953), pp. 174ff for a discussion of Bersuire's *Ovide moralisé* and its relation to Petrarch's mythography.

11. Cf. Bernardo's allegorical approach to the *Trionfi* and the allegorical approach advocated in Books XIV and XV of Boccaccio's *De genealogia deorum*. Similar views are set forth in Boccaccio's "Vita di Dante" in *Il commento alla "Divina Commedia" e gli altri scritti intorno a Dante*, ed. Domenico Guerri (Bari: G. Laterza e Figli, 1918). An English version of Books XIV and XV was prepared by Charles G. Osgood, *Boccaccio on Poetry* (Princeton: Princeton University Press, 1930).

12. Sig. A.i^v: "il preclarissimo Poeta Francesco Petrarca sotto legiadro & mirifico velamento poetico lo a dito ... cosi legiadramente introduce il nostro Poeta: sei gloriosi triumphi luno a laltro come superiore & dominatore designando. Nelli quali la clarissima intelligentia dogni stato deli homini e collocata e aperta."

13. See E. R. Curtius, *European Literature and the Latin Middle Ages*, trans. W. R. Trask (New York: Pantheon Books, 1953), p. 221.

14. Sig. A.i^v: "Quanto a dunque a la prima dico la intentione & subgetto essere lanima humana sotto consideratione di transito & varieta per rispecto & relatione a le humane opere & al iudicio di quelle dato a li homini."

15. Romans, 7:14-23.

16. Sig. A.ii: "Ladonde in tal stato pare che due qualita se li convengano, luna cioe e che delle opere virtuose·exercitate nella vita mentre era col corpo."

17. *Ibid.*: "Pare che etiamdo tale laudo & fama si habbi a denigrare secondo la sententia di Salamone al iii dello ecclesiastes quando disse. Omnia tempus habent & spatius suis transeunt universo sub celo."

18. *Ibid.*: "il tempo suo misura come in nel quarto de la physica Aristotele dimostra a una sempiterna & distantia infinita: alla quale poi che e condotta: non po piu lo intellecto nostro per non esserne capace suo stato considerare."

19. Sig. A.ii^v: "Severa e la sententia di tutti li morali che le operatione virtuose overo essa virtu sia summo bene: e quello si difinisse essere utile: che per destra via si conduce alla possessione di tal bene. Certamente niuna cosa a noi puo dimostrarsi piu utile che la presente doctrina."

20. Sig. A.iii: "Dividesi adunque principalmente la presente opera in sei parti si come dinanzi e dimostrato sei essere le variatione che a lanima nostra generalmente secondo il mondano intendere satribuiscono: della quali nella prima determina Missier Francescho del dominio dello appetito sensitivo: il quale secondo la poetica fantasia simula nella persona di Cupido. Nella seconda tratta il principato della ragione: la qual finge per persona di Madona Laura. Ne la terza parte descrive de lamorte terza varieta a laia atribuita. Nella quarta si iunge della fama a lanima doppo la morte riferita da li homini. Nella quinta aduce la longeza del tempo preditta fama obscurare. Nella sexta & ultima demostra al iudicio universale divino sequire la eternita."

21. See Patricia Thomson, "Wyatt and the Petrarchan Commentators," *Review of English Studies*, X (August 1959), 215–233. Miss Thomson's *Sir Thomas Wyatt and His Background* (London: Routledge and Kegan Paul, 1965) contains additional useful information on Wyatt's use of Petrarch.

22. Velutello, *Il Petrarca*, sig. X.

23. See Wilkins, "Petrarch's Map of Vaucluse" in *The Making*.

24. Velutello, *Il Petrarca*, sig. X^v.

25. Gesualdo, *Il Petrarca*, sig. a.2^{r-v}.

26. For a study of French translations of the *Trionfi*, see Giulio Bertoni, *Per la fortuna dei "Trionfi" in Francia* (Modena: Libreria Editrice Internazionale, 1904). Elie Golenistcheff-Koutouzoff, "La première traduction des 'Triomphes' de Pétrarque en France," in *Mélanges de Philologie, d'Histoire et de Litterature Offerts à Henri Hauvette* (Paris: Les Presses Françaises, 1934), pp. 107–112, describes a French translation of the *Trionfi* that appeared shortly after Bernardo's edition.

27. Morley's dedicatory epistle to the *Tryumphes* notes that he knew a French translation by "one of late dayes that was grome of the chaumber with that renowmed and valyaunte Prynce of hyghe memorye, Fraunces the Frenche kynge, whose name I have forgotten."

28. *Toutes les Euvres Vulgaires de Francoys Petrarque* (Paris, 1555). My translation.

29. *Sonnets, Chansons et Triomphes de M. F. Petrarque* (Paris, 1597).

30. Philieul, *Toutes les Euvres*, sigs. X5^v–X6.

31. *Francisco Petrarca con los seys triunfos de toscano sacados en castellano* (Madrid, n.d.), sig. A.vi.

32. *Los Triumphos de Francisco Petrarcha* (Medina del Campo. 1554).

33. *Sechs Triumph* (Basel, 1578).

34. The translation is included in *The Works of William Fowler*, ed. Henry W.

Meikle, 3 vols. (Edinburgh and London: The Scottish Text Society, 1914–1940), I, 13–134.

35. See Mary Fowler, *Catalog of the Petrarch Collection, passim,* and *Ca. Tr.,* pp. lxii–lxiv, for lists and studies of translations of the *Trionfi* into European vernaculars during the Renaissance and after.

36. *Le Rime del Petrarca brevemente sposte* (Basel, 1582), sig. ZZ^{r-v}.

37. "Discorso di Tomaso Costo" in *Il Petrarca Nuovamente Ridotto alla vera Lettione* (Venice, 1592), sig. R^8. My translation.

38. *The Arundel Harington Manuscript of Tudor Poetry,* 2 vols. (Columbus: Ohio State University Press, 1960).

39. See *The Poems of Queen Elizabeth I,* ed. Leicester Bradner (Providence: Brown University Press, 1964), p. xiv. This edition also reprints Elizabeth's translation in modern spelling (pp. 13–16).

40. *The Prayse of Nothing* is included in *The Writings in Verse and Prose of Sir Edward Dyer,* ed. A. B. Grosart, 4 vols. (Blackburn, 1870–1876).

41. The translation is included in its entirety in Frances Young, *Mary Sidney, Countess of Pembroke* (London: Nutt, 1912), Appendix A.

42. *Works,* I, 16. See *ibid.,* III, 5, for the argument that Fowler's translation is not at all indebted to Morley's.

43. Several translations of the work, none of them very successful, appeared after the sixteenth century. In 1644 Mrs. Anna Hume's translation of the first three trionfi appeared, accompanied by a promise to translate the remaining three if her initial attempt was well received. The remainder of the poem never appeared, perhaps because the first half had generated little enthusiasm. For reasons which remain unclear, the poem went practically unheeded by Italian as well as English readers throughout the eighteenth century, and it was not until the Romantic revival of interest in medievalism that it drew attention once more. In 1807 the Reverend Henry Boyd published a translation of the poem in rhymed couplets. Boyd was not without critical intelligence, for he saw the Petrarchan temper as similar to that of the pre-Romantics, and he made a special point of underlining the similarities between Petrarch's poetry and that of Young and Cowper. His preface includes an apology for "taking some liberties with his author by way of amplification" and an explanation that "by appropriate ornaments" he has attempted a "transfusion of the spirit rather than a servile adherence to the letter"; both statements indicate that he had as much difficulty with the complexities of diction and metaphor in the *Trionfi* as did his predecessors. Late in the century came several quasi-academic exercises in translation of the *Trionfi* from Italophiles such as Lady Barberina Dacre, Major MacGregor, and Lord Charlemont. As recently as 1962 Ernest Hatch Wilkins published a translation of the poem that was outstanding for its fidelity to the original, though perhaps that fidelity was achieved by resorting too often to archaisms and stilted phrases.

The *Trionfi* and Renaissance Iconography

1. The standard work on the subject is Victor Massena d'Essling's and Eugene Müntz's *Pétrarque, ses études d'art, son influence sur les artistes, ses portraits, et ceux de*

Laure (Paris: Gazette des beaux-arts, 1902)—cited hereafter as *Pétrarque.* D'Essling and Müntz point out (chap. iii) that though the *Trionfi* provided the main Petrarchan source of inspiration for artists, the *De viris illustribus,* the *Canzoniere,* and the *De remediis utriusque fortune* were also mined for subject matter and themes. Mantegna's great painting, *The Triumph of Caesar,* now hanging at Hampton Court, is classical rather than Petrarchan in subject matter.

2. For general discussions of the Renaissance doctrine that poetry is a "speaking picture," see R. W. Lee, "*Ut Pictura Poesis:* The Humanist Theory of Painting," *Art Bulletin,* XXII (1940), 97–269, and Robert John Clements, *Picta Poesis: Literary and Humanistic Theory in Renaissance Emblem Books* (Rome: Edizioni di storia e letteratura, 1960). Petrarch himself was interested in the graphic arts, both as a theorist and collector of paintings. His Latin works are scattered with reflections on art, and it is very possible that he intended to write a treatise on the origin and scope of the graphic arts and a series of lives of eminent artists. See Lionello Venturi, "La Critica d'Arte e F. Petrarca," *L'Arte,* XXV (1922), 238–244; Adolfo Venturi, "Il Petrarca e le arti rappresentative," *Fanfulla della Domenica,* XXV (1903), 52, and Arturo Farinelli, "Petrarca e le arti figurative" in *Michelangelo, Dante, e altri brevi saggi* (Turin: Bocca, 1918), pp. 421–444. We know of Petrarch's interest in emblematic poetry from the reflections on the subject found in his Latin works. See Mario Praz, *Studies in Seventeenth Century Imagery,* 2 vols. (London: The Warburg Institute, 1939–1947), I, 11. Petrarch was also a friend of painters and an admirer of their work. During the spring of 1336 he made the acquaintance of the Sienese painter Simone Martini, who had been summoned to Avignon by the pope to decorate the papal palace that was then being built. Petrarch got Martini to paint a miniature of Laura, and in gratitude the poet wrote two sonnets for Martini—77 and 78 in *Rime e Trionfi di Francesco Petrarca,* ed. Ferdinando Neri (Torino: Unione Tipografico-Editrice Torinese, 1963). Two years later Martini painted a frontispiece for Petrarch's copy of Vigil, and the poet himself may have had a hand in the planning of the picture, which includes figures of Virgil, Servius, and Aeneas. (See Wilkins, *Life of Petrarch,* p. 23.) He probably saw and admired Giotto's frescoes in the Royal Chapel in Naples, and he owned a painting of the madonna by Giotto, which he willed to his friend Francesco da Carrara. Lastly, we know that Petrarch saw actual representations of figures from his *De viris illustribus* and from his "Triumph of Fame" in the Sala Virorum Illustrium in Padua. See Theodor E. Mommsen, "Petrarch and the Decoration of the Sala Virorum Illustrium in Padua," *Art Bulletin,* XXXIV (1952), 95–116. Moreover, there is also evidence that the *Trionfi* may have been inspired by paintings of triumphal processions. The *Trionfo della Morte* at the Camposanto of Pisa (formerly attributed to Orcagna but now ascribed to Traini), the *Trionfo di San Tomaso* in the Capella Spagnuola of Santa Maria Nuova, and the *Trionfo del Buon Governo* by Ambrogio Lorenzetti at the Palazzo Pubblico in Siena are other paintings that antedate Petrarch's *Trionfi.* The origins of these pre-Petrarchan trionfi are unclear: on the one hand they may have been inspired by the Roman triumph or by triumphal pageants described in classical literature, but on the other hand they may have been modeled upon actual triumphal processions staged at various times in the course of the Middle Ages. Such triumphal processions, of a secular as well as of a religious kind, were extremely popular. For example,

Dante describes a trionfo of Beatrice in "Purgatorio," XXIX, in a way that suggests that he may have seen such processions. Jacob Burckhardt, *The Civilization of the Renaissance in Italy* (London; Phaidon Press, 1951), pp. 106–107, and René Schneider, "Le Thème des Triomphes dans les entrées solennelles en France à la Renaissance," *Gazette des beaux-arts*, IX (1913) 85–106, consider triumphal pageants in Italy and France and suggest the interesting possibility that reality imitated art and that the triumphal processions were fashioned after processions described in literature.

3. *Pétrarque*, pp. 121ff.

4. Dorothy C. Shorr, "Some Notes on the Iconography of Petrarch's 'Triumph of Fame,'" *Art Bulletin*, XX (1938), 101–105.

5. Liliane Guerry, *Le Thème du "Triomphe de la Mort" dans la Peinture Italienne* (Paris: G.-P. Maissonneuve and Co., 1950).

6. The most popular of these bestiaries was the *Physiologus* of Theobaldus (eleventh century), but the genre dated to the fourth century in Greece. *The Bestiary: A Book of Beasts* (New York: G. P. Putnam's Sons, 1954), a twelfth-century Latin bestiary translated and edited by T. H. White, is a good example of the kind of manual to which the illustrators might have turned. For an excellent "dictionnaire d'un langage perdu," see Guy de Tervarent, *Attributs et symboles dans l'art profane, 1450–1600* (Geneva: E. Droz, 1958).

7. For excellent photointaglio reproductions of representations of the *Trionfi* attributed to Fra Lippo Lippi, see George William Reid, *Works of the Italian Engravers of the Fifteenth Century* (London, 1884).

8. D'Essling and Müntz, *Pétrarque*, pp. 129–130.

9. BM MS. 28962.

10. See H. C. Marillier, *The Tapestries at Hampton Court Palace* (London: Her Majesty's Stationery Office, 1962), pp. 18–24.

11. There is a fourth panel, *The Triumph of Death over Chastity*, which now hangs in the adjoining Horn Room.

12. See below, pp. 52–53.

13. Bibliothèque Nationale, Fonds français, no. 22541.

14. Bibliothèque de l'Arsenal, MS. 5065.

15. Bibliothèque Nationale, Fonds français, no. 594, fol. 7^v.

16. Bibliothèque Nationale, Fonds français, no. 594, fol. 8^v.

17. Lydgate's translation is included in Hammond, *English Verse*, pp. 124–142.

18. *The Dance of Death in the Middle Ages and the Renaissance* (Glasgow: Jackson, Son and Co., 1950), pp. 40, 51–57.

The *Trionfi* and the Literature of the Early Tudor Period

1. In *The English Works of Sir Thomas More*, ed. W. E. Campbell and A. W. Reed (New York: Eyre, 1931). Rastell noted that More had composed four "things" in English "for his pastime"; these consisted of "A Mery jest how a Sergeant would learne to playe the frere," "Nyne Pageauntes," a lamentation on the death of Queen Elizabeth, and some verses to be prefaced to the Book of Fortune.

2. *Ibid.*, p. 332.

3. Samuel C. Chew, *The Pilgrimage of Life* (New Haven: Yale University Press, 1962), pp. 157–158, describes the conflation of the two themes.

4. Ed. W. E. Mead (Oxford: Early English Text Society, 1928).

5. *Ca. Tr.*, "Trionfo della Fama," I, 8–9.

6. *Pastime of Pleasure*, xlii, 5,527; 5,570.

7. *Ibid.*, xliv, 5,611–5,627.

8. Erwin Panofsky, *Studies in Iconology* (New York: Harper and Row, 1962), p. 91, and Chew, *Pilgrimage*, p. 158, n. 14.

9. *Ca. Tr.*, "Trionfo dell' Eternità," 1–6, 19–21. My translation.

10. *Pastime of Pleasure*, xlv, 5,747–5,753.

11. See William Nelson, *John Skelton, Laureate* (New York: Columbia University Press, 1939), pp. 158–190.

12. Skelton, *Works*, II, 347–348.

13. *Ibid.*, p. 348.

14. See A. K. Foxwell, *A Study of Sir Thomas Wyatt's Poems* (London: University of London Press, 1911), pp. 147–152, in which Wyatt's sources are tabulated. The most recent study of Wyatt's sources is Otto Hietsch's *Die Petrarcaübersetzungen Sir Thomas Wyatts: eine sprachvergleichende Studie* (Vienna: W. Braumüller, 1960), which fails to uncover any use of the *Trionfi* by Wyatt. See also Eva Katherine Hangen, *A Concordance to the Complete Poetical Works of Sir Thomas Wyatt* (Chicago: University of Chicago Press, 1941), p. 472, for Wyatt's use of the word "triumph" in its general sense.

15. This is number 13 in *Henry Howard, Earl of Surrey: Poems*, ed. Emrys Jones (Oxford: Clarendon Press, 1964). Surrey's poem, a direct translation of a passage in the "Trionfo d'Amore," III, 151–187, was first noticed by G. F. Knott in his edition of the works of Wyatt and Surrey, 2 vols. (London, 1816), II, 297–298. Knott also cited Morley's translation of the Petrarchan passage.

16. "The Scolemaster" in *Roger Ascham: English Works*, ed. William Aldis Wright, (Cambridge: Cambridge University Press, 1904), p. 232.

The Elizabethan Triumph

1. As early as 1189, for example, there was a formal royal entry at the coronation of Richard I; in 1236 a more elaborate Lord Mayor's pageant was presented on the occasion of the passage of Henry III and Eleanor of Provence through London to Westminster. These and hundreds of other pageants are included in Frederick William Fairholt, *Lord Mayors's Pageants* (London, 1843–1844); John Nichols, *The Progresses and Public Processions of Queen Elizabeth*, 3 vols. (London, 1823), and *The Progresses, Processions, and Magnificent Festivities of King James the First*, 4 vols. (London, 1828); Robert Withington, *English Pageantry: An Historical Outline*, 2 vols. (Cambridge, Mass.: Harvard University Press, 1918–1920).

2. We now have a considerably fuller understanding of the ways in which spectacle and pageantry made their way into Elizabethan drama. There is a full study of the subject by Alice S. Venezky, *Pageantry on the Shakespearian Stage* (New York: Twayne Publishers, 1951), which overemphasizes the direct connections between Petrarch's *Trionfi* and Elizabethan triumphal pageants. Useful, but more diffuse, are George

Kernodle's *From Art to Theatre* (Chicago: University of Chicago Press, 1944) and Arthur Henry Rolph Fairchild, *Shakespeare and the Arts of Design* (Columbia, Mo.: University of Missouri Press, 1937).

3. See Venezky, *Pageantry*, p. 194.

4. *Thesaurus Linguae Romanae et Brittanicae* (London, 1565).

5. *Principall Rules of the Italian Grammar* (London, 1567).

6. *An Alvearie, or Quadruple Dictionarie* (London, 1580).

7. *A Worlde of Wordes* (London, 1598) and *Queen Anna's New World of Words* (London, 1611).

8. *The Arte of English Poesie*, ed. G. D. Willcock and A. A. Walker (Cambridge: Cambridge University Press, 1936), p. 46.

9. *The Works of Francis Bacon*, ed. J. Spedding, R. L. Ellis, and D. D. Heath, 15 vols. (London, 1887–1902), VI, 467–468.

10. *The Countess of Pembroke's Arcadia*, vols. I and II in *The Complete Works of Sir Philip Sidney*, ed. A. Feuillerat, 4 vols. (Cambridge: Cambridge University Press, 1917–1926), I, 101ff.

11. All references to Shakespeare's plays are from *The Complete Plays and Poems of William Shakespeare*, ed. W. A. Neilson and C. J. Hill (Cambridge, Mass.: Houghton Mifflin Co., 1942), and will henceforth be given in the text.

12. See Fairchild, *Shakespeare and the Arts of Design*, p. 146, and W. Marschall, "Das Troja-Gemälde in Shakespeare's 'Lucrece,'" *Anglia*, LIV (1930), 83–96.

13. For a full discussion of Shakespeare's treatment of the Ovidian idea that "tempus edax rerum," see J. W. Lever, *The Elizabethan Love Sonnet* (London: Methuen and Co., 1966), pp. 246–272. The sonnets are numbers 12, 15, 16, 19, 55, 60, 63, 64, 65, 73, 74, 76, and 77.

14. See Panofsky, *Studies in Iconology*, pp. 69–93.

15. "The Visions of Bellay" and "The Visions of Petrarch" had appeared in substantially the same form in van der Noodt's *A Theatre for Worldings* (1569). Alfred W. Satterthwaite, *Spenser, Ronsard, and Du Bellay* (Princeton: Princeton University Press, 1960), studied the connections between Spenser and the French Petrarchists and attributed the translation of "Standomi un giorno" to Du Bellay (p. 28). W. L. Renwick, editor of the *Complaints* (London: Scholartis Press, 1928), and the Variorum editors agree, however, that the translation is from Marot's version. A useful study of sixteenth-century French Petrarchism is Joseph Vianey's *Le Pétrarquisme en France au XVIᵉ siècle* (Montpellier: Coulet et Fils, 1909).

16. See *The Faerie Queene*, I. v. 35–36; III. iii. 3. 1–2; IV. i. 50.9; all references to *The Faerie Queene* are from the edition by J. C. Smith (Oxford: Clarendon Press, 1909), and will henceforth be given in the text.

17. I. 2. 35.

18. *Orlando Furioso*, Canto XXXIII. See the translation by William Stewart Rose, ed. Stewart A. Baker and A. Bartlett Giamatti (New York: Bobbs-Merrill Co., 1968).

19. 3.1–13 and 4.23–26 in the Loeb Classical Library edition.

20. 2.25ff, in the Loeb Classical Library edition.

21. See Seznec, *The Survival of the Pagan Gods*, pp. 77, 127.

The Triumph: Late Renaissance and After

1. See *The Works of Thomas Nashe*, ed. R. B. McKerrow, 5 vols. (London: Sidgwick, 1904–1910), II, 7–175. There are scores of works by Nashe's contemporaries whose titles suggest a connection with Petrarch's *Trionfi* but which owe little to the poem or to the Renaissance illustrators. The best known of these are Robert Greene's *Pandosto: The Triumph of Time* (1588), a pastoral romance; Thomas Morley's *Triumphs of Oriana* (1601), a set of madrigals, and John Reynold's *The Triumphs of God's Revenge* (1621), a prose polemic.

2. See *The Complete Works of John Davies of Hereford*, ed. A. B. Grosart, 2 vols. (Blackburn, 1869–1876).

3. See *Giles and Phineas Fletcher: Poetical Works*, ed. F. S. Boas, 2 vols. (Cambridge: Cambridge University Press, 1908), I, 5–90.

4. See *The Non-Dramatic Works of Thomas Dekker*, ed. A. B. Grosart, 5 vols. (London, 1884–1886), II, 1–81. See also Marie Thérèse Jones-Davies, *Un peintre de la vie londonienne: Thomas Dekker* (Paris: Didier, 1958).

5. This and the other masques cited in this section are included in *Ben Jonson*, ed. C. H. Herford and Percy and Evelyn Simpson, 11 vols. (Oxford: Clarendon Press, 1925–1952), vol. III. See also *The Complete Masques of Ben Jonson*, ed. Stephen Orgel (New Haven: Yale University Press, 1969), and Dr. Orgel's excellent study *The Jonsonian Masque* (Cambridge, Mass.: Harvard University Press, 1965).

6. Herford and Simpson, *Ben Johnson*, VII, 305.

7. *Ibid.* See Panofsky, *Studies in Iconology*, pp. 81–85, for Ripa; see also Allan H. Gilbert, *The Symbolic Persons in the Masques of Ben Jonson* (Durham: Duke University Press, 1948), *passim*, for the influence of Ripa on Jonson, and pp. 127, 185, 196, 233, 242–243, and 250 for mention of Petrarch and the *Trionfi*.

8. Herford and Simpson, *Ben Jonson*, VIII, 134–135. Herford and Simpson argue (I, 53) that "Charis" was the lady who played Venus in the masque *The Hue and Cry after Cupid*.

9. Lines 119–120 in John Milton, *Complete Poems and Major Prose*, ed. Merritt Y. Hughes (New York: Odyssey Press, 1957). All quotations are from this edition.

10. XI, 721–723.

11. VI, 878–892.

12. Shelley's *Triumph of Life* is included in *The Complete Works of Percy Bysshe Shelley*, ed. Roger Ingpen and Walter E. Peck, 10 vols. (London: Gordian Press, 1965), IV, 167–185. See also Carlos Baker, *Shelley's Major Poetry: The Fabric of a Vision* (Princeton: Princeton University Press, 1948), pp. 161, 259–260, 262, and A. C. Bradley, "Notes on Shelley's 'Triumph of Life,'" *Modern Language Review*, IX (1914), 441–456; the latter lists nineteen parallels between the *Trionfi* and Shelley's poem. An excellent critical edition and study of the poem has been done by D. H. Reiman, *Shelley's "The Triumph of Life": A Critical Study* (Urbana: University of Illinois Press, 1965).

The Tryumphes of Fraunces Petrarcke

The Tryumphe of Love, I

1. *In the tyme.* April 6, 1327. In Sonnet 211 Petrarch noted that *Mille trecento ventisette, a punto / Su l'ora prima il dí sesto d'aprile, / Nel labirinto entrai; né veggio ond'esca:* "In thirteen hundred twenty-seven, at exactly the first hour of the sixth day of April, I entered the labyrinth of love and I cannot find my way out." See also Sonnet 3, which says the fatal day was Good Friday.

6. Added by Morley.

7. *Tytans child.* Tithonus's young bride, Aurora.

9–10. Morley changed the order, perhaps to force a rhyme. The original reads: *Amor, gli sdegni e'l pianto e la stagione;* "Love, disdain, tears, and the season." Morley added *oute of reason* and moved *season* to the next line. Curiously, he missed Petrarch's reference to the *chiuso loco* (the Enclosed Place, Valchiusa), and perhaps read *l'occhio* instead of *loco.*

14. Added by Morley.

15–17. Blurring of *vidi una gran luce, / e dentro assai dolor con breve gioco;* "I saw a great light, in which was much grief and little joy. 16. Added by Morley.

18. Added by Morley.

24. Added by Morley.

28–32. Added by Morley.

33. Petrarch describes him as *un garzon crudo,* "a cruel boy."

36. Misreading of the original, which notes that Cupid himself wore no armor and carried no shield. The misreading accounts for the padding in lines 37–38.

41–43. Expansion of *di color mille, tutto l'altro ignudo:* "of a thousand colors; the rest of his body was bare."

48–49. Added by Morley.

50–54. Misreading and blurring of the original. Petrarch describes how the poet, eager to hear news, moved in the direction of the throng and risked becoming one of those who were victims of love. *That as it lyked her* seems to refer to *love* in the previous lines.

57. For *del re sempre di lagrime digiuno,* a slightly obscure line which troubled even the sixteenth-century commentators. Wilkins (*Wi. Tr.,* p. 6) translates it as "Following the king n'er satisfied with tears," which is accurate but still obscure. Lines 61–62 in Morley's text are probably an attempt to make some sense of the line.

58–60. Morley's logic is slightly different from Petrarch's. Petrarch says that he recognized no one, and that if in fact one of his acquaintances was in the throng, Love had so transformed him that he was unrecognizable. 59. *By . . . payne.* Added by Morley. 58. *that he.* Read: "he who." 60. *As that.* Read: "So that."

61–64. Added by Morley.

65. *more sadde.* Misreading of *men che l'altre,* "less than the others." *for to regarde* and *that . . . harde.* Added by Morley.

66. *and . . . agayne.* For *dissi,* "I said."

67. *to . . . faine.* Added by Morley.

72–74. These words are spoken by the guide in the original.

76. *thou . . . dismayde.* Added by Morley.

77. *perdye.* Added by Morley for emphasis and rhyme.

78. *auncient.* For *vero amico,* "true friend." See *Ca. Tr.,* p. 7, for the attempts to identify the guide as Tommaso Caloiro, Guido Settimo, Cino da Pistoia, Convenevole da Prato, Sennuccio del Bene, or even Dante himself. Calcaterra, "La Prima ispirazione dei 'Trionfi'" in *Nella Selva di Petrarca* (Bologna, 1942), argued convincingly that the guide was Guido d'Arezzo. *if . . . se.* Added by Morley.

79–81. Adequate rendition of Petrarch's original, but Morley's syntax is clumsy. Read: "Although I could not see his face, I knew him by his words and by his noble intellect." *Ragionare* cannot be translated as "speech," because it would be redundant. *Antico* often signified "noble."

82–83. Added by Morley. The original read: *e così n'assidemmo in loco aprico,"* and so we seated ourselves in a high and open place."

87–88. *For . . . playne.* Blurring of the fateful quality of *da' primi anni / tal presagio di te tua vita dava,* "from your earliest years your life foretold that this would be your fate."

89. Added by Morley to separate the guide's words from those of the poet.

90. Expansion of *amorosi affanni,* "sufferings of love."

91. *daunger.* difficulty, disdain, lordship. See C. S. Lewis, *The Allegory of Love* (New York: Oxford University Press, 1958), pp. 364–366, for the complexities involved in this word.

97. Morley omitted the apostrophe *O figliuol mio,* "Oh, my son."

99–102. Misreading of the original. Read: "I did not understand him at that time, but now his words are firmly set in my mind, as if in marble."

103. Misreading of the original. Petrarch says: *E per la nova età, che ardita e presta / fa la mente e la lingua;* "And because of youth, which makes mind and tongue fervent and quick."

104–105. Morley used indirect address in place of the direct address of the original. He also changed Petrarch's present tense to the past tense.

106. Added by Morley for more effective transition between the words of the poet and those of the guide. Morley also put the guide's words into indirect address.

109. Added by Morley.

111. For *cangerai volto e capelli,* "Your face and your hair will change." Morley also omitted *dal collo e da'tuo'piedi anco ribelli,* "However much your neck and feet may rebel."

113. *thy yonge desyre.* Your youthful wish.

114. For *dirò di noi,* "I will tell you about us"; thus the guide includes himself among the servants of love.

115. *capteynes.* For *maggiore,* "chief," "master."

116. For *che così vita e libertà ne spoglia,* "Who deprive us of life and liberty."

118. In the present tense in the original.

120. Expansion of *quando fia tuo,* "When he shall be your [lord]"; Morley omitted *com'è nostro signore,* "As he is our lord."

124–126. Loosely translated from *ben sa chi 'l prova, e fiate cosa piana / anzi mill'anni;*

'*nfin ad or ti sveglio*, which is rendered by Wilkins as "As who makes trial knows, and thou shalt know / In less than a thousand years, I prophesy" (*Wi. Tr.*, p. 8).

127–131. Morley slightly altered the order of vices. Petrarch says that love is born of idleness and wantonness, nourished by vain thoughts, and made a god by vain persons.

130. Added by Morley.

135. Added by Morley.

136. *Cheke and chynne.* Added by Morley.

137–138. Added by Morley.

140. Added by Morley.

141. *valeaunte.* Morley's adjective. Petrarch describes Caesar's appearance as *superba*, "proud."

142. Added by Morley. Petrarch says Cleopatra enslaved Caesar with pleasures and enticements.

146. *even . . . se.* Padding to round out a rhyme.

148. *that . . . peare.* Added by Morley.

150. *Lyvyahe.* Livia, who was married to Tiberius Claudius Nero. Augustus compelled her husband to divorce her.

151. *dyspytefull.* Petrarch's adjective is *dispietato*, "pitiless." Petrarch adds that he was '*ngiusto*, "unjust."

152. Petrarch adds that he was full of disdain also.

154. Added by Morley to replace *e par tanto robusto*, "though he seems strong."

156. Petrarch describes Marcus Aurelius as *d'ogni laude degno*, "worthy of every praise."

159. *that . . . by.* Added by Morley.

160. Petrarch adds *sospetto*, "suspicion."

161. *Denyse.* Dionysius, tyrant of Syracuse; he kept two women at the same time and he was famous for his jealousy. *Alexander.* Tyrant of Pherae in Thessaly; he was also famous for his cruelty and jealousy. See *Ca. Tr.*, p. 11.

162. *sclaundre.* For *temer*, "fear." See *Ca. Tr.*, pp. 11–12.

163. *Aeneas.* Lines 163–168 are obscure because of Morley's expansions, his difficulties with the syntax of the original, and his omissions. Wilkins's translation reads: "The next is he who by Antrandos wept / Creusa's death, and took another bride / From that same prince who slew Evander's son" (*Wi. Tr.*, p. 9).

168. Added by Morley.

169. Morley mistook Petrarch's reversal of subject and verb in *Udito hai ragionar* for a question and put the following sentence in the interrogative. The reference is to Hippolytus.

171. *foull . . . desires.* For *furor*.

172. Added by Morley.

173. *But wo alas.* Added by Morley.

174. *as . . . fynde.* Added by Morley.

175. Petrarch adds *terribile e maligna*, "terrible and evil."

176. Added by Morley.

178. Added by Morley.

179. For *Ed ella ne morio: vendetta forse / d'Ippolito e di Teseo e d'Adrianna, / ch'a*

morte, tu 'l sai bene, amando corse, translated by Wilkins as "Herself she slew, perchance avenging thus / Theseus, Hippolytus, and Ariadne, / Who, as thou know'st, sped, loving, to her death" (*Wi. Tr.*, p. 10). *Adryan*. Ariadne.

180–188. Verbose and unclear. Read: "In blaming another, one condemns himself, and one who takes delight in committing fraud must not complain if he himself is deceived."

189. Theseus.

190–192. *two systers*. Phaedra and Ariadne. These lines are inaccurate renderings of the original, in which Petrarch says simply that both sisters are dead and that Theseus loved one sister and was loved by the other. See *Ca. Tr.*, pp. 12–13.

194. Petrarch's adjectives are *possente* and *forte*, "powerful" and "strong."

195. Morley's phrase; Petrarch says simply that Hercules was taken by Love.

197. *the . . . bolde*. Added by Morley.

198. Added by Morley.

200–202. *that . . . syde*. Added by Morley.

203–206. Loosely translated. Morley omitted the line *ch'Amor e lui seguí per tante ville*, "who followed Love and him to many lands." Morley also omitted Petrarch's description of Medea's wild and passionate nature. Lines 205–206 were added by Morley.

207. *Hysyphyle*. Hypsipyle.

208. *barbarouse*. See *Ca. Tr.*, p. 14. Misreading of the original. Petrarch says that Hypsipyle suffered because Medea, a woman from a barbarous nation, wooed Jason and won him.

210. Petrarch describes Helen first—she w. ⸺ holds the title to beauty, *colei ch'ha 'l titol d'esser bella*—and then Paris—the "shep erd" whose sight of her fair face was the cause of so much conflict.

212. Added by Morley.

214. Added by Morley.

217–218. *that . . . Helen awaye*. Added by Morley.

219. *the Grekysse kynge*. Added by Morley.

220–224. These pairs of lovers are simply catalogued in the original. Morley added descriptive details, but he omitted Petrarch's comment that Argia was more faithful than Amphiarus's covetous wife Eriphile. 221. *Hermon*. Hermione. 223. *Protheossolaus*. Protesilaus.

228. Added by Morley.

229. *are about to*. Petrarch uses the past tense.

230. For *a lui che 'n tal modo gli guida*, "to him who leads them thus."

232. Added by Morley.

235. For *empion del bosco e degli ombrosi mirti*, "fill the woods and shading myrtles."

236. Added by Morley.

238. For *i pie', le braccia e 'l collo*, "feet, arms, and neck."

240. *for . . . pryde*. Added by Morley.

241. *gaye golden lockes*. For Petrarch's *biondo*, "blond."

242–244. Read: "who used to scorn the bow [of love] that dealt him such a blow in Thessaly." 242. Expansion of Petrarch's *solea dispressar*, "used to scorn."

245. *And for conclusion.* For Petrarch's *Che debb'io dire? In un passo men varco:* "What shall I say? I'll clear myself with a pithy phrase."

246. *Of . . . rehearsall.* For *gli dei di Varro,* "Varro's gods." *Varro.* Marcus Terentius Varro, Roman poet and grammarian.

247. Petrarch says Jupiter leads the entire procession; Morley says that he is "amonge the other" and Morley omits Petrarch's phrase describing Jupiter as burdened by innumerable bonds of love.

248–250. *toppe to too . . . whiche is a marvelous thing.* Added by Morley.

Changes in Capitalization and Orthography. Epistle, p. 79 God] god. title First] first; 4 Bull] bull. 158 at] as.

The Tryumphe of Love, II

1. *All . . . admiration.* For *Stanco già di mirar,* "weary with gazing."

2. *As . . . fasshyon.* For *non sazio ancora,* "still not satisfied."

3. *To se . . . route.* For *guardando / cose ch'a ricontarle è breve l'ora,* "seeing things I do not have time to relate."

6. For *quando / tutto a sé il trasser due,* "when it [my heart, mind] was drawn by two."

7. *Hande in hand.* Morley's literal translation of *a mano a mano,* which is idiomatic for "together." *in the prease.* Added by Morley.

8. *Reasongynge . . . sease.* For *passavan dolcemente lagrimando,* "walking and gently weeping." Morley's reading of *ragionando* for *lagrimando* destroys the tender pathos of the original.

10. *language more strange.* For *'l parlar pellegrin,* "foreign speech."

11. *darke and obscure.* For *oscuro,* "unintelligble."

12. Added by Morley.

13–14. Expansion of *l'interprete mio mel facea piano,* "my interpreter [the guide] made it clear for me."

16. Petrarch adds *più securo,* "with more assurance."

18. *Frende . . . Romaynes.* For *amico / al nostro nome,* "Friendly to our people." The reference is to Masinissa. *that . . . passe.* Added by Morley.

19. *a perpetuall foo.* For *era empio e duro* "was harsh and cruel." The reference is to Sophonisba.

20–21. *I . . . sayde.* For *Fecemi al primo,* "I turned to the first."

22. *which . . . alway.* Added by Morley.

23. Expansion of *per costei,* "for him."

24. *That . . . bolde.* For *quel ch'i'dico,* "what I say."

25. Added by Morley.

26. *with . . . chere.* For *Mirommi,* "he looked at me."

27. *what . . . be.* For *chi tu se',* "who you are." Petrarch adds *innanzi,* "first."

28–31. For *da poi che sí bene / hai spiato ambeduo gli affetti miei,* "since you have so well discovered the two [Scipio and Sophonisba] to whom I was devoted."

32–33. Added by Morley. 32. *that . . . me.* Read: "Ask me."

34–35. For *L'esser mio, gli risposi, non sostene / tanto conoscitor,* "I [my being] am not worthy to be known by such a person."

38. *O noble knyght.* Added by Morley.

39. *blowen and spredde.* For *per tutto aggiunge,* "extends everywhere." Morley omitted the lines which follow.: *e tal, che mai non ti vedrà né vide, | con bel nodo d'amor teco congiunge,* "and binds to you with the fair knot of love people who shall never see you and people who have never seen you."

40. *This duke:* Love.

42. For *se colui 'n pace vi guide,* "as you hope for peace."

43. *You and Sophonysba.* Added by Morley.

44–45. For *che coppia è questa, | che mi par de le cose rare e fide?* "Who are the couple, who seem to be a rare example of fidelity?"

46–47. *He . . . sayde.* Added by Morley. *kind.* For *presta,* "ready." Line 47 confuses the sense of the original. Read: "Your words, so ready with my name, show that you know us."

48–49. Added by Morley.

50. *thy mind.* For *per sfogar l'anima mesta,* "to relieve the tortured soul." Masinissa's words imply that he speaks to relieve his own suffering, not that of the listener.

51. *Duke:* Scipio. Petrarch describes him as *quel sommo uom,* "that great man."

52. Added by Morley.

53. *Lelius.* Friend of Scipio Africanus.

55. *wyth . . . knyght.* Added by Morley.

58. Added by Morley.

62. Added by Morley.

64–66. Expansion of *ivi n'aggiunse e ne congiunse Amore,* "there Love found us and joined us together."

67–69. Blurring and expanding of *Né mai più dolce fiamma in duo cori arse,* "Never did a sweeter flame burn in two hearts."

70. Circumlocution, perhaps deliberate, for *Omè, ma poche notti | fur a tanti desir sí brevi e scarse,* literally, "Alas, to such passionate desires were given only a few short nights."

71–72. Added by Morley.

73. *albeit.* For *indarno,* "in vain."

74. Added by Morley, perhaps to replace *che del nostro furor scuse non false | . . . furon rotti,* "That all the honest reasons for our love were lost."

78. *and . . . place.* For *ché di nostri sospir nulla gli calse, | e ben che fosse onde mi dolse e dole,* rendered by Wilkins as "Nor could he heed the pity of our sighing, | And though it brought and brings me bitter dole" (*Wi. Tr.,* pp. 13–14).

81. Added by Morley.

83–84. Expansion of *Gran giustizia agli amanti è grave offesa,* translated by Wilkins as "To those who love, high justice is high doom" (*Wi. Tr.,* p. 14).

85. *his . . . councell.* Morley was kinder to Scipio than was Petrarch, who wrote *un tal consiglio | fu quasi un scoglio a l'amorosa impresa,* "such a verdict was a reef to the amorous enterprise."

88. *in yche degree.* Added by Morley. The original is equally obscure. What is probably intended is "He was like a son to me by virtue of the love he bore me."

90. *with . . . payned.* For *con turbato ciglio,* "with a distressed eye."

91. *Scipio.* Added by Morley. *my wyfe.* For *mia cara,* "my beloved."

92. For *a morte venne,* "met her death."

96. Expansion of *del dolor mio,* "of my own pain."

97–98. Blurring of *'l pregator e i preghi eran sí ardenti,* "the suppliant [Sophonisba] and her entreaties were so ardent."

100. For *offesi me per non offender lui,* "I suffered that she might not suffer."

102–106. Blurring of *com'io so bene, ed ella il crede; / e tu, se tanto o quanto d'amor senti,* "as I well know, as she knows, and as you must know if you know of love."

104. *brest.* Metathesis of *burst.*

107. *Pianto fu 'l mio di tanta sposa erede,* "Sorrow was the only inheritance I had from my wife," was omitted by Morley. Line 107 is a blurring of *lei, ed ogni mio bene, ogni speranza / perder elessi per non perder feder,* "I chose to lose her and all happiness and hope rather than break my faith [with Scipio]."

109. Added by Morley.

111. *this lovers daunce.* The Triumph of Love.

112. For *notabil cosa,* "thing of note."

113. Added by Morley.

118–119. Added by Morley.

121. Inaccurately translated. Sophonisba says *Costui certo per sé già non mi spiace,* "This fellow himself does not displease me." She adds, however, that her hatred is directed toward all Romans.

122–123. Expansion of *ferma son d'odiarli tutti quanti,* "I am determined to hate them all."

124. Added by Morley.

126. Added by Morley.

127. *Two times.* Petrarch says *tre volte,* "three times," referring to the three Punic wars.

128. Added by Morley.

129. For *a la terza giace,* "on the third occasion was utterly defeated."

130. Added by Morley.

131–132. Added by Morley. Morley overlooked *Altro vogl'io che tu mi mostre,* "I want you to show me other [Roman defeats]."

134. For *non ne rise,* "Had no cause for laughter."

136. Added by Morley.

138. *here and there.* Added by Morley.

141. *that . . . ride.* For *che per terren dubio cavalca,* "who rides in strange lands."

147. Added by Morley.

149–150. For *un fuor di strada, / a guisa di chi brami e trovi cosa / onde poi vergognoso e lieto vada,* "a man out of line, like one who seeks and finds something which gives him shame and joy."

152. *By pytie.* Added by Morley.

153. For *O sommo amore e nova cortesia,* "Oh greatest love, unparalleled courtesy." Morley omitted *Tal ch'ella stessa lieta e vergognosa / parea del cambio,* "So that she herself seemed happy and ashamed at the exchange."

155. *of . . . case.* For *de'lor dolci affetti,* "Of their sweet loves."

156. For *e sospirando il regno di Soria,* "And sighing for the land of Syria.'

158. *as . . . see.* Added by Morley.

162. Added by Morley.

163. For *al suon del ragionar latino,* "At the sound of Latin speech."

165. For *si rattenne un poco,* "He stayed his steps a bit."

166. Misreading of *del mio voler quasi indovino,* "almost guessing what I desired."

167–168. Added by Morley.

169. *brifely to discus.* Added by Morley.

171. *the Romaines nacion.* For *voi,* "you." For Petrarch's confusion of Antiochus I and Antiochus III, see *Ca. Tr.,* p. 25.

174. For *per scamparlo d'amorosa morte,* "To save him from dying of love."

175. *lefull.* Lawful. For *gliel'diedi; e 'l don fu lecito tra noi,* "I gave her to him, and the gift was permissable according to our laws."

176. *She . . . so.* Added by Morley.

177. Misreading. The original reads *Stratonica è 'l suo nome, e nostra sorte, / come vedi, indivisa,* "Her name is Stratonica, and [as you see] our destiny is inseparable."

178. A complete blurring of the original, which reads: *e per tal segno / si vede il nostro amor tenace e forte,* "by that sign it is evident that our love is firm and strong."

179–181. Blurring of the original, which reads: *è contenta costei lasciar me e il regno, / io il mio diletto, e questi la sua vita, / per far, via piú che sè, l'un l'altro degno;* "She was content to leave me and the kingdom, I to leave my delight, and he [Antiochus] his life. Each thought the other worthier than himself."

182–188. In the original these lines follow Petrarch's reference to the *fisico gentil,* "the gentle physician." See line 189 in Morley's translation.

190. *Disclosed to me.* Added by Morley.

192. Petrarch remarks that Antiochus's silence about his love for Stratonica was motivated by virtue and that Seleucus's action was motivated by paternal love.

194. Morley omitted *come uom che voler mute,* "like a man who changes his mind."

196. Added by Morley.

198–199. Blurring of the original, which reads: *rimasi grave è sospirando andai, / ché 'l mio cor dal suo dir non si disciolse,* "I remained pensive, and I moved on, sighing, and still thinking of his words."

200. Added by Morley, but perhaps taken in part from three lines not translated: *infin che mi fu detto: "Troppo stai / in un penser a le cose diverse; / e 'l tempo ch'è brevissimo ben sai,"* "Until a voice said to me, 'You linger too long on one thought; [there is much to see] and you know well that time is short.'" For a more logical connection between lines 200 and 201, read: "But as I stood thus musing apart, it occurred to me that Xerxes," etc.

202. Added by Morley.

203. *had . . . sort.* Added by Morley.

204. *barrayne of comforte.* The original reads *ignudi e presi,* "nude and captive."

205–206. Morley linked two ideas which were separate in the original. Petrarch says first: *tal che l'occhio la vista non sofferse,* "so that the eye could not see them all." He then adds that they spoke many languages and came from several countries.

208. *that there standes.* Added by Morley.

209. *theyr person.* Added by Morley. Read: "That of a thousand I knew not one by person or by name."

210. Added by Morley. The original reads *e fanno istoria quei pochi ch'intesi,* "the few I recognized were famous," or "my story is about those few I recognized."

211. *desyre.* For *saper,* "to know."

212. *Howe . . . attyre.* Added by Morley. The original reads *come Andromeda gli piacque,* "how he loved Andromeda."

213–215. Misreading of Petrarch's original, which says simply that Andromeda was *vergine, bruna i begli occhi e le chiome,* "a maiden with lovely dark eyes and dark hair." *that whote country* is also Morley's addition.

216–218. Added by Morley.

219. *the . . . playne.* For *il vano amador,* "the vain lover": Narcissus.

220. *pycter.* For *bellezza,* "beauty."

221. For *fu distrutto,* "was destroyed."

222–223. Added by Morley. Morley omitted *povero sol per troppo averne copia,* "poor only in having too much [beauty]."

226. For *e quella che,* "and she who": Echo.

228–229. Expansion for Petrarch's difficult *ignuda voce / fecesi* ("became a mere voice"), which is translated by Wilkins (*Wi. Tr.,* p. 18) as "a floating voice became." Petrarch's description of Echo's voice precedes his description of how she was turned to stone. Morley reversed the order.

230. Added by Morley, no doubt to identify Echo, who is not mentioned by name in the original.

231. The Iphis to whom Petrarch refers is the young prince of Cyprus who committed suicide when disdained by Anaxarete. Ovid tells the story in *Metamorphoses, XIV.* Petrarch says that he was *al suo mal sí veloce,* "quick to do himself ill," and that *amando altrui in odio s'ebbe,* "loving another, he hated himself." Morley may have confused this figure with another Iphis whose story is also told in Ovid's *Metamorphoses* (IX). This Iphis is a young girl, a Cretan, who was metamorphosed into a young man when she was betrothed against her will.

232. *in . . . state.* For *piú altri dannati a simil croce,* "others condemned to bear a similar cross."

233–235. Loosely rendered. Petrarch notes that among the throng of lovers who had no wish to live there were several moderns. He notes, too, that it would be useless to mention all of them. The sense of Morley's line 235 is implied, but not stated, in the original.

236–242. In the original two sets of lovers are mentioned—Ceyx and Halcyone and Aesacus and Hesperia—all of whom were transformed into birds. Morley took the whole passage to refer to Ceyx and Halcyone. *the kyngedome of Esperye* was, of course, a gross misreading of the original.

243–244. Added by Morley.

245. Scylla.

246. For *fuggir volando,* "flew away."

247. For *e correr Atalanta,* "and Atalanta running."

248. For *tre palle d'or,* "three golden balls."

249–252. A blurring of the original, translated by Wilkins (*Wi. Tr.*, p. 18) as "his rivals all / Lost both the fateful race and their own lives, / And he alone could boast of victory." Line 252 blurs Petrarch's *Fra questi fabulosi e vani amori*, "Among these famous and vain loves."

253. *Acys*. Petrarch obviously referred to the legend of Acis and Galathea, not to Atys (or Attis), a mythological figure in the worship of the Phrygian goddess Cybele-Agdistis.

255–256. Loose rendering of ll. 172–173 in the original: *Glauco ondeggiar per entro quella schiera / senza colei cui sola par che pregi*," "I saw Glaucus wandering in that throng, without her who alone was dear to him."

257. *Canente*. Canens. See *Ca. Tr.*, p. 30, for a discussion of Canens and Picus.

258. *which . . . thing*. Added by Morley. Morley omitted *e chi di stato il mosse / lasciogli 'l nome e l' real manto e i fregi*, "And she [Circe] who transformed him and left him his ornaments and his royal robe."

260. *Because*. Petrarch suggests no connection between Egeria and Scylla's metamorphosis.

263–264. Added by Morley. Petrarch does not mention Canace by name. 264. *by . . . oppressed*. Canace fell in love with her brother and was slain by her father.

265. *In . . . hande*. Petrarch says *da man destra*, "in her right hand."

266. *with . . . colde*. For *come dogliosa e disperata scriva*, "writes as one who is desperate and in grief."

267–268. Expansion of *Pigmalion con la sua donna viva*, "Pygmalion with his living wife."

269–272. Expansion of *e mille che Castalia ed Aganippe / udír cantar per l'una e l'altra riva*, "And a thousand more whose names have been sung by Helicon and the Castalian spring."

274. *scorned . . . apple*. See *Ca. Tr.*, p. 31.

Changes in Capitalization and Orthography. Title Second] second. 103 felte] feltes. 127 Cartage] cartage. 231 Yphys] yphys. 237 them] they. 248 three] theyr. 253 Acys] Atys. 257 Canente] Carmenite. 268 alyf] Alyf.

The Tryumphe of Love, III

3. *or . . . peace*. Added by Morley.

6. For *Che fai? che mire? che pensi?* "What are you doing? What do you gaze at? What are you thinking?"

7. Added by Morley.

9. Added by Morley.

11. *Myne entention*. For *l'esser mio*, "who I am." *and . . . feale*. Added by Morley.

12–14. Expansion and blurring of *l'amor del saper, che m'ha sí acceso, / che l'opra è ritardata dal desio*, "The desire to know has so taken me that the desire itself keeps me from learning."

15–16. Expansion of *I' t'avea giá, tacendo, inteso*, "Though you are silent, I understand your wish."

18. *yf . . . me.* Blurring of *se 'l dir non è conteso,* "If the telling is not interrupted."

20. *so . . . power.* Added by Morley.

21. *the chaste.* Added by Morley.

22. *Tholome.* Ptolemy. See *Ca. Tr.,* p. 33. *the unstedfast.* Added by Morley.

23. Added by Morley.

25. Added by Morley. Petrarch's *gran greco,* "the great Greek," refers to Agamemnon, not to Alexander.

26–29. Misreading of the original: *né vede Egisto e l'empia Clitemestra: | or puoi veder Amor s'egli è ben cieco,* "Nor did he [Agamemnon] see the evil Clytemnestra and Aegistus. Now can you see how blind love is!"

30. *Ipermistra.* Hypermnestra. See *Ca. Tr.,* p. 34. The remainder of the line was added by Morley.

32. *that . . . soo.* Added by Morley.

33. Added by Morley.

35. Morley omitted *affabile ombra,* "kindly spirit."

37. *from Troy.* Added by Morley.

38. Blurring of *ma Circe, amando gliel ritiene e 'ngombra,* "But Circe detains him with her love and keeps him from leaving."

39–40. Added by Morley.

41. *Amilcar's sonne.* Hannibal.

42. Loose rendering of *nol piega | in cotanti anni Italia tutta e Roma,* "Neither Rome nor all of Italy could bend him to their will." The reference is to the Second Punic War.

43. Added by Morley.

46. Expansion of *va seguitando,* "follows."

47. See *Ca. Tr.,* p. 35.

50. Added by Morley.

51. *the true.* Added by Morley.

52. Added by Morley.

53–54. See *Ca. Tr.,* p. 35. The two lines are expanded from *che 'l ferro e 'l foco affina,* "refined by steel and fire."

55. *Julia.* Julius Caesar's daughter and wife to Pompey.

56. Added by Morley.

60. *the . . . father.* Jacob the Patriarch. See *Ca. Tr.,* p. 36. Petrarch adds *non si muta,* "and does not change, is constant."

61–62. Inaccurate. Petrarch says that Jacob did not mind serving Rachel for *sette e sette anni,* "for seven years and then for seven more."

64. *the . . . Jacob.* Isaac.

65. *the graundefather.* Abraham. *of . . . delight.* Inaccurate rendering of *come di sua magion sol con Sara esce,* "How he [Abraham] left his home with [his wife] Sara."

66. Added by Morley.

68–69. *and . . . servaunt.* Expanded from *e sforzalo a far l'opra* "and made him do the deed." See *Ca. Tr.,* pp. 36–37.

70. *he . . . therefore.* Added by Morley.

71. *pyte . . . upon.* Added by Morley.

72. *Salomon.* Added by Morley for clarity. Petrarch refers to Solomon as *più saggio figliuol,* "the wisest son [of David]."

73. *That ... quenched.* Added by Morley.

74. For *De l'altro,* "the other," Amnon, David's other son, who fell in love with his sister Thamar and ravished her. He afterward conceived great hatred for her and hated her as much as he had loved her. Amnon was murdered by his brother Absolon.

75. *in a whyle.* For *che'n un punto ama e disama,* "who loves and hates at the same time."

76. Added by Morley.

78. Added by Morley.

80. *that ... repent.* Added by Morley. Petrarch says that Sampson was *più forte che saggio,* "stronger than he was wise."

81. *in ... lappe.* Petrarch specifies that Sampson *per ciance / in grembo a la nemica il capo pone,* "wantonly placed his head in the lap of a woman who was an enemy." For the use of the figure of Sampson by the Renaissance illustrators of the *Trionfi,* see Fig. 2.

82. Added by Morley.

83–88. Are understandably obscure because the syntax of the original is extremely complex. Read: "After this behold proud Holophernes, in spite of his swords and spears [i.e., his martial might], overcome by the widow Judith. Her weapons were love, sleep, soothing words, and a lovely face. See her, too, with her maidservant as she returns in haste at midnight bearing the horrid head of Holophernes and giving thanks to God." The passage is rendered even more obscure by Morley's omission of a number of key phrases. Even Wilkins (*Wi. Tr.,* p. 22) had considerable difficulty with the original. 88. *abrayde.* to speak out suddenly. *At ... abrayde* is idiomatic for "suddenly."

89. *Doest ... see.* Petrarch's sentence is in the imperative, not the interrogative. *Sychen.* Shechem. See *Ca. Tr.,* p. 38.

90–91. Misreading and blurring of *'l suo sangue, ch'è meschio / de la circoncisione e de la morte / e 'l padre colto e 'l popolo ad un veschio,* "and his blood was mixed with rite and with slaughter, and his father and his people were ensnared by both."

93. *Assuerus.* Ahasuerus. See *Ca. Tr.,* p. 39.

96–97. Misreading of the original. Petrarch does not say that the best remedy for love is finding another love; he says that trying to cure love by replacing one love object with another is like trying to knock out one nail with another.

98. Added by Morley.

99–100. Blurring of *Vuo'veder in un cor diletto e tedio, / dolce ed amaro?* "Do you want to see in one heart delight and weariness, sweetness and bitterness?" 100. *which ... parte.* I.e., which do not go together.

101. *howe ... complayne.* Added by Morley. Petrarch says *Amore e crudeltà gli han posto assedio,* "Love and cruelty have brought him low."

102. Added by Morley.

103. Blurring of *Vedi come arde prima, e poi si rode, / tardi pentito di sua feritate,* "See how first he burns and then he turns against himself, repenting too late for his sins."

104. Added by Morley. Read: "The deed once done, it cannot be undone."

106. Added by Morley. Petrarch says merely that Mariamne *non l'ode*, "does not hear him."

107. Expansion of *Vedi*, "see."

108. *where they be*. Added by Morley.

109–110. Expansion of *Procri, Artemisia con Deidamia*, "Procris, Artemisia, and Deidamia." See *Ca. Tr.*, pp. 39–40.

111–112. Expansion and blurring of *ed altrettante ardite e scellerate*, "and three others whose love was bold and evil."

113. *the gent*. Added by Morley. Petrarch calls her *ria*, "evil." See *Ca. Tr.*, p. 40. *Biblia*. Byblis, who fell in love with her brother. *Mirra*. Myrrha, who slept with her father.

115–116. Added by Morley.

117. *with lyes*. For Petrarch's *di sogni*, "with dreams."

118. *that . . . dyes*. Added by Morley. Petrarch says *e gli altri erranti*, "and the other knights errant." Isolde's name, however, is mentioned, along with Guinevere's, in the lines which follow.

119. *Gueynor*. Guinevere.

120–122. *the . . . Darmino*. Morley's misreading of Petrarch's *la coppia d'Arimino*, "the two from Rimini," Paolo Malatesta and Francesca da Polenta.

123–124. *and . . . tell*. Added by Morley.

128. *new . . . awaken*. Added by Morley.

130. *The . . . mayden*. Laura. See *Ca. Tr.*, p. 41. *of . . . mode* [mind]. Added by Morley.

132. Added by Morley.

133–134. Added by Morley.

136. *in . . . case*. Added by Morley.

138. *and . . . prysoner*. Added by Morley.

139. For *E come ricordar di vero parme*, "And as I seem to remember."

140. *smyling*. Petrarch says *con un riso, per più doglia darme*, "with a [sarcastic] laugh, to give me more pain."

142. *and . . . playe*. Added by Morley.

143. For *tutti siam*, "We are all."

144. *spottyd . . . maladye*. For *macchiati d'una pece*, "stained with the same pitch."

145. *of . . . arraye*. Added by Morley.

146–148. For *un di color cui più dispiace / de l'altrui ben che del suo mal*, "one of those who more regrets another's good than his own ill."

149–150. Expansion and blurring of *come tardi dopo 'l danno intendo*, "as I now know, after all my suffering."

154. *like . . . woo*. Added by Morley. In the original, *ardendo*, "burning," refers to the love, jealousy, and envy just mentioned. Morley also omitted *Gli occhi dal suo bel viso non torcea*, "I did not take my eyes from her lovely face." Line 155 is perhaps a loose rendering of this line.

162. Added by Morley.

164. Added by Morley.

165. For *Da quel tempo*, "since that time."

166. For *ebbi gli occhi umidi e bassi*, "my eyes were wet and downcast."

168–170. Expansion of *fonti, fiumi, montagne, boschi e sassi*, "fountains, streams, mountains, woods, and rocks." *I . . . goodes*. Added by Morley.

171. *And to this*. For *Da indi in qua*, "ever since then." *so . . . whyte*. Added by Morley.

172–174. Blurring of Petrarch's *cotante carte aspergo | di pensieri e di lagrime e d'inchiostro, | tante ne squarcio e n'apparecchio e vergo*, "I sprinkle so many pages with thoughts and tears and ink and destroy as many as I write."

175. Expansion and blurring of Petrarch's *Da indi in qua so che si fa nel chiostro | d'Amore*, "Ever since then I know what is done in the prison of love."

176. Added by Morley.

178. *and . . . thereto*. Added by Morley.

180. Added by Morley.

181–182. Expansion of *E veggio andar quella leggiadra fera*, translated by Wilkins (*Wi. Tr.*, p. 24) as "The fair one whom I hunt eludes me."

183. *Goeth afore me*. Added by Morley.

184. For *di mie pene*, "of my sufferings."

185. *set so hye*. Added by Morley.

186. Added by Morley.

188–189. Added by Morley.

191. For *teme di lei*, "fears her."

192. Added by Morley.

194. Blurring of *ch'a mia difesa non ho ardir né forza*, "that I have no courage or strength to defend myself." Here Morley also omitted two difficult lines: *e quello, in ch'io sperava, lei lusinga | che me e gli altri crudelmente scorza*, "He in whom I had hopes [Love] still leads her on / In cruelty to others and to me" (*Wi. Tr.*, p. 25).

195–197. Added by Morley.

198. Blurring of *Costei non è chi tanto o quanto stringa | cosí selvaggia e ribellante suole | da le 'nsegne d'Amore andar solinga*, "There is no one who can win her, so untamed and rebellious does she go her way, alone against Love's banners."

201. Morley omitted *suoi disdegni*, "her scorn."

202. Morley omitted *o sparse al vento*, "or free to the wind."

205–207. Misreading of the original. Read: "Who could speak of her benign and gentle bearing and of her virtue? My words are but as brooks are to the sea."

208. Added by Morley.

210. *so . . . sheene*. So sweet and fair. Added by Morley.

211. *hyr . . . expresse*. Added by Morley.

213. *and . . . tyde*. And bound, tied, to her. Compare with *ed ella è sciolta*, "and she is free."

214. *on every syde*. Added by Morley.

215. Expansion of *o stella iniqua*, "O evil star!"

216. Added by Morley.

217–220. Blurring of *io prego giorno e notte . . . ed ella a pena di mille uno ascolta*, "I pray both night and day, and she of a thousand prayers scarcely hears one."

221–226. Very loosely translated from the original. For clarity read: "Hard law of Love! But though unjust, it must be served, for that law extends from heaven to earth; it is universal and ancient." It is clear that Morley had only the vaguest notion of the sense of the original.

227. *He that is.* Incorrect. Petrarch says *or so.* "Now I know." The rest of the line is Morley's addition.

228. *from . . . departed.* I.e., transferred to the beloved.

229. Petrarch adds *tregua*, "truce."

230–231. Expanded from *coprir suo dolor quand'altri il punge*, "conceal its pain when another hurts it."

232–234. Added by Morley.

235. *to my harte.* For *le guance*, "cheeks."

236. *doth starte.* For *si dilegua*, "retreats." Morley also omitted Petrarch's remark that the rushing of the blood to the cheeks or its retreat was caused either by fear or shame.

238. *the . . . devoure.* Added by Morley.

239–242. Expansion of *come sempre tra due si vegghia e dorme*, translated by Wilkins (*Wi. Tr.*, p. 26) as "how uncertainty may banish sleep." Morley omitted *come senza languir si more e langue*, "how without illness one may languish and die."

244. *my love.* Petrarch refers to the beloved as *la mia nemica*, "my enemy."

246. Blurring of *so in qual guisa / l'amante ne l'amato si trasforme*, "I know how the lover is transformed into the beloved." Morley also omitted an entire terzina of the original: *So fra lunghi sospiri e brevi risa / stato, voglia, color cangiar spesso, / viver stando dal cor l'alma divisa*, translated by Wilkins, (*Wi. Tr.*, p. 26) as "I know the changing of my mood and will / And color, 'mid long sighs and brief delight, / My very soul divided from my heart."

247. Petrarch adds *mille volte il dí*, "a thousand times a day."

248. Added by Morley.

249–250. Complete blurring of the original: *so, seguendo 'l mio foco ovunque e'fugge, / arder da lunge ed agghiacciar da presso*, "I know that, following the flame of my love wherever it may fly, I will burn when I am far from her and freeze when I am near her."

251. *how . . . calles.* For *sopra la mente rugge*, "roars throughout the mind."

252. Added by Morley.

253. *and . . . away.* Added by Morley.

254. For *so in quante maniere il cor si strugge*, "I know in how many ways the heart may destroy itself."

256. *lace.* net, snare, for *canape*, "hemp." *and cannot start.* Added by Morley.

257–258. Added by Morley, perhaps for *quand'ella è sola, / e non v' è chi per lei difesa faccia*, "when it [the gentle heart] is alone and there is no one to help defend it."

260. *without gevyng boote.* without giving remedy.

262. Added by Morley.

263. *And . . . ignorant.* Added by Morley. *whele.* For *rote*, "wheels."

264. For *le mani armate, e gli occhi avvolti in fasce*, "his hands armed and his eyes blindfolded."

265. *The doloure sure.* Added by Morley.

266. Added by Morley.

267–270. Blurring of *come nell'ossa il suo foco si pasce, / e ne le vene vive occulta piaga, / onde morte e palese incendio nasce,* translated by Wilkins (*Wi. Tr.,* p. 27) as "And how his fire feeds still upon my frame / And lives, a hidden passion, in my veins, / Burning me evermore, and threatening death." *267. and . . . this.* Read: "And how in addition to this."

272. waveryng . . . me. Added by Morley.

277. Added by Morley.

278. is . . . songe. Added by Morley.

Changes in Capitalization and Orthography. Title Thyrde] thyrde; Chapter] chapter; Tryumphe] tryumphe. 24 Grecian] grecian. 38 Cyrces] Cyres. 40 Ytaly] ytaly. 41 Amilcars sonne] Amilcar sonne. 109 Procry] Pocry. 117 they] then. 119 Gueynor] Queynor. 158 his] this. 194 Love] love.

The Tryumphe of Love, IV

1. Petrarch adds *in forza altrui,* "into another's power."

2. Added by Morley.

3. vaynes. Petrarch says *nervi,* "nerves."

4. and . . . paynes. For *ov'alcun tempo fui,* "which I had enjoyed for some time."

6. for my parte. Added by Morley. Petrarch adds that he was tamed *ratto,* "swiftly."

7. For *con tutti / i miei infelici e miseri conservi,* "with all my unhappy companions in servitude."

9. For *per che torti sentieri e con qual arte / a l'amorosa greggia eran condutti,* "by what tortuous ways and with what deceits they had been led to the gathering of lovers."

10. Added by Morley.

12. among . . . route. Added by Morley.

14. Petrarch adds *per antiche o per moderne carte,* "for ancient or for modern writing."

15. call. Petrarch says *ama.* The reference is to Orpheus.

16. Added by Morley.

17. as . . . tell. Added by Morley.

19–20. Added by Morley.

21. Alceo. Alcaeus. Petrarch adds that he was *a dir d'Amor sí scorto,* "skilled in verse of love." The order in which the Greek poets are mentioned in the original is different from Morley's order. In the original, Alcaeus comes first, then Pindar (*wyse* is Morley's addition), and last Anacreon. Petrarch adds that Anacreon ("Nacreon" in Morley's translation) *rimesse / ha le sue muse sol d'Amore in porto,* "led his Muses into the one port of Love."

22. Added by Morley.

23. I . . . case. Added by Morley.

24. For *e parmi ch'egli avesse / compagni d'alto ingegno e da trastullo / di quei che volentier già 'l mondo lesse,* "and it seemed to me that he had companions whom the world read for delight and for wit."

27. For *che d'amor cantàro / fervidamente,* "who sang fervidly of love."

28. Added by Morley, perhaps for *a paro a paro,* "side by side."

29. Petrarch adds *e raro*, "and rare." The allusion is to Sappho.

30. Added by Morley.

32. *with sadde chere*. Added by Morley.

33. Petrarch adds *volgarmente*, "in the vulgar tongue."

34. *fayre and gent*. Added by Morley. Morley also omitted *ecco Selvaggia*, "and here is Selvaggia [Cino da Pistoia's love]."

35. Added by Morley.

36. *wyth . . . me*. Added by Morley.

37. *and . . . place*. Added by Morley, perhaps in place of *che di non esser primo par ch'ira aggia*, "who seems to be angry that he is not the first."

38. *Two other Guydos*. Guinicelli and Cavalcanti. *in lyke manner and case*. Added by Morley, perhaps for *già fur in prezzo*, "held in high esteem."

39–40. A serious misreading of the original. In Petrarch's catalog of love poets the two Guidos are followed by *Onesto Bolognese, e i ciciliani che fur già primi e quivi eran da sezzo*, "Ser Onesto di Bonacosa [a Bolognese] and the Sicilians [of the court of Frederick II] who were once first but now are last." Morley understood *Onesto* to be an adjective modifying *Bolognese*, which in turn he thought modified *Guido*. He committed the same error with *ciciliani*.

41. *Senicio*. The Florentine Sennuccio del Bene, a friend of Petrarch, to whom the poet addressed several sonnets and a humorous *epistola*. See *Ca. Tr.*, p. 51. *Francisco*. Franceschino degli Albizzi. See *Ca. Tr.*, p. 51. Morley omitted *come ogni uom vide; e poi v'era un drappello / di portamenti e di volgari strani*, "As all men know; then there was a troop foreign in dress and speech." The reference is probably to the Provençal poets mentioned in the lines that follow.

42. *And . . . Daniell*. Arnaut Daniel. Morley took the name to refer to two persons and added *in lyke facion* and omitted *fra tutti il primo*, "first among the rest."

43. Expansion of *gran maestro d'amor*, "great master of love."

44. Blurring of *ch'a la sua terra / ancor fa onor col suo dir strano e bello*, "who still brings honor to his native land with his beautiful foreign verse." Morley then omitted *Eranvi quei ch'Amor sí leve afferra*, "There were those whom love took easily."

45. *There was Peter*. For *l'un Piero e l'altro*, "both Peires," Peire Vidal and Peire Rogier. See *Ca. Tr.*, p. 52. *the clerke famouse*. For *e 'l men famoso Arnaldo*, "and the less famous Arnaut [de Marueill]." Morley also omitted *e quei che fur conquisi con piú guerra*, "and those who were conquered through greater battle."

46. *And Rambaldo*. For *i'dico l'uno e l'altro Raimbaldo*, "I mean the two Raimbauts [d'Orange and de Vaqueiras]." See *Ca. Tr.*, p. 52. *with his stile curiouse*. Added by Morley.

47. *That wrote*. Petrarch says that one of the Raimbauts (de Vaqueiras) sang of Beatrice and of Monferrato.

48. *The olde Peter*. Peire d'Auvergne. *Geraldo*. Giraut de Bornelh. See *Ca. Tr.*, p. 53.

49. *Filileto*. Folquet de Marseille. See *Ca. Tr.*, p. 53. Petrarch says Folco *a Marsilia il nome ha dato*, "who gave the name to Marseilles," i.e., brought fame to Marseilles.

50. Blurring of *ed a Genova tolto*, "[the name] taken from Genoa." Folquet was born in Genoa but lived and wrote in Marseilles. Morley also omitted *ed a l'estremo /*

cangiò per miglior patria abito e stato, "and near the end [of his life] changed dress and state for a better homeland."

51–52. *sought . . . water.* For *ch'usò la vela e 'l remo / a cercar la sua morte,* "who used both oar and sail in seeking out his death." See *Ca. Tr.,* p. 53. *as . . . passe.* Added by Morley.

63. *Wubon.* Guillem de Cabestanh. See *Ca. Tr.,* p. 54.

54–55. Misreading and blurring of *che per cantar ha 'l fior de' suoi dí scemo,* "who for singing lost the flower of his life." See *Ca. Tr.,* p. 54.

56. Added by Morley.

57. *Amerego.* Aimeric de Peguilhan. *Barnardo.* Bernard de Ventadour. *Hugo.* Uc de Saint Circ. *Anselme.* Guacelm Faidit. See *Ca. Tr.,* pp. 54–55.

58–59. Blurring of *a cui la lingua / lancia e spada fu sempre e targia e elmo,* translated by Wilkins (*Wi. Tr.,* p. 29) as "for whom the tongue / Was ever lance and sword, helmet and targe."

60. Added by Morley.

61. *from that companye.* Added by Morley.

62. For *e vidi,* "and I saw." Morley also omitted *poi convien che 'l mio dolor distingua,* "since I must express my grief." Petrarch also adds that he turned *a'nostri,* "to our [Italian] poets."

63. *Thomaso.* Tommaso Caloiro, Petrarch's close friend and fellow student at the University of Bologna. See *Ca. Tr.,* p. 55. *that . . . prayse.* Petrarch says that Tommaso gave fame to Bologna and *or Messina impingua,* "is now buried in Messina."

64. *in hys dayse.* Added by Morley.

65. *payneful.* Added by Morley.

66. For *Chi mi ti tolse sí tosto dinanzi,* "Who took you away from me?" Petrarch adds *senza 'l qual non sapea movere un passo,* "without whom I could not walk a step."

67. *These . . . fryndes.* In this and the following line Morley uses the plural. In the original Petrarch still refers to the death of Tommaso Caloiro.

68. For *Dove se'or, che meco eri pur dianzi,* "Where are you now, who lately were with me?"

69–74. Extensive expansion of two lines of the original: *Ben è 'l viver mortal, che sí n'aggrada, / sogno d'infermi e fola di romanzi,* translated by Wilkins (*Wi. Tr.,* p. 30) as "This mortal life, that we do cherish so, / Is an ill dream, a tale of vain romance."

75–76. Misreading and blurring of *Poco era fuor de la comune strada,* "I was not far from the common path."

77–78. *howe . . . agree.* Misreading. "Socrates" and "Lelius" are soubriquets for two of Petrarch's friends. For the identification of "Socrates" and "Laelius" as Louis de Kempen and Lello di Pietro di Stefano, see *Ca. Tr.,* p. 56.

80. Added by Morley. Petrarch says *O qual coppia d'amici,* "Oh what a pair of friends!"

83. *and . . . dayes.* Added by Morley.

84. *many dyvers wayes.* For *monti diversi,* "many lands." Morley also omitted *andando tutti tre sempre ad un giogo; / a questi le mie piaghe tutte apersi,* "one yoke [of friendship] binding the three of us together, to them I told of all my wounds."

85. *man.* Petrarch says *tempo né luogo,* "neither time nor place."

86. Added by Morley. Petrarch adds *sí come io spero e bramo*, "as I hope and pray."

88. Petrarch adds *forse anzi tempo*, "perhaps too soon."

91. *of . . . wryte.* Petrarch says *ch'io tanto amo*, "whom I love so much."

92. Added by Morley.

93. *which . . . commend.* For *che 'l cor di pensier m'empie*, "who fills my heart with thoughts."

94. Added by Morley.

96. Added by Morley, perhaps for *sí fur le sue radici acerbe ed empie*, "so bitter and unyielding were her roots."

97–103. Extreme blurring of the original. Wilkins's translation (*Wi. Tr.*, p. 31) reads:
Wherefore, though overcome with grief betimes,
Like one offended, what I now beheld
With mine own eyes bids me to grieve no more.
Matter for tragedy, not for comedy,
To see him captured who is held a god
By slow and blunted and deluded minds!
But first I'll tell of what he did with us
And then of all that he himself endured—
A tale for Homer, or for Orpheus.

104. Added by Morley.

105–106. Added by Morley. Petrarch says *Seguimmo il suon de le purpuree penne / de' volanti corsier per mille fosse*, "We followed the sound of the red wings of the flying coursers, through a thousand woes."

107. *chylde.* I.e., Cupid. *his kyngdome.* Cythera.

109. For *né rallentate le catene o scosse*, "nor were the chains loosened or removed."

110. For *ma straccati per selve e per montagne*, "drawn through woods and over mountains." *and other brayes.* Added by Morley.

112. Added by Morley.

113. *Egeo.* Aegean. *that grete see.* Added by Morley. Petrarch adds that the Aegean *sospira e piagne*, "sighs and cries."

114. *delectable.* For *dilicata e molle*, "gentle and soft." *to . . . see.* Added by Morley.

115. Petrarch adds *'l mar bagne*, "bathed by the sea."

116. Added by Morley.

117. *of . . . expressed.* Added by Morley.

118. *fayre ydressed.* For *un ombroso e chiuso colle*, "a hidden and shadowy hill."

119. *With fayre flowres.* For *con sí soavi odor*, "with sweet fragrances."

120. *sadde.* Petrarch says that the beauty of the place *ogni maschio pensier de l'alma tolle*, "banishes manly thoughts from the heart."

121. Added by Morley.

123–125. Misreading of the original: *e 'n quel tempo a lei fu sagra / che 'l ver nascoso e sconosciuto giacque*, "It was sacred to her in ancient times when truth lay hidden and unknown." 125. *I saye.* Added by Morley.

126. Blurring of the original: *tanto ritien del suo primo esser vile / che par dolce ai cattivi ed ai buoni agra*, "it retains a part of its pagan evil, which is sweet to the bad and sour to the good."

129. *Tyle.* Thule. See *Ca. Tr.*, p. 59.

130–134. Added by Morley. 130–131. Read: "Among innumerable men one may find this prince," etc.

135. Petrarch says *pensieri in grembo*, idiomatic for "thoughts in our bosoms."

136. Added by Morley.

137. *and . . . go.* Added by Morley.

138. *doth . . . also.* Added by Morley. Petrarch adds *e ferma noia*, "and constant weariness."

139. *he . . . about.* Added by Morley.

140. *this . . . stoute.* Added by Morley.

142. *waverynge and blynde.* Added by Morley.

144. *when . . . opprest.* Added by Morley.

145. Added by Morley.

147. *fayre and swete.* Added by Morley.

148. *that . . . strete.* Added by Morley.

149. *briefly to endyte.* Added by Morley.

151. *rynnyng . . . place.* For *di fontane vive*, "from live fountains."

152. For *al caldo tempo*, "in the summer heat."

153. *fayre greene flowres.* For *erba fresca*, "fresh grass." Read: "There were flowers upon the fresh fair green," etc.

154. Expansion of *l'ombra spessa*, "deep shadow."

156. Blurring and expansion of *l'aure dolci estive*, "sweet summer breezes." Morley omitted *quand'è 'l verno e l'äer si rinfresca*, "When winter comes and the air is cool."

157. Expansion of *tepidi soli*, "warm sun."

158. Expansion of *cibi*, "food." Petrarch adds *giuochi*, "games," and *ozio lento*, "torpid idleness."

159. Expansion and blurring of *che i semplicetti cori invesca*, translated by Wilkins (*Wi. Tr.*, p. 32) as "that casts its spell on foolish hearts."

160. Added by Morley.

161–163. Expansion of *Era ne la stagion che l'equinozio | fa vincitore il giorno*, "It was the season when the equinox gives victory to the day."

164–165. *early afore daye* and line 165. Added by Morley. Petrarch says that *Procne riede | con la sorella al suo dolce negozio*, "Procne came with her sister [Philomel] for their sweet work."

166–167. Added by Morley.

168. *for to se.* Added by Morley.

169–170. Misreading and blurring of *in quel loco, e 'n quel tempo ed in quell'ora, | che più largo tributo agli occhi chiede*, translated by Wilkins (*Wi. Tr.*, p. 33) as "For there, and at the very time and hour | That draws a tearful tribute from my eyes."

171. Expansion of *a qual servaggio ed a qual morte*, "what servitude and what death."

172. *his . . . attayne.* Added by Morley.

173. Added by Morley.

174. *This goddes chayre.* Petrarch says it is a triumphal arch. *where . . . hye.* Added by Morley.

176. *glosynge ymages*. For *imagini smorte*, "vain imaginings." *of . . . realmes*. Added by Morley. Petrarch adds *eran d'intorno a l'arco trionfale*, "were gathered around the triumphal arch."

177. *stode . . . theyr ate*. For *su per le scale*, "were on the stairs."

181. *was . . . there*. Added by Morley.

182. *alwayes in fere*. Added by Morley.

184. *lefte . . . warke*. Added by Morley.

186. *lacked . . . presse*. Added by Morley.

187. *entre who woulde*. For *ove si vien per strade aperte*, "which one may enter easily."

188. Blurring of *onde per strette a gran pena si migra*, "from which one escapes with great difficulty." Morley omitted *ratte scese a l'entrare, a l'uscir erte*, "easy descent for entering, but steep slopes for exit."

190. For *certe doglie*, "certain sorrows," and *allegrezze incerte*, "uncertain joys."

192. *Stronglie*. For *in tanta rabbia*, "with such rage." Petrarch also mentions Stromboli.

193. Added by Morley. Note that Petrarch's triumphal arch was first called a "chayre" and is now called a castle. Morley also omitted *Poco ama sé chi 'n tal gioco s'arrischia*, "He who risks such game has little love for himself."

194–195. Added by Morley.

196–197. Blurring of *In cosí tenebrosa e stretta gabbia*, "In such a dark and narrow cage."

198. Added by Morley. Morley omitted *le penne usate / mutai per tempo e la mia prima labbia*, "Before long I became grey, and my former looks were changed."

199. For *pur sognando libertate*, "dreaming of liberty."

200–202. Added by Morley.

203–210. Misreading, blurring, and expansion of *l'alma . . . consolai col veder le cose andate*, "I soothed my soul by thinking of the loves of olden times."

211–212. Expansion of *er'io fatto al sole di neve*, "I was like snow that melts in the sun."

213. *noble men*. Petrarch says *spirti*, "spirits."

214. *there and then*. Added by Morley.

215–216. Expansion of *quasi lunga pittura in tempo breve*, "like one who tries to see a large picture in a short time." Read: "Just as one who sees," etc.

219–220. Added by Morley.

Changes in Capitalization and Orthography. Title Fourth] fourth. 21 Nacreon] Macreon. 26 Tibullo] Tubullo. 34 Beatryce] beatryce. 36 Pistoia] Piscoia. 39 Boleyne] boleyne. 47 Beatryce] beatryce; Mont Ferrato] mont ferrato. 105 Folowed] Folowing. 164 Prougne] prougne. 174 he] they.

The Tryumphe of Chastitie

1. *even . . . face*. Added by Morley, perhaps for *quivi*, "there [in the prison of love]."

2. *in . . . place*. For *ad un giogo*, "under the same yoke."

3. For *domita l'alterezza degli Dei*, "the pride of the gods tamed."

4. *mortall*. For *divi*, "divine."

5. For *i'presi esempio de'lor stati rei*, "I took example from their sorry condition." *And . . . fall*. Added by Morley.

6. *then . . . call*. Added by Morley.

8. Added by Morley. Read: "That I was like others."

9. *When*. Read: "if." *taken . . . lure*. Petrarch says that Phoebus and Leander were wounded with one arrow from a single bow and that Juno and Dido were caught in the same snare.

10. *Leander*. Petrarch calls him *'l giovine d'Abido*, "the young man of Abydos."

12. *lasyd . . . parte*. For *ad un lacciuol*, "in one snare." Morley omitted *ch'amor pio del suo sposo a morte spinse*, "driven to death by love for her husband."

13–14. Expansion of *non quel d'Enea, com'è 'l publico grido*, "not for Aeneas, as is popularly believed." There were two versions of the story of Dido in the Renaissance. In one she was a passionate woman, a victim of her love for Aeneas; in the other she was a chaste woman whose brother Pygmalion slew her husband Sychaeus, to whom she had been devoted and faithful. Petrarch here insists on the latter version, and he mentions Dido again in the "Triumph of Chastity"; see lines 229–236.

15–16. Added by Morley. Petrarch does not mention Sychaeus.

17–20. Expansion and loose rendering of *non mi debb'io doler s'altri mi vinse / giovine, incauto, disarmato e solo*, translated by Wilkins (*Wi. Tr.*, p. 39) as "I should not grieve if I be overcome, / Being young, unarmed, incautious, and alone."

21. *my lady*. Petrarch says *la mia nemica*, "my enemy." *that . . . best*. Added by Morley.

22. For *Amor non strinse*, "was not conquered by Love."

23. Added by Morley.

25–28. Added by Morley.

29–30. Very loosely rendered from *'n abito il rividi ch'io ne piansi, / sí tolte gli eran l'ali e 'l gire a volo*, "I saw him [Love] in such a state that I could weep for him, captive and bereft of his wings."

31–32. Added by Morley.

33. Petrarch adds that the thunder cleaves the air, earth, and sea.

34. Added by Morley.

35. Petrarch's simile is stronger: *Non con altro romor di petto dansi / duo leon feri*, "Greater than the roar of two fierce lions when they clash." In the original this simile also precedes the simile in line 33 above.

36–44. An extremely loose rendering of a single Petrarchan terzina: *Ch'i'vidi Amor con tutt'i suoi argomenti / mover contra colei di ch'io ragiono, / e lei presta assai piú che fiamme o venti*, "I saw Love with all his armaments [not arguments] move against her of whom I speak, and she was swifter [in her own defense] than flames or winds." Lines 36 and 38 are virtually meaningless.

45. *What . . . say*. Added by Morley.

46. Added by Morley.

48. *Enchelado*. Enceladus. See *Ca. Tr.*, p. 69.

50–51. Blurring of lines 28–30 of the original: *che via maggiore in su la prima mossa / non fusse del dubbioso e grave assalto, / ch'i' non cre'che ridir sapea né possa*, translated by

Wilkins (*Wi. Tr.*, p. 40) as "Was the first clash of the two combatants— / The outcome of the dread assault unsure— / Nor have I words to tell of it aright."

52. Added by Morley.

54. *The . . . stryfe.* Added by Morley. *for to advert.* Petrarch says *per veder meglio,* "to see better."

56. Blurring of *e l'orror de l'impresa / i cori e gli occhi avea fatti di smalto,* "and the horror of the undertaking turned all hearts and eyes to stone."

57. *vanquer.* conqueror.

58. Added by Morley. Morley omitted *che primo era a l'offesa,* "who was the first to attack."

59. *sharpe and kene.* Added by Morley.

60. *bryght and shene.* Added by Morley.

61. *this . . . feare.* Added by Morley. Petrarch says *e la corda a l'orecchia avea già stesa,* "He had already drawn the bowstring to his ear."

62. *In . . . anger.* Added by Morley.

63. Added by Morley.

64. *that maketh pretence.* For *al varco,* "lying in wait." Morley omitted *libero in selva o di catene scarco,* "free in forest and unchained."

67–68. Blurring of *ch'al volto ha le faville ond'io tutto ardo,* "who has in her face the eyes that make me burn."

69. Added by Morley.

70–74. Blurring of *Combattea in me co la pietà il desire, / ché dolce m'era sì fatta compagna, / duro a vederla in tal modo perire,* "Pity contended in me with desire, for it would have been sweet to have such a companion and it would be difficult to see her perish in such a way."

75–79. Expansion, blurring, and misreading of *Ma virtú, che da'buon non si scompagna, / mostrò a quel punto ben come a gran torto / chi abbandona lei, d'altrui si lagna,* "But Virtue, which never forsakes the good, proved then how wrong is he who abandons Virtue and blames Fortune and the stars." Line 79 may be Morley's translation of Petrarch's reference to the deftness with which his lady warded off the attack of Love. The deftness is compared first to the skill of a fencer and then to the art of a ship's pilot in bringing a ship through harbor rocks.

82. *then . . . all.* Added by Morley.

84. *on . . . syde.* Added by Morley.

85. For *subito ricoverse quel bel viso / dal colpo,* "that sweet face quickly recovered from the blow." Read: "Which made it then appear that," etc.

86. Blurring of Petrarch's description of the blow of Love as *agro e funesto,* "sharp and disastrous."

87. *I . . . styll.* Petrarch says that he watched the battle to the end.

88. Added by Morley.

89. For *sperando la vittoria ond'esser sòle,* "hoping that victory would go to the one it usually goes to [i.e., to Love]."

90. For *e di non esser piú da lei diviso,* "and never be separated from her [Laura]."

91–94. Blurring of *Come chi smisuratamente vòle, / ch'ha scritte, innanzi ch'a parlar cominci, / negli occhi e ne la fronte le parole,* translated by Wilkins (*Wi. Tr.*, p. 41) as

"And like to one compelled by great desire / Whose words, before he even starts to speak, / Are written in his eyes and on his brow."

96. *for . . . yelde.* Added by Morley.

97–98. Added by Morley.

99. Petrarch says *s'io ne son degno,* "if I am worthy of it."

100–102. Blurring of *né temer che già mai mi scioglia quinci,* "and have no fear that I will ever seek release [from service to you]."

103–110. Complete misreading of the original: *Quand'io 'l vidi pien d'ira e di disdegno / sí grave, ch'a ridirlo sarien vinti / tutti i maggior, non che 'l mio basso ingegno,* translated by Wilkins (*Wi. Tr.,* p. 41) as "When I beheld him filled with wrath so fierce / Not e'en the greatest pens could tell of it, / Much less the little skill that is in me."

111. *and . . . shafte.* Petrarch says that the gilded shafts (*i dorati suoi strali*) were lit with the flame of amorous beauty (*accesi in fiamma / d'amorosa beltate*) and that they were dipped in pleasure (*'n piacer tinti*).

112–114. Expansion and blurring of *in fredda onestate erano estinti,* "were quenched by her cold honor."

115. *fayre . . . gent.* Added by Morley. Petrarch says *e l'altre,* "and the other [Amazons]."

116. Their right breasts were cut off so that they could better draw their bows. See *Ca. Tr.,* p. 72.

117. Petrarch says Pharsalia. He adds *contra 'l genero suo,* "against his son-in-law," but does not mention Pompey by name.

119–120. Expansion and blurring of *contra colui ch'ogni lorica smaglia,* translated by Wilkins (*Wi. Tr.,* p. 42) as "'Gainst him who shatters every coat of mail."

124. Added by Morley.

128. For *nobile par de le virtú divine,* "a noble pair of divine virtues."

129. *for . . . shyne.* For *sopra le donne altera,* "that set her above other women."

130. Added by Morley.

131. *Wyt and sobernes.* For *Senno e Modestia,* "Judgment and Modesty." Petrarch adds *a l'altre due confine,* "joined the other two." Morley added *without arrace.* In Petrarch's catalog, Judgment and Modesty are followed by *Abito con Diletto in mezzo 'l core,* translated by Wilkins (*Wi. Tr.,* p. 42) as "Benignity and Gladness of the Heart."

132. *without arrace.* I.e., so that it could not be uprooted.

133. Petrarch says that Perseverance is accompanied by Glory.

135. *Fayre Entreatynge.* For *Bella Accoglienza,* "Fair Welcome." Petrarch adds *Accorgimento,* "Prudence." *was not behynde.* Added by Morley.

136. *Clemesse.* Clemency, added by Morley, as was *that . . . kynde.* In the original Courtesy and Purity are linked.

137. Petrarch adds *Desio sol d'onore,* "Desire for Honor."

140–141. Blurring of *e (la concordia ch'è sí rara al mondo) / v'era con Castità somma Beltate,* "And, in a concord so rare in this world, there was Chastity at one with supreme Beauty."

144. For *le ben nate alme,* "well-born souls."

147. Added by Morley.

148–150. Misreading and blurring of *Mille e mille famose e care salme | tôrre gli vidi e scuotergli di mano | mille vittoriose e chiare palme*, translated by Wilkins as "Thousands of victims, famed and dear, from him | She rescued; and a thousand shining palms | Of victory she wrested from his hands" (*Wi. Tr.*, p. 43).

151. *throwe*. For *cader*, "fall." *fierse*. Added by Morley. Read: "Not the sudden fall of fierce Hannibal," etc.

152. Added by Morley. Petrarch refers to Scipio as *giovine romano*, "the young Roman."

153. *when*. For *dopo*, "after."

154. *mayned*. mixed.

155. *Colyas*. Goliath. Petrarch calls him *quel gran filisteo*, "the Philistine giant," and adds that the event took place in the vale of Terebinth (*ne la valle di Terebinto*).

157. *By David yonge*. For *garzon ebreo*, "Hebrew boy." Petrarch adds that Goliath was struck by the first stone (*primo sasso*). *and . . . age*. Added by Morley.

158. *more . . . rage*. Added by Morley. Petrarch adds *in Scizia*, "in Scythia."

159. *wydow*. Thomyris. Petrarch describes her as *orba*, "bereaved." *vengeaunce*. Petrarch describes it as *memorabile*, "unforgettable."

160–161. Added by Morley. Tomyris's son was Spargapises. See *Ca. Tr.*, p. 74.

162–166. For *Com'uom ch'è sano e 'n un momento ammorba, | che sbigottisce e duolsi, o colto in atto | che vergogna con man dagli occhi forba*, translated by Wilkins (*Wi. Tr.*, p. 43) as "Like one who, being well, falls suddenly ill, | And is afraid and troubled, or is caught | In an act so shameful that he hides his eyes."

167. Petrarch adds *e tanto a peggior patto*, "and in worse condition."

168. Petrarch adds *dolor* and *vergogna*, "pain" and "shame."

169. For *eran nel volto suo tutte ad un tratto*, "were all together in his face."

170. Read: "Neither the raging sea," etc. *ye . . . sure*. Added by Morley.

171. Petrarch adds *non Inarime allor che Tifeo piagne*, "not Ischia when Typhoeus weeps."

172. Added by Morley.

173–176. For *Passo qui cose gloriose e magne | ch'io vidi e dir non oso*, "I pass by great and glorious things that I saw but dare not tell."

178. *hyr chast company*. For *sue minor compagne*, "her lesser friends."

179. *this . . . victoriouse*. Added by Morley. Petrarch adds *il dí*, "that day."

180. *gaye and gloryouse*. Added by Morley.

181–182. Misreading of *lo scudo in man che mal vide Medusa*, translated by Wilkins (*Wi. Tr.*, p. 44) as "and held | The shield that brought Medusa to her death."

183–185. For *d'una in mezzo Lete infusa | catena di diamante e di topazio*, "and a chain of diamond and topaz, once dipped in Lethe."

186. *and . . . gone*. Added by Morley. Petrarch says *oggi non s'usa*, "it is not worn today."

187. Petrarch does not specify that Love is bound by Laura; he says simply *legarlo vidi*, "I saw him bound."

188. *in . . . wyse*. Added by Morley.

189–190. Blurring of *che bastò bene a mille altre vendette*, translated by Wilkins as "Enough to wreak a thousand vengeances" (*Wi. Tr.*, p. 44).

191–192. *And . . . dyd.* Added by Morley. *content.* Petrarch says *contento e sazio,* "content and satisfied."

193–194. Expansion and blurring of *I'non porria . . . chiudere in rima,* "I could not tell in rhyme."

195–198. Expansion and blurring of *le sacre e benedette / vergini, ch'ivi fur . . . non Calliope e Clio con l'altre sette,* "[I could not tell in rhyme], nor could Calliope and Clio and the other seven Muses, of the sacred and blessed virgins who were there."

200. *what . . . be.* Added by Morley.

201. *there she stode.* Added by Morley.

202. *swete and mylde of mode.* Added by Morley. Petrarch adds that Lucrece *era la prima,* "was the first."

203. *in pecis small.* Added by Morley.

204. For *strali,* "arrows," and *faretra,* "quiver."

205. For *spennacchiato l'ali,* "plucked the feathers from his wings."

206. Added by Morley.

207. *hir . . . father.* Virginius.

208. For *armato / di disdegno e di ferro e di pietate,* "armed with scorn and steel and piety."

209. Petrarch adds that he changed her daughter's state as well. See *Ca. Tr.,* p. 76.

210. For *l'una e l'altra ponendo in libertate,* "setting both free."

211. For *poi,* "then."

212. *a huge company.* Added by Morley.

213–214. Blurring of *che con aspra morte / servàro lor barbarica onestate,* "who chose death to preserve their barbaric honor." See *Ca. Tr.,* p. 76.

215. Petrarch adds *casta,* "chaste."

216. *she was amonge.* Added by Morley. See *Ca. Tr.,* p. 77.

217. *great perylious,* "great perilous"; added by Morley.

218. For *per morir netta,* "to die pure." Petrarch adds *e fuggir dura sorte,* "and to flee an evil fate."

219. *divers moo.* For *altre anime chiare,* "other famous souls."

220–221. Expansion of *trionfar vidi di colui che pria / veduto avea del mondo trionfare,* "I saw [her] triumph over him I had seen triumph over all the world."

222. For *Fra l'altre,* "among the others."

223. *meke* and *there she was.* Added by Morley. *Vesta.* The emendation from *Vesca* to *Vesta* is dictated by etymology. The Vestal Virgins were priestesses of the Roman goddess Vesta, whose name and nature were akin to the Greek goddess *Hestia.*

224–225. *by . . . case.* Added by Morley. Petrarch says *che baldanzosamente corse al Tibro / e . . . / portò del fiume acqua col cribro,* "who boldly ran to the Tiber and carried water in a sieve." See *Ca. Tr.,* p. 77.

227. *also . . . route.* Added by Morley. See *Ca Tr.,* p. 77.

228. *that . . . aboute.* Added by Morley. Morley omitted *schiera che del suo nome empie ogni libro,* "a troop whose names would fill many a volume."

229. *free.* Petrarch says *pellegrine,* "pilgrim, from other lands."

230. *hyr.* Dido.

231. *husbande.* Petrarch describes him as *diletto e fido,* "beloved and faithful."

234. *that . . . rehearse.* For *dico,* "I speak of."

236. *that . . . offende.* For *come è il publico grido,* "as is the public cry."

237. Piccarda Donati. See *Ca. Tr.,* p. 78.

239. For *si chiuse,* "shut herself up [in a convent]." Morley omitted *e non le valse,* "but it availed her not."

241. Blurring of *ché forza altrui il suo bel penser vinse,* "since another's force overcame her good intent."

242. Added by Morley.

243. *Excellent and whereof I wryte.* Added by Morley.

244-245. Blurring of *Era il trionfo dove l'onde salse / percoton Baia, ch'al tepido verno / giuns'e a man destra in terra ferma salse,* translated by Wilkins (*Wi. Tr.,* p. 46) as "The triumph now had come, in the warmth of Spring, / to Baia's shore, where beat the salty waves, / And landed there, and turned to the right hand."

246. *place . . . repayre.* Petrarch says *l'antichissimo albergo di Sibilla,* "Sybil's ancient home." Petrarch adds *fra monte Barbaro ed Averno,* "between Monte Barbaro and the Avernian lake." See *Ca. Tr.,* p. 78.

247. Added by Morley. *Linterna.* Linterno, in Campania, said to be Scipio Africanus Major's last home.

249. *that . . . went.* Added by Morley.

250. *smale citie.* Petrarch says *angusta e solitaria villa,* "in that narrow and solitary little city."

252. Petrarch adds that Scipio had earned the epithet because he was the first to open Africa with his sword (*perché prima col ferro al vivo aprilla*).

253-254. Blurring and misreading of *qui de l'ostile onor l'alta novella, / non scemato co gli occhi, a tutti piacque,* translated by Wilkins (*Wi. Tr.,* p. 46) as "And here the tidings of the victory, / Not lessened by beholding, gave delight."

255-256. Blurring and misreading of *e la più casta v'era la più bella,* "She who was most chaste was the most beautiful." Here Morley omitted a complete terzina: *Né 'l trionfo non suo seguire spiacque / a lui che, se credenza non e vana, / sol per trionfi e per imperii nacque,* translated by Wilkins (*Wi. Tr.,* p. 46) as "And he [Scipio] to join a triumph not his own / Was ready, who—as is believed of him—/ Was born for triumphs and imperial might."

257-258. Added by Morley. Petrarch says that the whole company, not Scipio alone, moved on to the temple of Sulpicia. See *Ca. Tr.,* p. 79.

260-261. Blurring of *per spegner ne la mente fiamma insana,* "to quench the flame of madness in the mind."

262. *wyth good entent.* Added by Morley. Read: "All went to that fair temple of honorable chastity," etc.

263. *honorable* and *so . . . name.* Added by Morley.

264. Added by Morley.

265. *To kyndle.* Read: "That kindles good will," etc.

266. For *non di gente plebeia ma di patrizia,* "not for common people, but for patricians."

267. *In . . . temple.* For *Ivi,* "there." *offered.* For *spiegò,* "spread out."

269. *laurell.* Petrarch calls it sacred.

270. Added by Morley.

271–274. Complete misreading and blurring of the original: *e 'l giovine toscan, che non ascose / le belle piaghe che 'l fèr non sospetto, / del comune nemico in guardia pose,* translated by Wilkins (*Wi. Tr.,* p. 47) as "And there to guard the common foe she set / The Tuscan youth who in his face displayed / The wounds that made him not a cause for fear." The Tuscan youth to whom Petrarch refers is Spurina, whose beauty attracted many women and who, rather than arouse desire in women, marred his beauty by slashing his face. See *Ca. Tr.,* p. 80.

275. Petrarch adds *e fummi il nome detto / d'alcun di lor, come mia scorta seppe,* "and the names of others were told to me by my guide, who knew them."

276. *gentle and faythfull true.* Added by Morley. Petrarch notes first that these were young men who had dared to challenge Love (*ch'avean fatto ad Amor chiaro disdetto*).

277. *the . . . juste.* Added by Morley.

278. Misreading and expansion of the original. See note for line 276 above.

Changes in Capitalization and Orthography. Title Excellent] excellent. 10 Leander] Leader. 23 enemy] enemies. 73 me] be. 90 be] he. 127 Shamefastnesse] shamefastnesse. 131 Sobernes] sobernes. 133 Perseveraunce] perseveraunce. 135 Entreatynge] entreatynge. 136 Clemesse] clemesse; Curtesy] curtesy. 137 Heart] heart; Feare] feare; Shame] shame. 138 Love] love. 139 Olde Wise Thoughtes] Olde wise thoughtes. 140 Gratiouse Concorde] gratiouse concorde. 141 Beuty] beuty; Chast Clene Thoughte] chast clene thoughte. 143 Heaven] heaven. 160 her son] Hermon. 223 Vesta] Vesca. 263 Chastitie] chastitie. 272 wyde] tyed. 273 Love] love. 274 Loves] loves.

The Tryumphe of Death, I

2. *in . . . lye.* For *è . . poco terra,* "is a little earth."

3. *valour.* worth.

6. *turneth . . . feet.* For *atterra,* "casts down."

7. *armour.* For *arme,* "arms." *she . . . deade.* Added by Morley.

8. *at . . . nede.* Added by Morley.

10. *this . . . wrought.* Added by Morley.

12. *to . . . degre.* Added by Morley.

13. *cast asyde.* Added by Morley. Petrarch says that both the bow and the arrows were broken.

14–15. Blurring and expanding of *e tal morti da lui, tal presi e vivi,* "and some were slain by him, and some were captive and alive."

16. Petrarch says *compagne elette,* "chosen friends."

17. Read: "Returning from her high victory." *as sayde is.* Added by Morley.

18. Misreading of *in un bel drappelletto ivan ristrette,* "went together in a small group."

19. *no . . . all.* Added by Morley.

20. *Vertuous.* For *vera,* "true." *and ever shall.* Added by Morley. *rath.* Soon, early, quick.

22. *it . . . case.* Added by Morley.

23–24. *of . . . verse.* Blurring of *di poema chiarissimo e d'istoria,* "of a famous poem or of historic fame."

25. *Hyr.* For *la lor,* "their."

26. *armyne.* Ermine. For the symbolism of the colors and insignia, see *Ca. Tr.,* p. 86.

29. Expansion of *non uman veramente,* "not really human."

30. *speche.* Petrarch says *sante parole,* "holy words."

31. *for . . . se.* Added by Morley.

32. For *nasce a tal destino,* "born to such destiny." Morley omits *di rose incoronate e di viole,* "decked with roses and with violets," but adds the phrase in line 37.

39. *for . . . lyfe.* Added by Morley.

40. For *quella brigata allegra,* "that joyous company." *without . . . stryfe.* Added by Morley.

41. *all sodenly.* Added by Morley. *there . . . appeare.* For *vidi,* "I saw."

42. *that approched nere.* Added by Morley.

44. *and . . . wracke.* Added by Morley. *wracke.* vengeance (?).

45. *I . . . tell.* Added by Morley.

46. *gyauntes.* Petrarch adds *a Flegra,* "in the Phlegraean fields."

47. Added by Morley.

48. *gastly.* Added by Morley.

49. *swete and excellent.* Added by Morley.

50. *moost perfytely arayde.* Added by Morley.

51. Petrarch describes both the youth and the beauty as proud.

52. Misreading of *e di tua vita il termine non sai,* "and do not know when your life will end."

54. *that doth arrest.* Added by Morley. Petrarch says that Death is called fierce and relentless only by *sorda e cieca gente,* "deaf and blind people."

55–56. Misreading of *a cui si fa notte innanzi sera,* "for whom it is dark before night comes." The reference in the original is to the deaf and blind of the previous line.

57. Expansion and blurring of *Io ho condutto al fin,* "I brought to their fate."

58. *and also hastyd.* Added by Morley.

59. *unto their decline.* Added by Morley.

60. *hath . . . fyne.* Added by Morley.

62. *all awaye cleane.* Added by Morley.

63. Petrarch adds *e strani,* "and strange."

64. Added by Morley.

65. Petrarch adds *giugnendo,* "arriving."

66. Added by Morley.

67. Petrarch describes the thoughts as vain. *frayle.* Added by Morley.

68. *this . . . certayne.* Added by Morley.

70–72. Blurring of *drizzo il mio corso, innanzi che Fortuna / nel vostro dolce qualche amaro metta,* translated by Wilkins (*Wi. Tr.,* p. 55) as "I take my course, ere Fortune strike at you, / Turning your sweetness into bitterness."

74. Added by Morley.

75. *unto . . . agayne.* Added by Morley.

76. Added by Morley.

78. *at this houre.* Added by Morley.

80. *chast* and *unto the grave.* Added by Morley.

81–84. Blurring of *Altri so che ne avrà più di me doglia, / la cui salute dal mio viver pende; / a me fia grazia che di qui mi scioglia,* "There is one who will suffer more than I, one whose health depends upon my living; I shall be grateful for my release."

85–86. Added by Morley.

87–91. Extreme blurring of *Qual è chi 'n cosa nova gli occhi intende, / e vede ond'al principio non s'accorse, / di che or si meraviglia e si riprende,* "As one who fixes his eyes on something strange, sees what he had not seen at first, and marvels and corrects himself."

94. Added by Morley. In the original these words are followed by the remark that she recognized the people in the throng, all of whom were her victims. Then, adds Petrarch, *col ciglio men torbido e men fosco,* "with her brow less troubled and less dark," she spoke.

96. *on every syde.* Added by Morley.

97. *fearefull stroke assayde.* For *sentisti mai del mio tosco,* "never felt my poisonous touch."

98. Blurring of *se del consiglio mio punto ti fidi,* "If you have any trust in what I say."

100. *age.* I.e., old age.

101–102. Added by Morley.

103. *And . . . present.* Added by Morley.

104. Added by Morley.

105. *present . . . place.* Petrarch says that the honor is an unusual one.

106. For *e che tu passi,* "to let you pass."

107. *or . . . all.* Added by Morley.

108. Added by Morley.

109–110. Added by Morley.

114. For *così rispose,* "thus she answered."

116. *that great place.* For *tutta la campagna,* "the whole countryside."

117. Added by Morley.

119. *Cateya.* Cathay. *Marow.* Morocco.

120. For *il mezzo avea già pieno e le pendici / per molti tempi quella turba magna,* "that great host had filled the plain and the slopes for a long time."

122. *Bysshoppes.* For *pontefici,* "popes."

123. Blurring of *or sono ignudi, miseri e mendici,* "now they are naked, poor, and mendicant."

126. For *le mitre e li purpurei colori,* "their mitres, and the purple that they wore."

127. Added by Morley.

128. *such thinges.* For *in cosa mortal,* "in mortal things." Petrarch adds *ma chi non ve la pone,* "but who does not [set his heart on mortal things]?"

129–132. Expansion and slight blurring of the original. Petrarch says *e se si trova / a la fine ingannato, è ben ragione,* "and if he finds himself deluded at the end, it is just."

133. *even . . . madde.* For *il tanto affaticar che giova?* "What is the use of striving so?"

134. Added by Morley.

135. *olde mother.* The earth. Petrarch calls her *la gran madre antica,* "the great old mother."

136. *and . . . was.* For *a pena si ritrova,* "hardly remembered." Here Morley omitted a complete terzina: *Pur de le mille è un'utile fatica, / che non sian tutte vanità palesi,* "Is there one task in a thousand that is useful, that is not merest vanity?"

137. *hath . . . you.* Added by Morley.

138. *Wyth . . . blode.* Added by Morley.

139. Blurring of *e tributarie far le genti strane / co gli animi al suo danno sempre accesi,* "and make their foreign people tributary, your will enkindled always for their harm?"

140–141. Morley omitted the two lines preceding these: *Dopo le 'mprese perigliose e vane / e col sangue, acquistar terre e tesoro,* translated by Wilkins (*Wi. Tr.,* p. 57) as "After emprises perilous and vain / And lands and treasures won with your own blood." *brown.* Added by Morley. Petrarch adds that one will find wood and glass better than gems and gold (*più dolce . . . 'l legno e 'l vetro che le gemme e l'oro*).

142. Petrarch adds *per non seguir più sí lunga tema,* "not to pursue such a long theme."

144. *of . . . lady.* Petrarch says *di quella breve vita gloriosa,* "of that brief and glorious life." *this . . . some.* Added by Morley.

146. Expansion of *di che il mondo trema,* "that the world dreads."

147. *women many one.* For *schiera di donne,* "throng of women." Petrarch adds *non dal corpo sciolta,* "not separated from the body," i.e., still alive.

148–149. Blurring of *per saper s'esser può Morte pietosa,* "to see if Death could be kind." Morley omitted the terzina immediately following this line: *Quella bella compagna era ivi accolta / pure a vedere e contemplare il fine / che far convensi e non più d'una volta,* "That good company was gathered there to see and contemplate the fatal end that comes, and comes but once."

151. Added by Morley.

152. Blurring of *Allor di quella bionda testa svelse / Morte co la sua man un aureo crine,* "Then Death plucked a single golden hair from her blond head."

154. *alas . . . alas.* Added by Morley.

155. *that . . . hadde.* Added by Morley.

156. Misreading and blurring of *ma per dimostrarsi / più chiaramente ne le cose eccelse,* "but to show more clearly [his sovereignty] over lofty creatures."

157–158. Expansion of *Quanti lamenti lagrimosi sparsi / fur ivi,* "What tearful laments were there."

159. *than . . . all.* Added by Morley.

160. Petrarch adds that only her eyes were dry.

161. For *per ch'io lunga stagion cantai ed arsi,* "for which I sang and burned for so long."

162–164. Added by Morley.

165–166. Morley misread *E fra tanti sospiri e tanti lutti / tacita e sola lieta si sedea, / del suo bel viver già cogliendo i frutti,* "Amid so many sighs and doleful cries, she sat alone, silent and content, gathering the fruit of her good life." Read: "Sat still . . . and gathered," etc.

167. *well content.* Added by Morley.

168. *with . . . excellent.* Added by Morley. Petrarch adds *dicean,* "they said." In the original these words are spoken by the women who attend Laura.

170. Added by Morley.

171–174. Expansion, misreading, and blurring of *Che fia de l'altre, se questa arse ed alse / in poche notti e si cangiò più volte?* translated by Wilkins (*Wi. Tr.,* p. 58) as "Night after night she had suffered burning pain, / Now less, now more: how then shall others fare?" Morley omitted *O umane speranze cieche e false,* "Oh blind, false human hopes."

175. Petrarch says *Se.* Read: "If so many tears fell," etc.

176. Added by Morley.

179. *sixe . . . Apryll.* Petrarch adds *L'ora prima,* "the first hour." Cf. Sonnet 3 ("Era il giorno") and Sonnet 211 ("Voglia mi sprona").

180. For *che già mi strinse,* "that I was bound."

181. Added by Morley, but implied in the original.

182. Added by Morley. Petrarch says *Come Fortuna va cangiando stile,* "How Fortune changes," which is perhaps the original of line 183.

184. Added by Morley. Here Morley omitted two terzine of the original. Wilkins (*Wi. Tr.,* pp. 58–59) translates the lines as follows:

> None ever grieved so much for servitude,
> Even for death, as I for liberty,
> And that my life was not now ta'en from me.
>   'Twas due this age of ours, and due the world,
> That I, who first had come, should first have gone,
> And that its brightest honor should remain.

185–187. Blurring of *Or qual fusse il dolor qui non si stima: / ch'a pena oso pensarne, non ch'io sia / ardito di parlarne in versi o 'n rima,* "The grief I felt could not be measured; I can scarcely think of it, much less be bold enough to speak of it in verse or in rhyme."

188. Added by Morley.

189. Petrarch adds that these words were spoken by *le belle donne intorno al casto letto,* "the beautiful women around her chaste bed."

192. Added by Morley.

195. Blurring of *Chi udirà il parlar di saver pieno / e 'l canto pien d'angelico diletto?* "Who will now hear her speech so full of wisdom or her song so full of angelic sweetness?"

196. Added by Morley.

197–200. Blurring of *Lo spirto per partir di quel bel seno / con tutte sue virtuti in sé romito, / fatto avea in quella parte il ciel sereno,* "Her spirit, ready to leave that sweet breast, was gathering her virtues to itself, and made the sky around her serene."

202. Added by Morley.

208. Added by Morley.

210. Morley omitted *ma che per sé medesma si consume,* "but like one that consumes itself."

211. *commeth to decay.* For *cui nutrimento a poco a poco manca,* "and slowly loses its

own nutriment."

212. For *tenendo al fine il suo usato costume*, "keeping its sweetness to the very end."
213–214. Added by Morley. 214. *byrth lycoure*. life fluid?
215. *she laye*. Added by Morley.
216. For *senza venti in un bel colle fiocchi*, "falls gently on a windless hill."
218. Added by Morley.

Changes in Capitalization and Orthography. 48 she] he. 54 Death] death. 58 Grekes] grekes. 75 Death] death. 82 taketh] take. 93 she] he; her] hym. 95 she] he. 110 Death] death. 113 me] her. 116 that] theyr. 154 She] He. 155 she] he. 160 those] that. 170 she] he. 173 nyghtes] myghtes. 180 Love] love.

The Tryumphe of Death, II

1–4. For *La notte che seguí l'orribil caso | che spense il sole, anzi 'l ripose in cielo, | di ch'io son qui come uom cieco rimaso*, "The night that followed the horrible event that quenched the sun—or rather lifted it to heaven—I was left here on earth like a blind man."
5–6. Added by Morley.
8–9. For *spargea per l'aere il dolce estivo gelo*, "the sweet coolness was spreading through the air."
10. For *con la bianca amica di Titone*, "with Tithonus's fair friend," Aurora. For *Afore* read "when."
11–12. Expansion and blurring of *da'sogni confusi tôrre il velo*, "takes the veil from confused dreams."
13. For *quando*, "when."
14. *fayre and cleare*. Added by Morley.
15. *Whyte*. Added by Morley.
16. Added by Morley, perhaps in place of *mosse vêr me da mille altre corone*, "she moved toward me from out of a company of a thousand other souls."
17. *fayre*. For *tanto desiata*, "greatly desired." Morley omitted *onde eterna dolcezza al cor m'è nata*, "which brought eternal sweetness to my heart."
19–22. Expansion and blurring of *Riconosci colei che 'n prima torse | i passi tuoi dal pubblico viaggio?* "Do you not know her who first guided your steps away from the common path?" 19. *Sayth . . . tell*. Read: "She said to me."
23. For *così, pensosa, in atto umile e saggio*, "pensive, humble, and wise."
24. *my . . . pleasaunce*. Added by Morley.
26. *me . . . were*. Added by Morley.
28. Petrarch says simply *ed un faggio*, "and a beech tree."
29. Added by Morley.
30. *a great pace*. Added by Morley.
31–32. Added by Morley.
33. Petrarch adds *l'alma mia diva*, "my heavenly spirit."
34. Added by Morley.
35. *I . . . knowe*. Added by Morley.

217

36. *sayes ... trowe.* Added by Morley.

39. *nowe ... saye.* Added by Morley.

42–44. Expansion and blurring of *'l tuo dir stringi e frena, / anzi che 'l giorno, già vicin, n'aggiunga,* translated by Wilkins (*Wi. Tr.,* p. 61) as "count and check thy words / Ere we be parted by the light of day."

45. Added by Morley.

46–47. Blurring and misreading of *Al fin di questa altra serena / ch'ha nome vita, che per prova il sai,* translated by Wilkins (*Wi. Tr.,* p. 61) as "When earthly life comes to its end, / pray tell me, thou who knowest it by proof."

49. For *Rispose,* "She answered."

50–51. Blurring of *Mentre al vulgo dietro vai / ed a la opinion sua cieca e dura, / esser felice non puoi tu già mai,* "As long as you follow the common herd and its blind and obdurate beliefs, you can never be happy."

52. *is ... dread.* Added by Morley.

53. *us.* Petrarch says that Death delivers *anime gentili,* "gentle souls," from dark imprisonment.

54. For *anime gentili?*

55–57. Blurring and expansion of *all'altre è noia, / ch'hanno posto nel fango ogni lor `ura,* "to those whose cares do not rise above the mire, it is an agony."

59. For *il morir mio,* "my death."

61. *and ... heale.* Added by Morley.

62. *halfe the joye.* For *la millesima parte,* "a thousandth part."

63. *celestyall.* Added by Morley.

65–66. Blurring of the original: *poi mosse in silenzio / quelle labbra rosate, infin ch'i' dissi,* "then in silence she moved her rosy lips, until I said."

67–68. Cruel men who made death painful for their enemies. See *Ca. Tr.,* p. 101. *Cayus.* Gaius Caligula. *Maxentius.* Mezentius, Etruscan tyrant. He appears in the *Aeneid* and in Livy. See *Ca. Tr.,* p. 101. *With ... put.* Added by Morley.

70. *Payne of burnyng.* Added by Morley.

72. Added by Morley.

76. *this ... some.* Added by Morley.

78. *of ... eternall.* For *eterno danno,* "eternal damnation."

79–80. Blurring and expansion of *ma, pur che l'alma in Dio si riconforte,* "but if the soul has placed its trust in God."

81. *Unto ... say.* Added by Morley.

82. For *ch'un sospir breve,* "but a short sigh."

83. Added by Morley.

85. Blurring of *la carne inferma, e l'anima ancor pronta,* "the spirit willing, though the flesh was weak." See Sonnet 208, in which Petrarch sets forth the same idea.

86. Petrarch adds *in un sòn tristo e basso,* "in a voice sad and low."

88–90. Expansion of *pargli l'un mille anni,* "each one seems like a thousand years."

91–92. Misreading of *Indarno vive, / ché seco in terra mai non si raffronta,* "He who never meets her on this earth has lived in vain." 92. Read: "And should never after see his comfort."

93–98. Expansion and blurring of *E' cerca il mare e tutte le sue rive, / e sempre un stil, ovunqu'e'fosse, tenne; / sol di lei pensa, o di lei parla, o scrive,* "He seeks the sea and all its shores, and he behaves the same no matter where he is: he thinks only of her, speaks only of her, writes only of her."

99. *This heryng.* For *Allora in quella parte, onde 'l suon venne,* "[I turned] to the place from which these words came."

100. *her.* See *Ca. Tr.,* pp. 101–102, for a discussion of Laura's friend.

101. *That . . . me.* For *che amò noi,* "who loved us."

102–103. For *me sospinse e te ritenne,* "sustained me and restrained you."

104. *that . . . she.* Petrarch adds *al volto e a la favella,* "by her face and by her voice."

105. *or I dyed.* Added by Morley.

106. Blurring of *or grave e saggia, allor onesta e bella,* "now grave and wise, then fair and chaste."

107. *and . . . the.* Added by Morley.

108. *and . . . case.* Added by Morley.

110–111. Expansion and blurring of *ch'a dire ed a pensare a molti ha dato,* "which gave many cause to think and speak."

112–113. Blurring of *mi fu la vita poco men ch'amara,* "my life was hardly less than bitter."

114. *To the respecte.* Literal translation of *a rispetto di,* "compared to."

116–120. Expansion and blurring of *ché 'n tutto quel mio passo er'io più lieta / che qual d'esilio al dolce albergo riede,* translated by Wilkins (*Wi. Tr.,* p. 63) as "In all my passing I was more content, / Than one from exile coming to a dear home." 118–119. Morley perhaps meant: "Except for the great compassion I felt for you when I had to leave this world."

121. Added by Morley.

122–126. Misreading and blurring of *Deh, madonna, diss'io, per quella fede / che vi fu, credo, al tempo manifesta, / or più nel volto di Chi tutto vede,* translated by Wilkins as "Prithee, Madonna, by the faithfulness / That while you lived was manifest to you / And in the sight of God is now confirmed" (*Wi. Tr.,* p. 63). 125. *Seynge.* I.e., having seen.

127–128. Petrarch asks *creovvi Amor pensier mai nella testa,* "did love ever inspire in your mind?"

130. Added by Morley.

132. *to . . . payne.* Added by Morley.

133. *peax.* peace.

134–135. For *tenner molti anni in dubbio il mio desire,* "Kept my desire in doubt for many years."

136. Added by Morley.

138. *even . . . brayde.* "Suddenly"; added by Morley.

139. *smylyng.* For *lampeggiar quel dolce riso,* "that sweet smile flash." *and fayre countenaunce.* Added by Morley.

140. Blurring of *ch'un sol fu già di mie virtuti afflitte,* "which had been a comfort to my afflicted spirit."

141. Added by Morley.

142. For *Poi disse sospirando,* "Then she said with a sigh."

143–144. For *Mai diviso / da te non fu 'l mio cor, né già mai fia,* "Never was my heart divided from you, nor shall it ever be."

144–145. *but . . . regard.* Added by Morley.

145. *that . . . marde.* Added by Morley.

148. *with . . . stay.* Added by Morley.

149–151. Expansion of *né per ferza è però madre men pia,* "a mother loves, though she uses the lash." 151. *good frame.* good conclusion, end.

152. Added by Morley.

153. *full . . . season.* For *Quante volte,* "how often."

154. *but.* Petrarch says *anzi,* "rather," "in fact." *out of reason.* Added by Morley.

156. Added by Morley.

157. For *e mal può provveder chi teme o brama,* "and one who hopes and fears provides badly."

158–160. Blurring of *Quel di fuor miri, e quel dentro non veggia,* "Let him see my face; let him not see what is in my heart."

162. Read: "As thou seest by the example of a horse being controlled by a man."

163. For *più di mille fiate ira dipinse / il volto mio,* "More than a thousand times anger showed on my face."

164. Added by Morley.

165. For *ch' Amor ardeva il core,* "but Love burned in my heart."

166–167. Added by Morley.

169. Added by Morley.

170. For *se vinto ti vidi dal dolore,* "if I saw you overcome with grief."

172–174. For *salvando la tua vita e 'l nostro onore,* "Safeguarding your life and our honor."

175. Morley omitted the two terzine which precede this line. Wilkins (*Wi. Tr.,* p. 65) translates the verses as follows:

> And if thy suffering were too intense
> Making me sorrowful or timorous,
> My brow and voice more gently greeted thee.
>   These my devices were, and these my arts,
> Now benign welcoming, and now disdain—
> Thou knowest, who hast often sung thereof.

176. *like . . . hayle.* Added by Morley.

177. *Then . . . then.* Added by Morley.

178. Petrarch adds *Questi è corso,* "he is undone."

179–180. Added by Morley. Petrarch adds *Allor provvidi d'onesto soccorso,* "And then I helped you as best I could."

181–183. In the original, these lines are preceded by the statement that *Talor ti vidi tali sproni a fianco, / ch'i' dissi,* "At other times I saw your desire so strong that I said."

184. *with . . . mo.* Added by Morley.

185. *golde.* Petrarch says *freddo.*

186. For *or tristo or lieto infin qui t'ho condutto | salvo (ond'io mi rallegro) benché stanco,* "Now sad, now glad, I have conducted you safe (for which I rejoice) but weary."

189. Added by Morley.

190. Petrarch adds *e non col viso asciutto,* "and my face was not dry." *I . . . agayne.* Added by Morley.

191. *passyng swete.* For *gran frutto,* "great reward."

192–193. Added by Morley.

195. *then answered she.* Added by Morley.

198. For *Rispose (e 'n vista parve s'accendessi),* "She answered (and her face seemed flushed to me)."

199. *lyving . . . sight.* Added by Morley. From this point to the end of the chapter Morley's translation deteriorates; he omits large segments of the original and replaces them with loose and imprecise verbiage. Portions of Wilkins's translation are provided to lend some meaning to the hazy segments of Morley's translation.

201–203. Between these lines read:

> Whether thou didst bring pleasure to my eyes
> I will not say; but pleasure that sweet knot
> Did give me that thou hadst around thy heart.
> And pleasure the fair name thy poetry
> Hath won for me, I ween, both near and far.
> All that I sought was measure in thy love:
> I never found it. While in sorrowful guise
> Thou wouldst have shown me what I always saw,
> Thou didst reveal thy heart to all the world.
> Thence came the coolness that still troubles thee,
> For in all else we were as much at one
> As love comports, within the bounds of honor.   (*Wi. Tr.,* pp. 65–66)

204–215. Morley barely captured the tenor of these lines. Read:

> The flames of love burned almost equally
> In us, after I knew the fire in thee:
> But one of us revealed them, one did not.
> Thou wast already hoarse, calling for mercy,
> While I was silent, since my fear and shame
> Combined to make my great desire seem small.
> Dole that is hidden is no less a pain,
> Nor is it made the larger by laments,
> For no pretense greatens or lessens truth.
> But was not every veil between us rent
> When in thy presence I received thy verse
> And sang, "Our love dares not say more than this?"
> My heart was thine, but I controlled mine eyes.
> For this thou grievest, thinking I was wrong:

What I withheld was least, what I gave, best.
    Knowest thou not that though mine eyes were turned
Away from thee a thousand times and more,
They were restored, and looked on thee with pity?
    And peacefully would I have let them turn
Ever to thee, had I not been afraid
Of the parlous flames that shone within thine eyes.
    Now that the time of parting is so near
I will say more, to leave thee not without
A final word that thou mayst cherish still.

(Wi. Tr., pp. 66–67)

216. Added by Morley.

218. *By . . . citie.* Petrarch says *almen piú presso,* "nearer, at least." *I . . . therforne.* Added by Morley.

219. Petrarch says *ma assai fu bel paese ond'io ti piacqui,* translated by Wilkins (*Wi. Tr.*, p. 67) as "But if it pleased thee, coming hence, 'tis well."

220–222. Misreading and blurring of *ché potea il cor, del qual sol io mi fido,* / *volgersi altrove, a te essendo ignota,* / *ond'io fôra men chiara e di men grido,* translated by Wilkins (*Wi. Tr.*, p. 67) as "For had I been unknown to thee, thy heart, / Wherein I trust, might not have turned to me, / And less renown and fame would have been mine."

223–226. Misreading of the original; Petrarch says *Questo non, rispos'io, perché la rota* / *terza del ciel m'alzava a tanto amore,* / *ovunque fusse, stabile ed immota,* "'Not so,' I answered, 'since the third heavenly sphere [of Venus], which is stable and eternal, destined me for a love as great as this, no matter where we might dwell.'"

227. For *diss'ella,* "she said."

228–229. Misreading and blurring of *i'n'ebbi onore,* / *ch'ancor mi segue. Ma per tuo diletto* / *tu non t'accorgi del fuggir de l'ore,* "I have had honor, and still have. But in your joy [in speaking to me] you do not notice how the hours fly."

230. For *Vedi l'aurora de l'aurato letto* / *rimenar ai mortali il giorno, e 'l sole* / *gia fuor de l'oceano infin al petto,* "See how Aurora from her golden bed / Brings the day back to mortals, while the sun / Is lifting now his breast above the sea" (*Wi. Tr.*, p. 67). Morley omitted *Questa vien per partirne, onde mi dole,* "She comes to part us, and this gives me pain."

232. *Be . . . byd.* In the original, this phrase is preceded by *S' a dire hai altro,* "If you have more to say." *for . . . departe.* Added by Morley.

233. *O sayde I.* Added by Morley. *myne . . . dere.* Morley misunderstood the syntax of the original. *Quant'io soffersi mai, soave e leve* / *dissi, m'ha fatto il parlar dolce e pio* should be translated as "'Your sweet and pious words,' I said, 'have made it seem that all my sufferings were light and tender.'" Morley suggests this idea in lines 235–236.

237. Added by Morley.

240. Added by Morley.

243. For *Ella, già mossa, disse,* "She, departing, said."

Changes in Capitalization and Orthography. Title Seconde] seconde; Death] death. 11 her] his. 47 That] what. 65 those] that. 98 her] hye. 148 honesty] honest. 151 it] her. 162 seest a horse] seest by a horse.

The Tryumphe of Fame, I

3. *dead and past.* For *tolto,* "taken away."

6. Added by Morley.

8. *Of perfyt* and *the . . . lyght.* Added by Morley.

9. *on every part.* For *su per l'erba,* "on the grass."

13. *this . . . ladye.* Added by Morley.

14–15. *goeth . . . orient.* For *venir d'oriente,* "comes from the east." Petrarch adds *innanzi al sole,* "before the [rising] sun." Morley also omitted *che s'accompagna volontier con ella,* translated by Wilkins (*Wi. Tr.,* p. 73) as "Who gladly enters her companionship."

16. For *cotal venía,* "so she came."

17. *master . . . scole.* I.e., poet in a rhetorician's school. Petrarch's statement is in the interrogative: "From what rhetoricians school," etc.

20. Added by Morley.

22. For *che, per tutto il desir ch'ardea nel core | l'occhio mio non potea non venir meno,* "so that, in spite of the desire that burned in my heart, my eyes could not help being dazzled."

23–28. Expansion and blurring of *Scolpito per le fronti era il valore | de l'onorata gente, dov'io scorsi | molti di quei che legar vidi Amore,* translated by Wilkins (*Wi. Tr.,* p. 74) as "Those who attended her bore on their brows | The signs of worthiness: among them were | Some I had seen aforetime bound by Love." The last statement probably means that some of those in the "Triumph of Fame" had already appeared in the "Triumph of Love."

30. *that honorable knyghte.* Added by Morley.

31. *next.* For *più presso,* "closer."

32. *remember.* For *accorsi,* "noticed discerned." *but . . . pas.* Added by Morley.

33. For *L'un di virtute e non d'amor mancipio, | l'altro d'entrambi,* "One [Scipio] was the servant of virtue and not of love; the other [Caesar] served both love and virtue."

34. Added by Morley.

36. *these . . . be.* Petrarch says *dopo sí glorioso e bel principio,* "after this glorious and beautiful opening."

37. For *gente di ferro e di valore armata,* "people armed with valor and with steel."

38–40. Misreading and blurring of *sí come in Campidoglio al tempo antico | talora o per Via Sacra o per Via Lata,* "As in ancient times were seen proceeding to Campidoglio or through the Via Sacra or the Via Lata." 38. *full ryghte.* directly.

41. *honest.* Added by Morley.

42. Blurring and expansion of *e leggeasi a ciascuno intorno al ciglio,* "and there could be read in each one's face."

43. For *il nome al mondo più di gloria amico,* "the name that is the most glorious of all," i.e., Romans. A list of famous Romans follows.

44. For *Io era intento al nobile pispiglio,* "I was intent upon their noble talk." *Pispiglia* is *bisbiglio* in modern Italian and means quiet and serious talk.

45. Blurring and expansion of Petrarch's statement that he was also gazing *ai volti, agli atti,* "at their faces and their actions."

47. *to hym dere.* Added by Morley. The reference is to Scipio Africanus's grandson Scipio Africanus Minor. See *Ca. Tr., p.* 118. *nevew.* grandson.

48. The reference is to Julius Caesar's adopted son Octavius. See *Ca. Tr.,* p. 118.

49. Added by Morley, perhaps for *che volsero a'nemici armati / chiudere il passo co le membra sue,* "who willed to block the armed enemy with their bodies." The reference is to Publius Cornelius Scipio and to Gnaeus Scipio, who were killed in Spain during the Second Punic War while attempting to prevent Hasdrubal, Hannibal's brother, from entering Italy. See *Ca. Tr.,* p. 118.

50. *The twayn fathers.* Refers to *And those* above. *the sonnes.* Petrarch says *tre figli,* "three sons." These three sons are Scipio Africanus Major, Scipio Asiaticus (sons of Publius Cornelius Scipio), and Scipio Nasica (son of Gnaeus Scipio). See *Ca. Tr.,* p. 118.

51–52. Added by Morley.

53. Petrarch, still referring to the three sons, says *l'un giva innanzi,* "One [Scipio Africanus] went before" and *duo venian dopo,* "two [Africanus's brother Scipio Asiaticus and their cousin Scipio Nasica] followed after."

54. *laste.* I.e., Scipio Nasica.

56. *of . . . fame.* Added by Morley.

58. Petrarch adds *a tutta Italia giunse al maggior uopo,* "who came to the aid of Italy in her greatest need." Claudius prevented Hasdrubal from joining Hannibal. See *Ca. Tr.,* p. 119. *with his hand.* I.e., with force of arms.

59–64. Expansion and blurring of *di Claudio dico, che notturno e piano, / come il Metauro vide, a purgar venne / di ria semenza il buon campo romano,* "I speak of Claudius, who, quietly by night, when he saw the Metaurus, purged the fields of Rome of evil seeds." The reference is to Claudius's exploits at the Battle of Metaurus. See *Ca. Tr.,* p. 119.

65. *after . . . race.* Added by Morley.

66. *The great old captayne.* Quintus Fabius Maximus, called "the Delayer" for his harassing actions against Hannibal. The line blurs Petrarch's *che con arte Annibale a bada tenne,* "who with his art held Hannibal at bay." *to byde bace.* To challenge to a chase in the game of base, a game played with three (and sometimes four) persons, two of whom cover bases and attempt to catch the baserunner off base by tagging him with a ball.

68. For *Duo altri Fabii,* "two other Fabii," Quintus Fabius Maximus Rullianus, who fought in the Second and Third Punic wars and who defeated the Samnites in 295 B.C., and Quintus Fabius Maximus Allobrogicus, who was granted a triumph for his defeat of the Allobroges and the southern Gauls. See *Ca. Tr.,* p. 119.

69. *Twayne named Catones.* Cato the Censor and Cato of Utica.

70. Paulus Aemilius, who fell at the Battle of Cannae in Apulia in 216 B.C., and his son Paulus Aemilius of Macedonia. *wyse . . . intent.* Added by Morley.

71. *Two Brutus.* Lucius Junius Brutus, who liberated Rome by ousting the Tarquins, and Marcus Junius Brutus, Caesar's assassin. *Twayne Marcellus.* Marcus Claudius Marcellus, who captured Syracuse, and his son, who defeated the Gauls. See *Ca. Tr.,* p. 119.

72–74. Misreading and expansion of the original. Petrarch says *un Regol ch'amò*

Roma e non se stesso, "a Regulus, who loved Rome but not himself." The reference is to Marcus Atilius Regulus, who sacrificed his life rather than commit treason against Rome. See *Ca. Tr.*, p. 119.

75. *Curio and Fabricius*. Curius Dentatus and Fabricius Luscinus; the former refused bribes offered by the Samnites and the latter could not be corrupted by Pyrrhus.

77. *Myde*. Midas.

80. Probably added by Morley, though it perhaps translates Petrarch's *assai più belli / con la lor povertà*, "nobler in their poverty."

81. Added by Morley.

82–84. *to ... dede*. Added by Morley. Petrarch includes Attilius Regulus Serran with Cincinnatus. Both were farmers who were called to defend Rome in times of danger.

85. *Camillus*. Marcus Furius Camillus, who returned from exile to help Rome defeat the Gauls, then voluntarily returned to exile in order not to incur the ill will of the Roman senate. See *Ca. Tr.*, p. 120. *ensued ... knyght*. Added by Morley.

86–87. Misreading of *di viver prima che di ben far lasso*, "Weary of life, but not of doing good."

88–90. Blurring of *perch'a sí alto grado il ciel sortillo / che sua virtute chiara il ricondusse / onde altrui cieca rabbia dipartillo*, translated by Wilkins (*Wi. Tr.*, p. 75) as "For he so highly won the honor of heaven / That his clear virtue lead him to return / Thither whence a blind rage had driven him." 89. *where*. from which.

91. *There ... fresh*. Added by Morley.

92. *welbeloved son Chevalerus*. Added by Morley.

93–94. Blurring of *e viver orbo per amor sofferse / della milizia, per che orba non fusse*, translated by Wilkins (*Wi. Tr.*, p. 75) as "Preferring to be reft of him than that / His troops be reft of spirit and of strength." He had given orders to his troops forbidding single combat with the enemy. When his son disobeyed the order, he had him executed.

95. *were ... place*. Added by Morley. *Decius*. Publius Decius Mus and his son, of the same name, who died bravely in battle. See *Ca. Tr.*, pp. 120–121.

96–98. Blurring of *che col petto aperse / le schiere de'nemici: o fiero voto, / che 'l padre e 'l figlio ad una morte offerse!* "who with their [bare] breasts opened the enemy ranks. Oh fierce vow, that offered father and son to the same death."

99. *vallyaunt hardy*. Added by Morley. *Curio*. Marcus Curtius, who leaped, armed and on his horse, into a chasm which had opened in the Forum and which soothsayers claimed would not close until a sacrifice was made. Curtius is, then, another noble Roman who sacrificed his life for his country.

103–105. All minor Roman warriors. See *Ca. Tr.*, p. 121, for detailed descriptions of their exploits.

106. Added by Morley. Petrarch says that Flaminius defeated the Greeks with force and with generosity.

107. *There ... presse*. Added by Morley. *he*. Popilius Laenus. See *Ca. Tr.*, pp. 121–122.

108. See *Ca. Tr.*, p. 121.

109. *hardy and ferse*. Added by Morley. *loke and countenaunce*. Petrarch says *co la fronte / e co la lingua*, "with his brow and with his tongue."

110–111. Expansion of *a sua voglia lo strinse,* "bent him to his will."

113. Added by Morley.

114–116. Manlius Capitolinus, who drove the Gauls back from the Campidoglio; afterward, accused of trying to win power, he was thrown from the Tarpeian Rock.

117. Expansion of *e quel che,* "and he who." Publius Horatius Cocles, who is said to have held off the whole Etruscan army while, behind him, a bridge leading to Rome was being destroyed.

119. Added by Morley.

120. *that ferse warrear.* For *e quel che,* "and he who." The reference is to Gaius Mucius Scaevola, who attempted to assassinate King Porsena, who was besieging Rome, but stabbed his secretary instead. Scaevola thrust his hand into a fire, and the king, amazed at his firmness, allowed him to go free. See *Ca. Tr.,* p. 122.

121–122. Blurring of *mosse la mano indarno, e poscia l'arse, | sí seco irato che non sentí il duolo,* "moved his hand in vain, and then burned it and was angry that he felt no pain."

124–125. Added by Morley.

126. *He that.* Gaius Duilius Nepos, who won a naval victory over the Carthaginians in 260 B.C.

127–128. In the original, Petrarch refers to a second naval hero, Quintus Lutatius Catulus, who in 241 B.C. defeated a Carthaginian fleet near the Aegates Islands and put an end to the First Punic War. 128. *Cycell.* Sicily.

129. *him . . . sight.* For *agli occhi,* "by his eyes."

130. *that . . . myght.* For *e' suoi,* "and his kindred." See *Ca. Tr.,* p. 122.

131. *men . . . people.* For *l'umil plebe,* "the humble plebs."

132. Added by Morley.

133. For *poi vidi un grande con atti soavi,* "then I saw a great man of gentle manners." The reference is to Pompey the Great.

134–143. Expansion and blurring of *E, se non che 'l suo lume allo estremo ebe, | forse era il primo, e certo fu fra noi | qual Bacco, Alcide, Epaminonda a Tebe; | ma 'l peggio e viver troppo!* "Who would have been the first had not his great light grown dim. He surely was for us what Bacchus, Hercules, and Epaminondas were for Thebes. But the worst fate is to live too long." 142. *Alcides.* Name applied to Hercules because he was the grandson of Alceus. 143. *Impammunda.* Epaminondas, Theban statesman. See *Ca. Tr.,* pp. 122–123.

144–145. Added by Morley.

146. For *E vidi poi,* "and then I saw."

147–148. *Hym that.* Lucius Papirius Cursor. *in . . . age.* For *fu 'l fior de gli anni suoi,* "was the flower of his age." Line 148 is a misreading of *quel che da l'esser suo destro e leggiero | ebbe nome,* "who from his skill and swiftness had his name."

150. *in . . . regyon.* Added by Morley.

152. For *non so se miglior duce o cavaliero,* "I cannot tell whether he was worthier as a leader or as a man-at-arms." The allusion is to M. Valerius Corvus.

153. For *Poi venía que',* "then came he who."

154–156. Misreading and blurring of *che livido maligno | tumor di sangue, bene oprando, oppresse,* "who removed a bleeding tumor, livid and malign." For the conflict between Volumnius and Appius Claudius, see *Ca. Tr.*, pp. 123–124. 155. *he . . . prese*. Added by Morley. 156. *and . . . sease*. Added by Morley.

157. Minor Roman heroes. See *Ca. Tr.*, p. 124.

158. *And . . . captayne*. Added by Morley. Petrarch's mention of Dentatus, Marcus Sergius, and Scaeva is preceded by the statement that *in disparte tre soli ir vedeva, / rotti i membri e smagliate l'arme e fesse*, "at one side I saw three lone men, their bodies broken, and their armor torn and cleft." All three men sustained horrible wounds in battle. See *Ca. Tr.*, p. 124.

160. Probably added by Morley, but perhaps his rendition of *quei tre folgori e tre scogli di guerra*, "those three thunderbolts and three rocks in war."

162. Added by Morley.

163–164. Blurring and expansion of *ma l'un rio successor di fama leva*, "but one [Marcus Sergius] is deprived of fame by an unworthy descendant." See *Ca. Tr.*, p. 125.

165–166. *these . . . ferse*. Added by Morley.

167. *of . . . king*. Added by Morley.

168–169. Petrarch notes that Marius defeated Jugurtha and the Cimbri and crushed the German rage (*'l tedesco furore*).

170–171. Added by Morley.

172–173. Misreading and blurring of *ch'a gl'ingrati troncar a bel studio erra*, translated by Wilkins (*Wi. Tr.*, p. 77) as "Who against orders puts ingrates to death." For Fulvius Flaccus's murder of Capuan prisoners in the Second Punic War against the orders of the Roman senate, see *Ca. Tr.*, p. 125.

174. For *il più nobil Fulvio*, "the nobler Fulvius," perhaps a pun on the name of Fulvius Nobilior, who fought in Spain and Greece.

175–176. Added by Morley.

177–180. Blurring of *e solo un Gracco / du quel gran nido garrulo inquieto, / che fe il popol roman più volte stracco*, "and only one Gracchus of that garrulous and restless brood that tired the people of Rome many times." The reference is to Tiberius Sempronius Gracchus. Petrarch excluded his two sons Tiberius and Gaius. See *Ca. Tr.*, p. 125.

181–190. Misreading and blurring of two terzine of the original. Wilkins (*Wi. Tr.*, p. 78) translates them as follows:

> Metullus, who to all seemed glad and blest—
> I do not say he was, for one sees not
> Into a heart shut close in secrecy;
> His father and his heirs were there as well:
> From Macedon and from Numidia
> They brought their booty, and from Crete and Spain.

See *Ca. Tr.*, pp. 125–126, for the identity of the Metelli mentioned by Petrarch.

191. Added by Morley.

192. *and . . . syde*. Added by Morley.

193. *eldest sonne*. Titus. Petrarch describes him as *buono e bello*, "good and fair." *cruell brother*. Domitian, Vespasian's other son. He is described by Petrarch as *bello e*

rio, "fair and evil." See *Ca. Tr.*, p. 126.

194. Added by Morley.

196. Petrarch adds *principi fidi*, "trusty princes."

197. *Helio and Adrian*. Morley misread *Elio Adriano*, "Aelius Hadrianus," as two separate names. *and . . . Antonius*. Petrarch says *Antonin Pio*, Pius Antoninus, who was the adopted son of the emperor Hadrian.

198. *Macronius*. For *Marco*, Marcus Aurelius. Petrarch adds *ché bono a buono ha natural desio*, "the good seek out the good," i.e., each good emperor assured himself that another good emperor would succeed him.

199–200. Added by Morley.

202–204. Blurring and misreading of *vidi il gran fondatore e i regi cinque; | l'altro era in terra di mal peso carco, come addivien a chi virtù relinque*, "I saw the founder of Rome and the next five kings; the last [i.e., the seventh] was weighed down by his burden of evil, as happens to those who abandon virtue."

Changes in Capitalization and Orthography. Title Excellent] excellent. 1 Deathe] deathe. 26 Fame] fame. 31 Fame] fame. 38 Capitall] capitall. 39 Sacra] sacra. 40 Via Lata] via lata. 50 them] him. 73 loved] layde. 77 Myde] myde. 103 Mummio] Munnio. 104 Attilio] Attibio. 105 Flaminius] Flamius; Grekes] grekes. 110 Romaines] romaines. 125 huge] hugh. 127 Carthagines] Cathagines. 155 Volumines] volumines. 172 Flaccus] Faccus. 176 Fame] fame.

The Tryumphe of Fame, II

4–5. Blurring of *giungea la vista con l'antiche carte | ove son gli alti nomi e' sommi pregi*, "I compared what I saw with [what I had read] in old books, where great names and high virtues are recorded."

6–7. For *e sentiv' al mio dir mancar gran parte*, translated by Wilkins (*Wi. Tr.*, p. 78) as "And found that much was lacking to my tale."

8–9. Expansion and blurring of *Ma disviârmi i pellegrini egregi*, "Illustrious foreigners distracted me [from these thoughts]."

10. *that . . . went*. Added by Morley.

11–14. Morley was led into absurdity by misreading the original; Petrarch says *e quel cantato in versi | Achille, che di fama ebbe gran fregi*, "And Achilles, whose exploits were sung in verse, and who gained great fame."

15. *Twayne . . . Troyans*. Hector and Aeneas. Petrarch calls them *chiari*, "famous." *were there also*. Added by Morley.

16. *And . . . Persiens*. Cyrus and Darius. *In . . . go*. Added by Morley.

17. *of Macedon*. Added by Morley.

18–21. Expansion and blurring of *che, da Pella a gl'Indi | correndo, vinse paesi diversi*, "who with great speed won many countries from Pella [in Macedonia] to the Indies." *as . . . fynde* in line 19 and all of line 21 are Morley's additions.

22. *folowed a pace*. Added by Morley. The reference is to Alexander I, king of Epirus; he was surnamed Molossus. See *Ca. Tr.*, p. 128.

23. Petrarch adds *non già correr cosí, ch'ebbe altro intoppo*, "moving less swiftly because he had greater obstacles.

24–26. Expansion and blurring of *quanto del vero onor, Fortuna, scindi*, translated by Wilkins (*Wi. Tr.*, p. 79) as "How much true honor Fortune tears away." Read: "How dost thou evermore divide from true honor those who put their trust in thee!"

27. Added by Morley.

28–29. Petrarch says *I tre Teban, ch'i'dissi*, "the three Thebans, already named." The three are Bacchus, Hercules, and Epaminondas, mentioned in the "Triumph of Fame," I, 142–143.

30. Added by Morley.

31. *And twayne Achilles*. Added by Morley. Petrarch says *Aiace*, Ajax. *the wyse Ulixes.* Petrarch says *che desiò del mondo veder troppo*, "who sought to see too much of the world."

32. *the . . . Greke.* Added by Morley.

33. *Nestor . . . yeares.* Petrarch says *che tanto seppe e tanto visse*, "who knew so much and lived so long."

34. Added by Morley.

35. *the great and the kynge.* Added by Morley.

37. *they.* I.e., Agamemnon and Menelaus.

39–41. *but . . . dede.* For *una terribil cena, / e 'n poca piazza fe'mirabil cose*, "an awesome supper [with the dead] and in a narrow pass [Thermopylae] did wondrous things." See *Ca. Tr.*, p. 129.

43. *There . . . knyght.* Added by Morley.

44–45. Blurring of *che sí spesso Atena, / come fu suo piacer, volse e rivolse / con dolce lingua e con fronte serena*, translated by Wilkins (*Wi. Tr.*, p. 79) as "who so many times / Turned Athens back and forth, to suit his will, / By his fair face and his honeyed words."

46. Added by Morley.

47. *that . . . free.* For *che 'l gran gioco a Grecia tolse*, "who removed the great yoke from Greece." *Melciedes.* Miltiades. See *Ca. Tr.*, p. 129.

48–49. Loose rendering of *e 'l buon figliuol, che con pietà perfetta / legò sé vivo e 'l padre morto sciolse*, "and his good son, who, loving perfectly, binding himself, set his father free." Miltiades's son was Cimon. See *Ca. Tr.*, p. 129.

50. Added by Morley.

51. *the valyaunt.* Added by Morley. Petrarch adds *con questa setta*, "with this group."

52. Petrarch says *Aristides che fu un greco Fabrizio*, "Aristides, who was a Greek Fabricius."

53. *I do saye.* Added by Morley.

54. I.e., they were denied burial.

55–56. Misreading of *e 'l altrui vizio / illustra lor, ché nulla meglio scopre / contrari due com' piccolo interstizio*, translated by Wilkins (*Wi. Tr.*, p. 80) as "Their excellence illumined by the vice / Of others: nought so well contrasts two acts / As brevity of intervening time."

57–58. For *Focion va con questi tre di sopra, / che di sua terra fu scacciato morto: molto diverso il guiderdon da l'opre*, "Focion goes with these three [Theseus, Themosticles, and Aristides]; even in death he was banished from his country; his reward was far different from his deeds."

229

60. *that . . . knyght.* Added by Morley.

61. *Masinises.* Masinissa.

62–63. I.e., because he had been friendly to the Romans until the time of his death. See *Ca. Tr.*, p. 130.

64. *the greate.* Added by Morley. This Hiero is not to be confused with Hiero the tyrant of Syracuse. See *Harper's Dictionary of Classical Literature and Antiquities*, ed. Harry Thurston Peck (New York: Harper and Brothers, 1897), under "Hiero" for an account of his exploits. Petrarch adds *mirando quinci e guindi*, "gazing here and there."

66–68. In the original these lines refer not to Hamilcar but to Croesus, king of Lydia. See *Ca. Tr.*, p. 130, for an account of how Croesus was spared being burned at the stake. Morley misread the original, which reads: *Vidi, qual uscí già del foco, ignudo / il re di Lidia, manifesto esempio / che poco val contra Fortuna scudo*, "I saw the king of Lydia as he came, naked, from the fire, living example that little avails against the will of Fate."

69. *Sciphas.* Syphax, king of the Numidians and contemporary and rival of Masinissa. He was taken prisoner by Masinissa and sent by Scipio to Rome, where he died.

70. *Brennius.* Brennus, Gallic leader. See *Ca. Tr.*, p. 131. *for . . . porte.* For *sotto cui cadde gente molta*, "under whom fell many men."

73. Blurring of *In abito diversa, in popol folta*, "In various dress, in a thick crowd."

74. For *fu quella schiera*, "went that throng."

75. Petrarch says that he looked up. The reference is to the Hebrew nation.

76. Blurring of *vidi una parte tutta in sé raccolta*, "I saw a group gathered by itself."

77. *one . . . make.* David.

78. Added by Morley.

80. *he . . . worke.* Solomon. *out of doubte.* Added by Morley.

81. *of . . . meane.* Added by Morley.

83. Added by Morley.

84. For *poi quel*, "then he." The allusion is to Moses.

87. For *e quel che*, "and he who."

88. *he.* Joshua. Petrarch adds *come uno animal s'allaccia*, "As one would bind an animal." This was accomplished, Petrarch says, *co la lingua possente*, "by the power of his speech."

91–92. Blurring of *chi Dio ben còle, / quanto Dio ha creato aver soggetto / e 'l ciel tener con semplici parole*, "he who worships God masters all that has been created by God and with simple words can stay the heavens."

93. *hym . . . wente.* Added by Morley.

94. *Our olde father.* Abraham. *whiche . . . entent.* Added by Morley.

96. For *e gisse*, "and that he should go."

98. *Electe of God.* In the original, *eletto*, "elected," modifies, *loco*, "place" (Palestine), not Abraham.

99–100. Expansion and misreading of *seco il figlio e 'l nipote*, "with his son and his son's son," Isaac and Jacob.

101. Petrarch says *a cui fu il gioco / fatto de le due spose*, "on whom was wrought the trick of the two wives." The reference is to Laban's trick of giving his eldest daughter

to Jacob. Morley's difficulty with the passage grew out of his misreading of *gioco*, which usually means "yoke" but in this case is used to mean *giuoco*, "trick."

102–103. Misreading of *e 'l saggio e casto | Iosef dal padre lontanarsi un poco*, "and the wise and chaste Joseph, somewhat apart from his father."

104. *alwaye*. For *quant'io basto*, "as far as I could."

105–106. These lines are a translation of *Vidi il giusto Ezechia e Sanson vasto*, "I saw the just Ezechiel and the mighty Sampson." Calcaterra omitted the lines in his edition of the *Trionfi* (*Ca. Tr.*, p. 133), but he noted that several of the MSS of the poem contain them, and that Appel's edition retained the reading (as did the sixteenth-century editions by Velutello, Gesualdo, Dolce, and Daniello). Calcaterra's edition reads *vidi lui, la cui gola ha il mondo guasto*, "I saw him [Adam] whose greed despoiled the world."

106–107. Expansion of *Di qua da lui, chi fece la grande arca*, "Not far from him, I saw the builder of the Ark."

109. *he*. Nembrot, the architect of the Tower of Babel.

111–114. Expansion and blurring of *Poi quel buon Juda, a cui nessun può torre | le sue leggi paterne, invitto e franco | come uom che per giustizia a morte corre*, "Then that good Judas [Maccabaeus], whom no one could constrain to disobey his father's teachings; he remained unconquered and free, and was like a man who rushed at death in a just cause." See *Ca. Tr.*, p. 133.

116. Slight blurring of the original; Petrarch says that his desire to see more was *stanco*, "weary." Petrarch also adds *mi fece una leggiadra vista | più vago di mirar ch'i'ne fossi anco*, "when another lovely sight made me more desirous of seeing than before." These lines are perhaps the original of Morley's lines 119–120.

118. For *alquante donne ad una lista*, "several [warrior] women in a troop." There follows a catalog of Amazon heroines.

122. *well armyd stand*. Petrarch says that Orithia, Antiope's sister, is *armata e bella*, "armed and beautiful."

124. Added by Morley.

125. *Manylipe*. Menalippe. *that vanquished Hercules*. Inaccurate. Petrarch says *e ciascuna sí snella | che vincerle fu gloria al grande Alcide*, "both [Hippolyta and Menalippe] were so swift that their defeat by Hercules [Alcides] was a great glory." The defeat of the Amazons was one of the twelve labors of Hercules.

126. Added by Morley. In the original, it is assumed that Menalippe and Hippolyta were sisters. Morley does not seem to understand that the two were sisters.

127–128. Expansion of *e l'una ebbe, e Teseo l'altra sorella*, "he kept one and gave the other to Theseus."

129. *wydowe*. Thomyris.

130. *most constantly*. Added by Morley.

132–134. Blurring of *però che, udendo ancora il suo fin reo, | par che di novo a sua gran colpa muoia; | tanto quel dí del suo nome perdeo!* translated by Wilkins (*Wi. Tr.*, p. 82) as "For even now, hearing his dreadful end, / He seems again to be dying in his guilt, / So much of honor did he lose that day!"

135–136. Expansion and blurring of *Poi vidi quella che mal vide Troia*, translated by Wilkins (*Wi. Tr.*, p. 82) as "Then I saw her who in an evil hour / Saw Troy." The allusion is to Penthesilea, queen of the Amazons, who went to the aid of Priam in the last year of the Trojan War. She was slain by Achilles.

137. *lady of Italye*. For *vergine latina*, "the Latin maid."

138. For *ch'in Italia a' Troian fe' molta noia*, "who did great damage to the Trojans in Italy." Petrarch refers to Camilla, queen of the Volsci, who fought bravely against Aeneas. She was slain by an obscure soldier named Aruns.

139. *that hardy lady*. For *magnanima reina*, "great queen."

140–142. See *Ca. Tr.*, p. 134. Petrarch alludes to Semiramis, who helped quell the rebellion of the Babylonians.

143–144. Misreading and expansion of the original. Petrarch notes that both Semiramis and Cleopatra were slaves of desire (*l'un'e l'altra er'arsa | d'indegno foco*).

146. *which was doutelesse*. For *del suo onore assai più scarsa* "much more careful of her honor [than Semiramis or Cleopatra]."

147. For *Bella era, e nell'età fiorita e fresca: | quanto in più gioventute e 'n più bellezza, | tanto par ch'onestà sua laude accresca*, "She was fair and fresh and in the flower of youth, and to cherish chastity in the time of youth and beauty is to merit great praise."

148. *high harte*. Petrarch says *cor femineo*, "woman's heart."

150. *danger . . . dreade*. Expansion of *fece temer*, "she brought fear." Petrarch adds *chi per natura sprezza*, "those who are fearless by nature."

151. For *io parlo de l'imperio alto di Roma, | che con arme assalío*, "I speak of the imperial might of Rome which she assailed with arms." See *Ca. Tr.*, p. 135, for this reference to Julius Caesar.

152–154. Expansion and blurring of *ben ch'a l'estremo | fosse al nostro trionfo ricca soma*, "although in the end she was a rich prize for the Roman triumph." Zenobia was finally defeated, and she was bound in golden chains and forced to take part in the Emperor Aurelian's triumph in A.D. 274.

155–157. For *Fra' nomi, che in dir breve ascondo e premo, | non fia Judith*, "Among the names I must abbreviate and speak of briefly must not be that of Judith." *chast.* Petrarch calls her *vedovetta ardita*, "fearless young widow." 155. *and albeit.* lest.

158–160. Added by Morley. Petrarch says simply *che fe' il folle amador del capo scemo*, "who reft her foolish lover of his head."

161–164. Morley conflated Petrarch's description of two kings: Ninus, legendary founder of the city of Nineveh, and Nebuchadnezzar, king of Babylon and conqueror of Jerusalem. See *Ca. Tr.*, p. 136. For the sake of clarity, I cite Wilkins's translation (*Wi. Tr.*, p. 83):

> But Ninus, with whom history begins,
> Where leave I him? And where his great successor?
> Whose pride reduced him to a bestial life?

165. For *Dov'e*, "Where is?"

167. *of . . . ground*. Added by Morley.

168–169. Blurring and misreading of *E chi de' nostri dogi, che 'n duro astro | passàr l'Eufrate, fece il mal governo, | a l'italiche doglie féro impiastro?* Wilkins translated the lines as follows (*Wi. Tr.*, p. 84):

And where is he who, east of the Euphrates,
So fiercely dealt with our ill-starred commanders—
A sorry plaster for Italic woes!

Petrarch alludes here to Orodes, king of Parthia, who defeated Crassus and the Romans in Mesopotamia in 53 B.C. See *Ca. Tr.*, p. 136.

170. *both . . . morowe.* Added by Morley. *Metridates.* Mithridates the Great, the sixth of that name, king of Pontus and, after Hannibal, fiercest enemy of the Romans. See *Ca. Tr.*, p. 137.

174. *that dyd excell.* Added by Morley.

176–178. Expansion of *un d'Affrica, un di Spagna, un Lottoringo,* "an African, a Spaniard, and a Gaul." These are Septimus Severus, Theodosius the Great, and Charlemagne.

179. For *Cingean costu'i suo'dodici robusti* "He [Charlemagne] was surrounded by the twelve peers."

180. *after . . . hyed.* For *poi venía solo,* "then came alone." Petrarch adds *che fe'l'impresa santa e i passi giusti,* "who fought the holy war and took righteous steps." See *Ca. Tr.*, p. 137.

181–183. Blurring and expansion of *Questo (di ch'io mi sdegno e 'ndarno grido) / fece in Jerusalem colle sue mani / il mal guardato e già negletto nido,* "With his own hands he built in Jerusalem that very nest which is now badly guarded and neglected. My cries of wrath go unheeded!" See *Ca. Tr.*, p. 137.

184. Added by Morley.

187. *for . . . all.* Added by Morley.

188. *the sepulcre royall.* Petrarch says *'l sepolcro di Cristo,* "the tomb of Christ." *dogges.* Perhaps referring to infidels, particularly the Turks.

189. Added by Morley.

190–191. Misreading and blurring of the original. Petrarch, still referring to Godfrey of Boulogne, says *Raro o nessun che 'n alta fama saglia / vidi dopo costui (s'io non m'inganno), / o per arte di pace o di battaglia,* "I saw few men [if any] rise after him to high fame, if I do not deceive myself, either through arts of peace or arts of war."

192. Blurring of *Pur, come uomini eletti ultimi vanno,* "And, since illustrious men come last [in triumphs]."

193–195. Misreading and expansion of the original; the Saracen and Saladin are the same person. Petrarch alludes to the sultan of Egypt who captured Jerusalem and opposed the Crusades. He adds that Saladin was followed by *Quel di Luria,* "He of Loria," Ruggero di Lauria. See *Ca. Tr.*, p. 138.

196. *Duke of Lancaster.* Probably Henry of Lancaster, cousin of Edward III. See *Ca. Tr.*, p. 138.

197. *with . . . launce.* Added by Morley.

198. *sharpe scourge.* For *aspro vicino,* "harsh neighbor." See *Ca. Tr.*, p. 138.

199–201. Blurring and expansion of *Miro, come uom che volontier s'avanzi, / s'alcuno vi vedessi qual egli era / altrove agli occhi miei veduto innanzi,* "Like a man who willingly presses forward, I looked to see if there were any there whom I had seen before."

202. For *e vidi,* "and I saw."

203. Blurring of *duo che si partir iersera / di questa nostra etate e del paese*, "two who had lately left our life and our country."

204. For *costor chiudean quella onorata schiera*, "these two closed that honorable troop."

205. *Cecyll.* Sicily. Petrarch alludes to Robert d'Anjou, king of Naples. *he was there.* Added by Morley.

206. For *ch 'n alto intese, / e lunge vide*, "of noble intent and far vision." Petrarch adds *e fu veramente Argo*, "and was a veritable Argus."

207. *And my.* Petrarch says *dall'altra parte*, "on his other side." *Columnes.* For *il mio gran Colonnese*, "my great Colonnese," Petrarch's friend Stefano Colonna il Vecchio.

208. For *magnanimo, gentil, costante e largo*, "great, noble, constant, and generous."

Changes in Capitalization and Orthography. Title Seconde] seconde. 21 Fame] fame. 32 Greke] greke. 36 their] his. 51 Themistocles] Thenustoctes. 122 Orithia] Arithia. 142 Babilonicall] babilonicall. 180 Fame] fame. 185 Christen] christen. 194 Christen] christen. 198 Fraunce] fraunce. 204 honorable] honorably.

The Tryumphe of Fame, III

1. *away put.* For *levarme*, "take my."

2. Added by Morley. Petrarch says simply *da tal vista*, "from such a sight."

3. For *quand'io udi'*, "when I heard."

4. *on . . . hande.* For *a l'altro lato*, "on the other side." This is followed in the original by a phrase which establishes the mood and subject matter of the whole capitolo; the guide reminds Petrarch that if he looks to the other side he will see *ché s'acquista ben pregio altro che d'arme*, "that it is not by arms alone that fame is won." Petrarch then adds that *Volsimi da man manca*, "I turned to the left." The catalog of men of letters follows.

5. *The dyvyne* and *that . . . nye.* Added by Morley.

6. Blurring of *che 'n quella schiera andò presso al segno / al qual aggiunge cui dal ciel è data*, "who of all that company went closest to that knowledge of truth which is achieved only by those who have divine grace." For Petrarch's attitudes toward Plato, see *Ca. Tr.*, p. 140.

7. Petrarch places him after Plato (*Aristotele poi*) and adds *pien d'alto ingegno*, "full of high intellect." Though Dante had judged Aristotle *il maestro di color che sanno*, "the master of those who know," Petrarch had strong reservations about the excesses of medieval scholastics. These attitudes are eloquently set forth in *De sui ipsius . . . ignorantia.* See *Ca. Tr.*, p. 141.

9. See *Ca. Tr.*, p. 141.

10. *folowed the same.* Added by Morley. *Xenophontes.* Xenophon.

11–13. Blurring of *e quello ardente / vecchio a cui fur le Muse tanto amiche, / ch'Argo e Micena e Troia se ne sente*, "and that fiery old man [Homer] to whom the Muses were so kind and who gave fame to Argus, Mycenae, and Troy."

14. Added by Morley.

15–16. Blurring of *Questo cantò gli errori e le fatiche | del figliuol di Laerte e de la Diva*, "He sang of the wanderings and the travails of the son of Laertes [Ulysses] and the son of the goddess [Achilles, Thetis's son]."

17–18. Expansion of *primo pintor delle memorie antiche*, "first painter of ancient memories."

19. Petrarch adds *cantando*, "singing."

20. *I . . . understand*. Added by Morley.

21. Blurring of *che di par seco giostra*, "who equals him in the poetic contest."

22–24. Expansion of *ed un al cui passar l'erba fioriva*, "and one whose passing made the grass bloom." 23. *passe*. pace, step?

25–27. Blurring and expansion of *questo è quel Marco Tullio, in cui si mostra | chiaro quanti eloquenzia ha frutti e fiori; | questi son gli occhi de la lingua nostra*, "This is that Marcus Tullius in whom the fruits and flowers of eloquence are seen. These [i.e., Virgil and Cicero] are the eyes of our language."

29–32. Expansion and blurring of *che fòri | e di speranza omai del primo loco, | non ben contento de' secondi onori*, "who no longer hopes to be first and is ill content with second honors."

34. Added by Morley.

35–36. For *Eschine il dica, che 'l potéo sentire | quando presso al suo tuon parve già fioco*, "Let Aeschines [Demosthenes's adversary in oratory] tell of it, for his voice next to that of Demosthenes seemed weak." See *Ca. Tr.*, p. 142.

37. *nether wryte nor*. Added by Morley.

38. *that . . . exell*. Added by Morley.

41–44. Expansion and blurring of *ché, cose innumerabili pensando | e mirando la turba tale e tanta, | l'occhio e 'l pensier m'andava disviando*, "For, thinking of many things and gazing at the great and noble throng, my eyes and my thoughts strayed constantly."

45. For *Vidi Solon*, "I saw Solon."

46–47. Blurring of *di cui fu l'util pianta | che, se mal colta è, mal frutto produce*, translated by Wilkins (*Wi. Tr.*, p. 87) as "who nursed the useful plant | That if it be ill tended, bears but ill." Petrarch refers here to Solon's fame as lawgiver.

48–49. For *co gli altri sei di che Grecia si vanta*, "With the other six of whom Greece is proud." The other six sages were Cleobulus, Periander, Pittacus, Bias, Thales, and Chilon.

50. Added by Morley.

51–56. Expansion and blurring of *Qui vid'io nostra gente aver per duce | Varrone, il terzo gran lume romano, | che, quando il miri piú, tanto piú luce*, "I saw Varro, the third of the great lights of Rome, leading our people; the more one looks at him, the more he shines."

57–60. Blurring of the original. Petrarch does not say that Sallust went hand in hand with Varro; he says *Crispo Sallustio e seco a mano a mano | un che già l'ebbe a schifo e 'l vide torto, | cioè 'l gran Tito Livio padovano*, "Then Crispus Sallustius, and with him nearby one who scorned him and looked at him askance. This was the great Titus Livy of Padua."

61. *on . . . Livius*. Added by Morley.

62. For *quel Plinio veronese suo vicino,* "his neighbor, Pliny of Verona."

63. *a scriver molto, a morir poco accorto,* "very wise in his writings, but less wise in his death." Petrarch's allusion is to Pliny the Elder's insistence on seeing Vesuvius in eruption and his resulting death (A.D. 79). See *Ca. Tr.,* p. 144.

64. Added by Morley.

65. *the great clarcke.* For *il gran platonico,* "the great Platonist."

68. For *il qual seco venía dal materno alvo,* "which followed him from the maternal womb."

70–71. Added by Morley.

72–73. These were all Roman orators. Petrarch lists them as follows: *poi Crasso, Antonio, Ortensio, Galba e Calvo / con Pollion,* "then [Lucius Licinius] Crassus, [Marcus] Antonius, [Quintus] Hortensius, [Sergius] Galba, and [Gaius Licinius] Calvus with [Gaius Asinius] Pollio." Morley called Calvus by his given name, "Licinius," and omitted Pollio entirely.

74–76. In the original, Petrarch speaks of the pride of only two of the six orators, Calvus and Pollio: *che 'n tal superbia salse / che contra quel d'Arpino armâr le lingue, / cercando ambeduo fame indegne e false,* "who grew so proud that they made verbal war against the Arpinian [Cicero], seeking a fame they did not deserve." *and . . . curiouse* and *that . . . trust.* Added by Morley.

77. For *Tucide vid'io,* "I saw Thucydides."

78–79. Loose rendering of *che ben distingue / i tempi e'luoghi e l'opere leggiadre / e di che sangue qual campo s'impingue,* translated by Wilkins as "who clearly tells / The times and places and the valiant deeds / Of war, and who it was that fought and bled" (*Wi. Tr.,* p. 87).

80. For *Erodoto, di greca istoria padre,* "Herodotus, the father of Greek history."

81–83. For *e dipinto il nobil geometra / di triangoli e tondi e forme quadre,* "and the noble geometer [Euclid] was bedecked with triangles, circles, and squares." 81. *And he beganne.* Read: "And he who began," etc. 82. *Orball.* Like an orb or circle.

84–85. Blurring of *e quel, che 'nvêr di noi divenne petra, / Porfirio, che d'acuti sillogismi / empié la dialettica faretra, / facendo contra 'l vero arme i sofismi,* translated by Wilkins (*Wi. Tr.,* p. 88) as "Then Porphyry, a stone against our faith, / Who with the sharpness of his syllogisms / His quiver filled, and used his sophistries / As weapons in his fight against the truth." See *Ca. Tr.,* pp. 145–146.

86–87. Complete blurring of the original. Petrarch says *e quel di Coo, che fe've miglior l'opra, / se bene intesi fusser gli aforismi,* "and he of Coo [Hippocrates], who improved the art [of medicine]; if only his aphorisms were heeded." See *Ca. Tr.,* p. 146. 87. *Amphorisomis.* Aphorisms.

88–90. Blurring of *Apollo ed Esculapio gli son sopra, / chiusi ch'a pena il viso gli comprende, / sí par che i nomi il tempo limi e copra,* "Apollo and Aesculapius went before him, so shrouded that their faces could scarcely be seen, so did time wear and cover their names." 89. *Howbeit.* Although.

91. For *Un di Pergamo il segue,* "He was followed by one from Pergamo [Galen]." See *Ca. Tr.,* p. 146.

92–93. Blurring of *ed in lui pende / l'arte guasta fra noi, allor non vile, / ma breve e scura; e'la dichiara e stende,* "and in him is seen that art [medicine] which is in disrepute among us; at that time it was not a base art, but limited and obscure. He explained and amplified it."

94. For *Vidi Anassarco intrepido e virile*, "I saw Anaxarchus, fearless and manly." For Anaxarchus, philosopher of the school of Democritus, see *Ca. Tr.*, p. 147.

96–98. Expansion of *che nulla forza volse ad atto vile*, "who could not be compelled to do a shameful act."

99. *There . . . there.* For *Vidi*, "I saw." *Archemenides.* Archimedes.

101. *pensyfe.* For *pensoso*, "thoughtful," or, more accurately, "speculative." Democritus, however, has been called "the Laughing Philosopher" because according to Seneca and Juvenal he never appeared in public without expressing his contempt for the follies of mankind by laughter.

102. Inaccurate rendering of *per suo voler di lume e d'oro casso*, "deprived of his gold and his sight of his own will." See *Ca. Tr.*, p. 147.

103. *Hyppia.* Hyppias, Greek Sophist and contemporary of Socrates. *of . . . age.* For *il vecchiarel*, "the old man."

106–108. Expansion, blurring, and misreading of *e poi di nulla certo | ma d'ogni cosa Archesilao dubbioso*, "and then Arcesilaus, certain of nothing and doubtfull of everything."

109. *with . . . close.* I.e., obscure in his teachings.

110–111. Blurring of *e Diogene cinico, in suo'fatti | assai più che non vuol vergogna aperto*, "and Diogenes the cynic much more open in his deeds than shame dictated." Diogenes and his father were charged with debasing the public coin; Diogenes escaped to Athens and his father went to prison.

112. Added by Morley.

113–114. Blurring of *e quel che lieto i suo'campi disfatti | vide e deserti, d'altre merci carco, | credendo averne invidiosi patti*, translated by Wilkins (*Wi. Tr.*, p.. 89) as "And one who, coming home with foreign lore, / Felt himself enviable and well content / E'en though his fields were all despoiled and bare." Petrarch alludes to Anaxagoras of Clazomenae. See *Ca. Tr.*, p. 148.

115. *Dicearco the Curyouse.* Dicaearchus the Inquisitive. Dicaearchus was a peripatetic philosopher; he was also a geographer, orator, and mathematician. See *Ca. Tr.*, p. 148. In fourteenth-century Italian *curioso* meant "learned, erudite."

116. In the original, these three names are preceded by *ed in suo'magisteri assai dispari*, "and very different in their works." The first was a rhetorician, the second a poet and philosopher, and the third a historian. See *Ca. Tr.*, pp. 148–150, for the disputed meaning of the word *magisteri*. *the famouse.* Added by Morley.

117–127. Expansion and blurring of two terzine of the original. Wilkins's translation (*Wi. Tr.*, p. 89) reads:

> And some I saw who have disturbed the seas
> With adverse winds and wanderings of the mind,
> Famed for contention, not for what they knew.
>
> Like lions or like dragons did they fight
> That lash with their tails: what good is there in this,
> Each being well content with what he knows?

129–131. Blurring of *parlando egli, il vero e 'l falso a pena / si discernea: cosí nel dir fu presto!* "when he spoke it was scarcely possible to tell the true from the false, so crafty was his speech!" Carneades of Cyrene in Africa was a neo-Platonist and founder of the Third, or New, Academy. See *Ca. Tr.*, p. 150.

132–136. Blurring and misreading of two terzine of the original. These were translated by Wilkins (*Wi. Tr.*, p. 89) as follows:

> He spent his lengthy life and his thoughtfulness
> Seeking to win accord between the sects
> Fiercely engaged in literary war;
> But he could not prevail: as doctrines grew
> So envy grew, and with the rise of learning
> Diffused its poisons into swollen hearts.

137–139. Blurring of *Contra 'l buon Siro, che l'umana speme / alzò, ponendo l'anima immortale, / s'armò Epicuro (onde sua fame geme),* "Against him of Syros, who raised human hopes by stating that the soul is immortal, came Epicurus, whose fame now suffers." The philosopher of Syros to whom Petrarch refers is Pherecydes of Syros (*c.* 600–500 B.C.). He was the teacher of Pythagoras and reputedly the first to maintain the doctrine of the transmigration of souls.

140–144. Expansion and blurring of *ardito a dir ch'ella non fusse tale; / cosí al suo lume fu famoso e lippo,* "who dared to say it [Pherecydes's teaching] was not true—so infamous and blinded was his vision." See *Ca. Tr.*, p. 151. Petrarch uses *famoso* in its Latin sense to mean "infamous."

145. *thys secte.* I.e., the followers of Epicurus.

146. Petrarch names two followers of Epicurus, Metrodorus and Aristippus. Lyppo is Morley's misreading of *lippo*, "blind, bleary-eyed" (see note for ll. 140–144, above). *the electe.* Added by Morley.

147–148. Added by Morley.

149–152. Expansion and blurring of *Poi con gran subbio e con mirabil fuso / vidi tela sottil tesser Crisippo,* "Then with a great weaver's beam and with a marvelous spindle I saw Chrysippus weaving a subtle web." Chrysippus was a Stoic philosopher famous for subtle dialectic and nice distinctions rather than for solid arguments. See *Ca. Tr.*, p. 152.

156. Zeno was said to have shown the difference between rhetoric and logic by comparing the former to an open palm and the latter to a closed fist. See *Ca. Tr.*, p. 152.

Changes in Capitalization and Orthography. Title Thirde] thirde; Fame] fame. 27 there was] there there was. 31 Fame] fame. 48 Grekes] grekes. 62 Plinius] Pluvius. 77 Thucides] Lucides. 82 Orball] Arball. 95 Xenocrates] Denocrates. 115 Curyouse] curyouse. 124 ragynge] raygne. 138 Syros] Cirus. 142 perysshe] perysshes. 144 Fame] fame 153 Zenone] zemone.

The Tryumphe of Tyme

1. For *De l'aureo albergo,* "From the golden resting place."

2. For *co l'aurora innanzi,* "with the dawn before it."

3–4. Expansion of *sí ratto usciva il sol cinto di raggi,* "so swiftly rose the sun, circled with rays."

5. *even . . . thought.* Added by Morley.

6. For *E' si corcò pur dianzi,* "It had just set."

7. *in . . . guyse.* Added by Morley.

8. For *come fanno i saggi,* "as wise men do."

10–13. Expansion and blurring of *Che pensi? omai convien che piú cura aggi,* "What are you thinking? You should take greater care."

14–18. Expansion and slight blurring of *s'un, che famoso in terra visse, / de la sua fama per morir non esce, / che sarà della legge che 'l ciel fisse?* "If a man who was famous while alive does not lose his fame through death, what will become of the law that heaven made?"

19. *forever do encrease.* For *morendo, cresce,* "in dying, increases."

20. For *che spegner si doveva in breve,* "that should have been quickly extinguished."

21. For *veggio / nostra eccellenzia al fine; onde m'incresce,* "I see our excellence come to an end, which gives me pain."

22–26. Expansion and blurring of a terzina made up of three questions: *Che piú s'aspetta? e che puote esser peggio? / che piú nel ciel ho io che 'n terra un uomo, / a cui esser egual per grazia cheggio?* translated by Wilkins (*Wi. Tr.,* p. 95) as "What more is to befall? What could be worse? / What more have I in the heavens than man on earth? / Must I then plead for equality with him?"

29. Petrarch adds *e sprono e sferzo,* "and spur and whip."

30. Added by Morley.

31–33. Expansion of *e pur la fama d'un mortal non domo,* "and yet I cannot overpower man's fame."

34–36. Misreading and blurring of *Ingiuria da corruccio e non da scherzo / avvenir questo a me, s'i'fossi in cielo, / non dirò primo, ma secondo o terzo!* "An injury for anger, not for jest, that this should happen to me, even if I were the second or the third in heaven and not [as I am] the first."

37–40. Expansion and blurring of *Or convien che s'accenda ogni mio zelo, / sí ch'al mio volo l'ira addoppi i vanni, / ch'io porto invidia agli uomini, e nol celo,* "Now I must kindle all my zeal, and let my anger double my wings, for I hate men, and I do not conceal it." 39. *In doubling.* Read: "By doubling."

42–43. Expansion of *piú chiari che 'n vita,* "more famous than when alive."

44. Misreading of *ed io m'avanzo di perpetui affanni,* "and I continue in perpetual anguish."

45–46. Expansion of *tal son qual era, anzi che stabilita / fosse la terra,* "I am what I was before the earth was established."

47–48. Blurring of *di e notte rotando / per la strada ritonda ch'è infinita,* translated by Wilkins (*Wi. Tr.,* p. 96) as "wheeling ever, day and night, / In my round course, that never comes to an end." 47. *going in compasse.* circling.

50. *Dysdaynyng.* Disdainfully. *furthwith . . . brayde,* "instantly," added by Morley.

51. *toke.* For *riprese,* "resumed." *I say.* Added by Morley.

53–56. Expansion and blurring of *né pensier porria già mai / seguir suo volo, non che lingua o stile, | tal che con gran paura il rimirai,* "nor could thought follow its flight, much less tongue or pen, and I gazed at him in great fright."

57. Added by Morley. *wyttely I minded.* I understood.

58. For *Allor tenn'io il viver nostro a vile | per la mirabil sua velocitate, | vie piú ch'innanzi nol tenea gentile,* "Then, seeing its marvelous speed, I held our life in as low esteem as it had once seemed high in dignity."

59–62. Expansion and blurring of *e parvemi terribil vanitate | fermare in cose il cor che 'l Tempo preme, | che, mentre piú le stringi, son passate,* "and it seemed to me a foolish vanity to set one's heart on things that Time moves, for while one thinks he possesses them they are gone."

63. For *chi di suo stato cura o teme,* "he who cares or fears for his state."

66. *delyght.* Petrarch says *speme,* "hope."

68. *After his guyde.* I.e., after the sun. *that . . . hast.* For *che mai non posa,* "which never rests."

71. *one . . . other.* Added by Morley.

72. *even . . . tother.* Added by Morley. 71–72. I.e., I saw the seasons following one another.

73. Petrarch says *che, pur udendo, par mirabil cosa,* "that it is a wondrous thing even to hear."

74. Added by Morley.

76. For *vedrà esser cosí,* "shall see that it is so."

77. Petrarch says simply *Ché nol vidi io?* "Why did I not see it?"

79–80. Expansion of *Segui' già le speranze e 'l van desio,* "I then followed my hopes and my vain desires."

81. *feble.* Added by Morley.

82. For *ov'io veggio me stesso e 'l fallir mio,* "in which I see myself and my failings."

83. For *e, quanto posso, al fine m'apparecchio,* "and, as best I can, I prepare myself for death."

84. For *pensando al breve viver mio,* "thinking of the brevity of my life."

85–86. Expansion of *stamani era un fanciullo ed or son vecchio,* "this morn I was a child and now am old."

87. Added by Morley.

91. For *Qui l'umana speranza e qui la gioia,* "Here is human hope and joy."

92. For *qui miseri mortali alzan la testa,* "Here miserable mortals raise their heads [in pride]."

94–95. Blurring of *Veggio or la fuga del mio viver presta, | anzi di tutti,* "I now see how fleeting is my life and the life of all men."

96–98. For *e nel fuggir del sole | la ruina del mondo manifesta,* "and in the flight of the sun the manifest ruin of the world."

99. For *Or vi riconfortate in vostre fole, | gioveni,* "Take comfort, young people, in your silly fables."

100. For *e misurate il tempo largo!* "measure time slowly," i.e., give yourselves many years, spoken with sarcasm in the Italian.

101. Added by Morley.

102. Read: "A hurt that is foreseen hurts less."

103. *Onles.* For *Forse,* "perhaps."

104. *note . . . certayne.* Added by Morley.

105. For *che voi séte offesi,* "that you are afflicted."

106. For *da un grave e mortifero letargo,* "with a deadly lethargy."

110. Added by Morley.

111. Petrarch says *cercar altri paesi,* "seek other lands."

112. Added by Morley.

113. For *Non fate contra 'l vero al core un callo, come séte usi,* "Do not harden your hearts against the truth, as you are wont to do."

115–118. Expansion and blurring of *Non aspettate che la morte scocchi, / come fa la più parte, ché per certo / infinita è la schiera degli sciocchi,* "Do not wait until death transfixes you, as most do, for certainly the throng of fools is infinite."

119–122. Expansion and blurring of *Poi ch'io ebbi veduto e veggio aperto / il volar e 'l fuggir del gran pianeta, / ond'io ho danni ed inganni assai sofferto,* "When I had seen, as still I see, the flying and fleeing of the great planet, when I had suffered great harm and deceit." 121. Read: "When I could have made most of time, I did not."

123. *amonge . . . all.* Added by Morley.

124–128. Misreading, expansion, and blurring of *vidi una gente andarsen queta queta, / senza temer di Tempo o di sua rabbia, / ché gli avea in guardia istorico e poeta,* "I saw a group of people moving quietly, without fear of Time and its rage, for they were guarded by poets and historians." 125. *course rabidouse.* angry curse.

129. *had envye.* Petrarch adds *più d'altri,* "more than others."

131. *madde vulgar.* Petrarch says *la comune gabbia,* "the common cage."

132. Added by Morley.

133–134. Blurring of *Contra costor colui che splende solo, / s'apparecchiava con maggiore sforzo, / e riprendeva un più spedito volo,* "Against these, then, he who shines alone prepared a greater effort and made his flight swifter than before."

135. *doubled the meate.* Petrarch says *l'orzo,* "barley."

136. Added by Morley.

137. *quene.* Lady Fame.

138. For *d'alcun de'suoi già volea far divorzo,* "[the sun] wanted to separate itelf from [her] followers." *at the brayde.* instantly.

139. *I . . . saye.* Petrarch says *Udi'dir,* "I heard a voice." He adds *'l detto scrissi,* "whose words were fixed in my mind." In the original, the following passage is in direct address.

140–142. For *In questi umani, a dir proprio, ligustri / di cieca oblivion che scuri abissi!* translated by Wilkins (*Wi. Tr.,* p. 99) as "What dark abyss of blind oblivion / Awaits these slight and tender human flowers!"

143. *And . . . that.* Added by Morley.

144–146. For *ma lustri / e secoli, vittor d'ogni cerebro, / e vedrà il vaneggiar di questi illustri,* "for lustra and for centuries, victorious over the human mind, it will witness the loss of their fame."

147–150. Expansion and blurring of *Quanti fur chiari fra Peneo ed Ebro, / che son venuti e verran tosto meno! Quanti sul Xanto e quanti in val di Tebro!* "How many were famous between Peneus and Hebrus and are famous no more! How many by the

Xanthus or the valley of the Tiber!" *Peneo.* The river Peneus in Thessaly. *Hebro.* The river Hebrus in Thrace. *Zanto.* The river Xanthus (Scamander) in Sicily. See *Ca. Tr.*, p. 163.

151-156. Expansion and blurring of *Un dubbio iberno, instabile sereno / è vostra fama, e poca nebbia il rompe, / e 'l gran tempo a'gran nomi è gran veneno,* translated by Wilkins (*Wi. Tr.*, p. 99) as "Your fame is nothing more than a sunlit day, / Or a doubtful winter: clouds may end it all. / Great length of time is poisonous to great names."

161-162. Misreading of *e ritolta a'men buon, non dà a'piú degni,* "and that which he takes from the evil he does not give to the good," i.e., he treats all alike.

165. Misreading of *Cosí fuggendo, il mondo seco volve,* "And fleeing thus, it turns the world around."

166. *it . . . so.* Added by Morley.

167-168. Expansion of *fin che v'ha ricondotti in poca polve,* "until he has reduced you to a little dust."

169-178. Extreme blurring of two terzine of the original. Wilkins (*Wi. Tr.*, p. 100) translates them as follows:

> Many indeed are the horns of human pride,
> Nor is it strange if some of them remain,
> Outlasting others, more than the common wont:
> But whatsoever men may think or say,
> If the span of this life of yours were not so brief,
> You soon would see them fade away in smoke.

179-181. Expansion of *Udito questo (perché al ver si deve / non contrastar, ma dar perfetta fede),* "Having heard this—for to truth we owe no opposition but only perfect trust."

182. For *vidi ogni nostra gloria al sol di neve,* "I saw our glory melt like snow in the sun."

183-185. For *E vidi il Tempo rimenar tal prede / de'nostri nomi ch'io gli ebbi per nulla, / benché la gente ciò non sa né crede,* "And I saw Time bear away such trophies of our fame that I held Fame to be nothing, even though men neither know this nor believe it."

188. *to . . . passage.* Added by Morley.

189. Added by Morley.

190-191. For *Quanti son già felici morti in fasce!* "How happy are they who died in swaddling clothes!" Petrarch adds *quanti miseri in ultima vecchiezza!* "How wretched are they who die in old age!"

192. Added by Morley, perhaps his expansion of *Alcun dice,* "Many say."

193-194. Expansion of *Beato è chi non nasce!* "Blessed is he who is not born!"

195-198. Expansion and blurring of *Ma per la turba a'grandi errori avvezza / dopo la lunga età sia il nome chiaro: / che è questo però che sí s'apprezza?* translated by Wilkins (*Wi. Tr.*, p. 101) as "And even though the errant crowd may hold / That for long ages Fame may still endure, / What is it that so highly is esteemed?"

199. *turneth . . . doune.* For *Tutto vince e ritoglie,* "Conquers all and takes all back."

200–201. Expansion and blurring of *chiamasi Fama, ed è morir secondo,* "it is called Fame, but it is a second death." Petrarch adds *né piú che contra 'l primo è alcun riparo,* "and there is no more remedy against it than against the first."

203–204. Expansion and blurring of *Cosi il Tempo trionfa nomi e 'l mondo,* "So does Time triumph over Fame and over the world."

Changes in Capitalization and Orthography. Title Excellent] excellent; Most] most; Dyvyne] dyvyne. 25 thynke] thynkes. 30 infinite] infinitie. 55 Nor] Noo. 107 flye] flyes. 108 folowe] folowes. 149 Zanto] zanto.

The Tryumphe of Dyvynitie

1. *I se.* For *vidi,* "I saw."
2. *but . . . vanitie.* Added by Morley. Petrarch adds *tutto sbigottito,* "full of dismay."
3. For *mi volsi al cor e dissi,* "I turned to my heart and said."
4. *I the pray.* Added by Morley.
5. *Softly . . . answered.* Added by Morley.
12. Blurring of *e doler mi vorrei, né so di cui,* "and though I would complain, I know not of whom."
13–14. Added by Morley.
15. *longe . . . this.* Added by Morley.
16. Added by Morley.
17–20. Expansion and blurring of *deve' aprir li occhi, e non tardar al fine, / ch', a dir il vero, omai troppo m'attempo,* "I should have opened my eyes instead of waiting to the end, and it is true that I have delayed too long."
21–22. Expansion of *Ma tarde non fur mai grazie divine,* "But divine mercies never come too late."
23–24. Blurring of *in quelle spero che 'n me ancor faranno / alte operazioni e pellegrine,* "I hope that they [divine mercies] will work rare and lofty changes in me." *it.* I.e., divine mercy.
25–26. *Thus . . . thus.* Misreading and expansion of *Così detto e risposto,* "Thus I said and thus my heart responded."
27–30. Misreading, expansion, and blurring of *Or, se non stanno / queste cose che 'l ciel volge e governa, / dopo molto voltar che fine avranno?* translated by Wilkins (*Wi. Tr.,* p. 107) as "If all things / That are beneath the heavens are to fail, / How, after many circlings, will they end?"
31. For *Questo pensava: e mentre piú s'interna / la mente mia,* "So I thought, and as I pondered deeply."
34. Added by Morley.
37. *To vanyshe.* Petrarch says *disfar,* "to unmake." *clene . . . place.* Added by Morley.
38. *made . . . grace.* Added by Morley.
39. *trowe ye then.* Added by Morley.
40–43. Serious misreading of the original. Petrarch says that Time, not its symbol, the sun, stood still: *Qual meraviglia ebb'io, quando ristare / vidi in un punto quel che mai non stette, / ma discorrendo suol tutto cangiare!* "How I marveled when I saw stand still that which had never done so but was wont in its course to change all things."

44–45. His thre partes. Past, present, and future. Petrarch adds *e quella una esser ferma, / sí che, come solea, piú non s'affrette,* "and that one immutable so that it [Time] had no longer any need to hurry, as it used to."

46–50. Misreading, expansion, and blurring of *e, quasi in terra d'erbe ignuda ed erma, / né "fia" né "fu" né "mai" né "innanzi" o "'ndietro,"* "And, as on a plain barren of grass, I now could see no 'shall be,' no 'was,' no 'ever,' no 'before,' no 'after,' all of which make human life mutable and infirm."

54–58. Expansion and blurring of *O qual grazia mi fia, se mai l'impetro, / ch'i' veggia ivi presente il Sommo Bene, / non alcun mal, che solo il tempo mesce / e con lui si diparte e con lui vene!* "Oh, what grace shall be mine, if I pray for it. I may there behold the Highest Good, and none of the harm that comes with Time and that goes with Time." *56.* Read: "And none of the evils that come with furious Time."

59–64. Expansion and blurring of *Non avrà albergo il sol Tauro né Pesce; / per lo cui variar nostro lavoro / or nasce, or more, ed ora scema, or cresce,* "The sun will no longer pause in the Bull or the Fish, through whose variation our labor is born or dies, increases or decreases."

65. But happye and. Added by Morley.

66. in . . . eternally. For *nel sommo coro,* "in the supreme choir."

67–68. For *si troveranno o trovano in tal grado / che sia in memoria in nome loro,* translated by Wilkins (*Wi. Tr.,* p. 109) as "Shall be or are already honored so / That memory eternal holds their names."

69. that way. For *guado,* "ford."

70. passage. For *torrente,* "stream."

72. For *e a molti è sí a grado!* "which men hold so dear!"

74. that . . . fall. Added by Morley.

76. Added by Morley.

77. unwise. For *ignudi,* "naked."

78. counsayle. For *consiglio,* "prudence," "judgment."

79. For *egri del tutto e miseri mortali,* "mortals who are infirm of purpose and wretched in everything."

80. Added by Morley.

82. as . . . please. Added by Morley.

83. For *al cui saver non pur io non m'appiglio,* "whose wisdom I cannot grasp."

84. Read: "Even the angels that sit," etc. *that . . . hye.* Added by Morley.

85. thousand . . . one. I.e., they are contented to grasp a thousandth part of the godhead.

86. Added by Morley.

88–92. Expansion and blurring of *O mente vaga, al fin sempre digiuna, / a che tanti pensieri? un'ora sgombra / quanto in molti anni a pena si raguna,* "Oh, wandering mind, hungering even at the last, why so many thoughts? A single hour can dispel all that was gathered painfully over many years."

93–95. Blurring of *Quel che l'anima nostra preme e 'ngombra, / "dianzi, adesso, ier, deman, mattino e sera" / tutti in un punto passeran com'ombra,* "All that oppresses and encumbers the soul, 'before' and 'soon,' 'yesterday' and 'tomorrow,' 'morning' and 'evening,' will pass like a shadow."

98. Added by Morley.

99–100. For *Non avrà loco "fu," "sarà" ned "era"; | ma "è" solo, "in presente,"* *ed "ora" ed "oggi" | e sola "eternità" raccolta e 'ntera,* translated by Wilkins (*Wi. Tr.*, p. 110) as "'Has been,' 'shall be,' and 'was' exist no more, / But 'is' and 'now,' 'the present' and 'today,' / 'Eternity' alone, one and complete."

101–102. Misreading, expansion, and blurring of *Quasi spianati dietro e 'nanzi i poggi, | ch'occupavan la vista, non fia in cui | vostro sperare e rimembrar s'appoggi,* translated by Wilkins (*Wi. Tr.*, p. 110) as "Future and past, like hills that hid our view, / Are leveled now, and nothing still remains / Whereupon hope or memory may lean."

103–104. Expansion of *fa spesso altrui | vaneggiar,* "often leads men astray."

106. For *pensando pur: che sarò io? che fui?* "Thinking 'What shall I be?' 'What have I been?'"

107–110. Slight blurring of *Non sarà più diviso a poco a poco, | ma tutto insieme, e non più state o verno, | ma morto il tempo, e variato il loco,* "Time shall not be broken into bits; all will be one; Time being dead, there will be no summer and no winter and all the world will be transformed."

111. *that . . . name.* Added by Morley.

113–114. Expansion and blurring of *chi fia | chiaro un volta, fia chiaro in eterno,* rendered by Wilkins (*Wi. Tr.*, p. 110) as "the glorious / Will glorious be to all eternity."

117–118. Added by Morley.

119. *that . . . be.* For *leggiadre e pellegrine,* "rare and beautiful."

124. *in . . . past.* Added by Morley.

125–128. Misreading and blurring of *Tanti volti, che Morte e 'l Tempo ha guasti, | torneranno al suo più fiorito stato, | e vedrassi ove, Amor, tu mi legasti,* "So many countenances, damaged by Death and Time, will return to their perfect flowering. The bond in which love bound me will be seen."

129–130. Expansion and blurring of *a dito ne sarò mostrato,* "[some] will point to me."

131–134. Expansion and slight blurring of *ecco chi pianse sempre, e nel suo pianto | sovra 'l riso d'ogni altro fu beato,* "Here is he who ever wept and who, amid his tears, was blest above the joys of other men."

137. *and . . . degre.* Added by Morley.

138. For *fra tutte dar il vanto,* "be praised above all others."

139. *God wote.* Added by Morley.

140–142. Misreading of *se fu soppressa | tanta credenza a più fidi compagni, | a si alto segreto chi s'appressa?* "If this knowledge [of the date of the Resurrection] was kept from His most trusted friends [the Apostles], who can presume to know such a high secret?" See *Ca. Tr.*, p. 177.

143–144. Petrarch adds *e de'guadagni | veri e de'falsi si farà ragione, | che tutti fien allor opre d'aragni,* "true values shall be separated from the false, and worldly goods will be as transparent as a spider's web."

145–148. Expansion and blurring of *Vedrassi quanto in van cura si pone, | e quanto indarno s'affatica e suda; | come sono ingannate le persone,* "It will be seen how vain are human cares, how we labor and sweat in vain, and how men are deceived."

149–150. Added by Morley.

151–154. Expansion and slight blurring of *Nessun segreto fia chi copra o chiuda; | fia ogni coscienza, o chiara o fosca, | dinanzi a tutto 'l mondo aperta e nuda,* "No secret will be covered or hidden, and every conscience, be it pure or sullied with sin, will stand open and naked before the world." See *Ca. Tr.,* p. 178.

155–159. Expansion and clarification of *e fia Chi ragion giudichi e conosca,* "and there will be One who shall know and judge the good and the evil." See *Ca. Tr.,* p. 178.

160–164. Expansion of *Ciascun poi vedrem prender suo viaggio, | come fiera scacciata che s'imbosca,* "And then we shall see each [sinner] going his way, hiding like a driven beast."

165–166. Blurring of a difficult terzina in the original: *e vedrassi quel poco di paraggio, | che vi far ir superbi, e oro e terreno | esservi stato danno e non vantaggio,* translated by Wilkins (*Wi. Tr.,* p. 112) as "Then shall we see how slight the greatness is / That we are proud of, and that gold and land / have brought to us not benefit, but harm."

167–172. Expansion and slight blurring of *e 'n disparte color che sotto 'l freno | di modesta fortuna ebbero in uso, | senz'altra pompa, di godersi in seno,* "and to one side those who, under the check of modest fortune, were content to live peacefully and without pomp." 170. Read: "Shall be merry together," etc.

173–176. Misreading, expansion, and blurring of *Questi Trionfi, i cinque in terra giuso | avem veduto, ed a la fin il sesto, | Dio permettente, vederem lassuso,* "We have seen five of these Triumphs here on earth, and (God willing) we shall see the sixth in heaven above."

177–182. Expansion and blurring of a single terzina of the original: *e 'l Tempo a disfar tutto cosí presto, | e Morte in sua ragion cotanto avara | morti insieme saranno e quella e questo,* "and Time, so ready to destroy all things, and Death, so greedy in her evil, shall die together."

183–186. Conflation of two terzine of the original. These are rendered by Wilkins (*Wi. Tr.,* p. 112) as follows:

> And those who merited illustrious fame
> That Time had quenched, and countenances fair
> Made pale and wan by Time and bitter Death,
>   Becoming still more beauteous than before
> Will leave to raging Death and thieving Time
> Oblivion, and aspects dark and sad.

187–189. For *Ne l'età piú fiorita e verde avranno | con immortal bellezza eterna fama,* "In the full flower of youth they shall have immortal beauty and eternal fame." 190. Added by Morley.

191–192. For *Ma innanzi a tutte, ch'a rifar si vanno,* "Before all those who go to be made new."

193–194. Blurring of *è quella che piangendo il mondo chiama | con la mia lingua e con la stanca penna: | ma 'l ciel pur di vederla intera brama,* translated by Wilkins (*Wi. Tr.,* p. 112) as "Is she for whom the world is weeping still, / Calling her with my tongue and weary pen, / But heaven too desires her, body and soul."

195. For *A riva un fiume, che nasce in Gebenna,* "by the banks of a river whose source is in Gebenna." *Gebenna.* A range of mountains, the modern Cévennes, situated northwest of Avignon and extending as far north as Lyon and south almost to the Pyrenees.

196. Added by Morley.

198. For *che la memoria ancora il cor accenna,* "that my heart still remembers it."

200. For *Che poi che avrà ripreso il suo bel velo,* translated by Wilkins (*Wi. Tr.,* p. 113) as "And now that she her beauty hath resumed."

201–206. Expansion of *se fu beato chi la vide in terra, / Or che fia dunque a rivederla in cielo?* "if he who saw her here on earth was blest, what joy will he experience in seeing her in heaven?"

Changes in Capitalization and Orthography. Title Excellent] excellent; Moste] moste. 5 Lord] lord. 18 trouthe] troughe. 23 it] hym. 28 guide] guides; governe] governes. 38 Godes] godes. 55 God] god. 56 Tyme] tyme. 60 Bull] bull. 61 Fyshe] fyshe. 80 Hym] hym. 81 His] his. 82 Hym] hym. 98 Goddes] goddes. 140 Goddes] goddes. 156 His] his. 175 Godes] godes. 178 Tyme] tyme. 180 Death] death. 185 Death] death; Tyme] tyme. 196 chaunced] chaunched. 197 warre] awarre.

Vyrgyll in his Epigrames of Cupide and Dronkenesse

1. The text of the original reads as follows:

Nec Veneris, nec tu Vini capieris amore.
Uno namquae modo Vina, Venusquae nocent
Ut Venus enervat vires, sic copia Bacchi:
Et tentat gressus, debilitatquae pedes:
Multos caecus Amor cogit secreta fateri:
Arcanum demens detegit ebrietas
Bellum saepe petit ferus exitiale Cupido.
Saepe manus itidem Bacchus ad arma vocat.
Perdidit horrendo Troiam Venus improba bello:
Et Lapythas bello perdis Iacche gravi.
Deniquae quum menteis hominum furiarit uterquae
Et pudor, & probitas, & metus omnis abest.
Compedibus Venerem, vinclis constringe Lyaeum.
Nec te muneribus laedut uterquae suis.
Vina sitim sedant, natis Venus alma creandis
Servit: sinem horum transiluisse nocet.

(*Opera Virgiliana cum decem commentis . . . ab Servio, Donato, Mancinello,*
Leiden, 1529)

Changes in Capitalization and Orthography. Epigraph capieris] capiares.

Bibliographical History of Morley's *Tryumphes*

1. *A Finding List of English Books to 1640 in Libraries in the British Isles* (Durham: Council of the Durham Colleges, 1958).

2. *Biblioteca Grenvilliana*, ed. John Thomas Payne and Henry Foss, 2 vols. (London, 1842), II, 539. The volume is described as "wood cut capital letters, 4° A–N in fours, 52 leaves Bl.l."

3. I am indebted to Mr. B. P. Robinson of the Bodleian Library for checking the Bodleian catalogs and for suggesting this explanation of the history of the Bodleian Library copy.

4. *Biblioteca Heberiana*, compiled by J. Payne Collier (London, 1834), Part IV, Day 9, pp. 231–232.

5. See Sydney Richardson Christie-Miller, *Catalogue . . . of Extremely Rare Works . . . from . . . Britwell Court* (London, 1923), p. 67.

6. See William Thomas Lowndes, *Bibliographers's Manual of English Literature*, 6 vols. (London, 1864), IV, 1,841; and William Carew Hazlitt, *Handbook to the Popular, Poetical, and Dramatic Literature of Great Britain from the Invention of Printing to the Restoration* (London, 1867), p. 455. Both Lowndes and Hazlitt listed only the two British Museum copies, the Bodleian copy, and the (then) Britwell copy.

7. Miss Elizabeth Edmondston, who graciously provided the facts about the Sion College Library copy. An account of the "discovery" of the volume appeared in the *Times Literary Supplement*, January 27, 1940, p. 52.

8. *Bibliothecae cleri Londinensis in Collegio Sionensi Catalogus* (London, 1724), sig. Ooo02^v. The work is listed under books on "Philosophia Ethica in Octavo et Duodecimo."

9. See Thomas Warton, *A History of English Poetry from the Twelfth to the Close of the Sixteenth Century*, ed. W. C. Hazlitt, 4 vols. (London, 1871), IV, 79–80. Warton's history first appeared in 1774–1781.

10. *Bibliographia Poetica, A Catalog of Engleish Poets of the 12, 13, 14, 15, and 16th Centurys* (London, 1802), p. 291.

11. 2 vols. (Edinburgh, 1820), I, 77ff. Morley's translation is also mentioned in Collier's *A Bibliographical and Critical Account of the Rarest Books in the English Language*, 6 vols. (New York, 1866), IV, 77.

Glossary

abashed: cast down, surprised

abatyd: beat down, demolished, destroyed, defeated; humbled, degraded

abjecte (v.): to cast or throw down; to degrade, abase, debase

abrayde, at that: suddenly, breaking forth abruptly

abroade: at large, freely moving about

abyde: to submit to, endure

abyde: to wait, wait for

accompted: reckoned, deemed, considered, valued

admiration: astonishment, surprise, wonder

adventure: hap, fortune, luck

adventure, at: at hazard, at random; recklessly

advert: to turn one's attention; to take notice, heed; to pay attention; to observe, note, notice

advyse (n.): opinion, judgment

advysed: counseled

afearde: afraid

agayne: against, in the opposite direction

agre (v.): to be pleased; to accept favorably; to bring into harmony

aknowen: known, recognized

algate: always, continually, in every way, at all events

all and some: the sum total, completely

alledge: to declare, plead

allegorye (adj.): allegorical

allgate: see *algate*

alway: all along, all the time; perpetually, throughout all time

alyf: alive

a merveld: struck with wonder; surprised, astonished

amphorisomis: aphorisms

apall: appalled, made pale or pallid; weak, faint

aparte: to one side, aside

appertayneth: belongs, is suited; is proper, appropriate

armyne: ermine

arrace: obliteration

arrest (v.): to sentence, decree; also in modern sense, to stop in its course, to arrest

arrest, standeth at: stands at attention

a sondre: asunder, apart

assaute: assault, attack, onslaught

assayde: tried, attempted; tested

asswage: to soften, assuage, mitigate, diminish

astonied: stunned, stupified

attayne: to reach, arrive at; touch

attyres: personal adornment, decoration; demands

avayle: to fall down

ay: ever, always, continuously

bare: bore, carried

bearde, in the: in the face, face to face

beguyldynge: beguiling, deceiving

beguyle: to beguile, deceive, cheat

be kynde: by nature, naturally, by natural disposition

bekynde (v.): to beget

beryth down: pushes to the ground, overwhelms, overthrows, vanquishes

bet: shaped by beating; ornamented, decorated

blowe: to breathe

blowen: proclaimed, spread abroad

bole: ball, sphere, globe

boote: (n.): relief, remedy

brased: brazen, shameless

brayde, at the: in a short space of time; instantly, suddenly

brayde, at this: at this instant, immediately

brayde, so short: so suddenly

brayes: steep banks, hillsides

brest: burst

busynes: anxiety, solicitude, care, distress, uneasiness

bynde: to tie up, join, unite; make prisoner; also to restrain, confine

by prove: by experience

Glossary

calde: named, gave a designation to

call: to summon, bring

canapye: canopy, covering

captayne: chief, leader

case: condition, state, plight

caste, at a: by fortune, chance; in extremities, near to death or ruin; at a glance(?)

certayne (v.): to make certain, reassure

chafed: vexed, irritated

chaufes: warmed, excited

chaunce: fortune, luck, lot, destiny

chaunce, hard: bad luck

chayre: throne, raised seat; chariot

cheke and chynne: cheek by jowl; side by side; in the closest intimacy

chere: aspect, facial expression, mien, disposition

chevalerus: chivalrous

choyce (adj.): select, exquisite

chylder: children

clam: climbed

clappe: noise, chatter, clatter

clarcke: scholar; cleric

clateryng: rapid, noisy talk

cleane: entirely, completely: also modern sense of cleanliness

cleare: clear, bright, well-sounding, free, noble, splendid, famous

clemesse: clemency, mildness, mercy, leniency

clepe: call, cry; call the name of

clepyng: embracing

clerckely: clerical, scholarly, erudite

cleres: becomes clear or bright

close (adj.): hidden, secluded, secret, covert

colour: rhetorical mode or figure, ornament of style or diction; rhythm, meter

coloures: color, appearance, complexion

combred: cumbered, overwhelmed, confounded, benumbed

comforte. (v.): to invigorate, refresh, gladden, cheer

compase (v.): to encircle, besiege

complaynt: grief, lamentation

comprehend: to grasp with the mind, understand: also to comprise, include, contain

compted: esteemed, accounted, reckoned, considered

compteth: counts

condicion: character, disposition, nature

condiscend: concede, consent, concur, agree

conformitye: conformity, harmony, agreement

conninge: wit, wisdom, intelligence, skill; as an adj., learned

conscience: consciousness, inward thought, mind

consent (n.): harmony, consort

constrayned: forced, compelled, obliged

consumynge: vanishing

contrariouse: contrary, repugnant, hostile; full of opposition

corde: cord, rope

councel: secret, purpose, design, opinion

councell: judgment, decision

courage: heart, mind, nature, disposition; desire, will, ardor; courage, encouragement

course: curse

craft: skill, art; device, artifice; also fraud, deceit, guile

cranckes: sicknesses, diseases; aches and pains

creasynge: increasing

cryspe: closely and stiffly curled

cumbrance: trouble of mind, perplexity, distress, annoyance

curiouse: fastidious, difficult to satisfy; intricate, elaborate, erudite(?)

curiously: with careful art, elaborately, exquisitely

dale: small valley

dalyeng: light or idle conversation, chatter, gossip

dartes: arrows

daunce: course of action, game

daunger: lordship, power, control; ungraciousness, disdain, difficulty

daungerouse: difficult, severe; haughty, proud

dead, in: indeed, in fact; also *in deade*

debarres: excludes, shuts out

debate: strife, quarrel, conflict

debatyd: brought down

decay: downfall, wasting away, dwindling

declyne (v.): to reduce, cause to dwindle

dected: decked, covered, adorned

deface: to destroy the reputation or credit of; to discredit, defame

defyne: describe

demaunde (v.): to ask

demure (n.): modesty, shyness, reserved or composed demeanor

demyde: deemed, judged, considered

denayde: denied, contradicted; negated

departed: separated, parted

deprave: to pervert the meaning; slander, calumniate; vilify, debase

derkyd: darkened, eclipsed

descryve: describe, write down

desire: to ask, request

devyde: to separate

differing: deferring, postponing

dilection: love, affection

discresing: decreasing

dispoyle: to take forcibly

dispyte: contempt, scorn, disdain

dispytefull: contemptuous; cruel, fierce, malicious; also *dyspytefull*

dissever: separate, part, disunite

dissolyynge: destroying, undoing; resolving

divers: diverse, different; also *dyvers*

domagid: injured, damaged

doubtfull: perilous, fearful, dubious

dowe: due, propriety; debt, duty

dulse: sweet, pleasing, agreeable

dure: persist, last, continue

durst: dared

duryng: duration, lifetime

dyamount: adamant, diamond

dyke: narrow ditch, trench

dyscryved: described

dyspyse: to scorn, show disdain or contempt for

dyssolved: melted away, died

dyte: recorded, put in writing(?)

enbrase: entwine, encircle, surround

endite: to write, compose, narrate, relate; also *endyte*

entent: attention, heed; intent, observation

eterne: eternal

expresse: to reveal, declare, relate

extincte: extinguished

extreme: last, final

eyen: eyes; also *eyne*

facion, of this: in this manner

facyons: actions, gestures, ways

fain: glad, well-pleased

fancy: delusive imagination: illusion of the senses

farde: fared

farme: firm, durable

farvente: fervent, hot, burning

fasshyon: manners and customs; outward action or ceremony; see *facyons*

fatherly: paternal

feare, to: to frighten, terrify

fearefull: timorous, apprehensive; inspiring terror; dreadful

felowe: friend, companion

fenester: window

ferde: feared, frightened, terrified

fervent: hot, burning, boiling

feste: feast, banquet

fierce (n.): fierceness; force(?)

flanckes: sides

flete: to float, swim

fleyng: fleeting

forbyde: forbad, denied

forehead: face, visage

forth ryght: straightforwardly

forth with all: at the same moment that

frandely: friendly

frayde: frightened, afraid

fraye: fear

fresh: bright, lively, brisk

fret: devoured, consumed, destroyed

fructe: fruit; advantage, benefit, enjoyment, profit

fugitive (adj.): fleeting, ephemeral, fickle, shifting

fulfyll: to satisfy

fyle: to string together; to spin, weave(?)

fyne: conclusion, end

fyrme: firm, stable

game: game, sport, fun, amusement; joke, jest; contest

Glossary

gate: got; also gait, manner of walking

gayne: profit, reward

gent: noble, high-born, graceful; elegant, pretty

gere: possessions, property, money

glasse: mirror

glosynge: flattering, having a fair appearance

gorgeous: brilliantly colored; magnificent, resplendent

grave sight: serious aspect

graven: engraved, carved

grevith: causes grief, pain, or annoyance

grevouse: burdensome, oppressive, heavy, severe

grovets: little groves or arbors

guyse: manner, method, way

habyts: apparel, attire; bearing, demeanor

halpe: helped

hand, in: in company, presence

hand, out of: at once, immediately

happe: hap, chance, fortune, luck; also *heape*

harboroughe: harbor, haven

harde: heard

hardines: boldness, daring, audacity

hardy: bold, daring, audacious

harnes: armor, military equipment

hastyd: hastened, accelerated

hastyth: hastens, hurries

havynge: greedy, covetous, grasping; living

helme: helmet

hent: seized, clutched, grasped

herbers: green plots, flower gardens, orchards

hete: heat, fervor, ardor, passion

hied, hyed: hurried, hastened

high: proud, noble, exalted

holde (n.): stronghold, fort

holden: confined, imprisoned

honest: honorable, worthy

hoote: unpleasantly vivid color(?)

hurl: to rush impetuously, dash

hyeth a pase: hastens at a good pace

hyght: was called, named

hylde: held, confined

hynmost: hindmost, last

importune (adj.): troublesome, burdensome, severe

infenyte (n.): infinity, eternity

intent: intention, purpose; will, inclination

intente, to myne: to the end that I; in order that I; to my aim, purpose

iwys: certainly, assuredly, indeed

joly: merry, lively, pretty

keale: to cool

kepe: to guard, defend, preserve

knewe: recognized, was aware of

kynde: race, species; nature

lappe, in one's: to be within the reach or power of; to thrust upon one's notice

lasyd: caught, entangled, ensnared

laude: praise, praiseworthiness, high commendation, cause or subject for praise; also *lawde*

lealtie: faithfulness, loyalty

lefte: neglected, omitted to perform; abstained from, refrained from

lefull: permissible, right, lawful, just

lernars: pupils, scholars; men of learning

lese: to lose

lesse: not so great; least of all things; unless

lest: least

let: to hinder; to quit, abandon, forsake; to hesitate, delay

liver: sooner, rather; dearly, gladly, willingly

loked: sought

lordely: nobly, magnificently, haughtily

losed: loosened, undid, set free, released from bonds

lust: pleasure, delight, attraction, charm; desire, appetite; sexual passion; vigor, lustiness

luste: wish, desire; that which gives pleasure

lusters: lustra(?); glory, that which adds luster; glass balls placed among artificial lights to increase brightness

lustye: joyful, cheerful, lively; pleasant, pleasing; lustful; healthy, vigorous *lyfte*: left; also lifted, raised

lyke: similar, in like manner; to the same extent as; in the manner of; in like degree, equally

lyked: pleased, delighted, gave pleasure to

lyst: to please, like, care, desire

lyvely: lively, sprightly, pertaining to life

magyke: sorcery; as an adj., magical

marveld: was filled with wonder, astonishment

mayned: maltreated; conducted, managed; conducted one's self in a particular way

meade: meed, reward, recompense, gift; also *mede*

meanly: moderately, tolerably; indifferently, poorly, badly; at a moderate speed

measure: moderation, temperance

memoriall: memory, remembrance, recollection; reminder

men: mean, base, common

mengled: mingled, mixed

merciable: merciful, compassionate

mete: suitable, fit, proper; also mild, gentle; equal, on the same level

mockes: jeers, jibes

mode: manner, mind; dress, habit of life

much: as an adv. greatly; as an adj., great

musynge: gazing intently, staring; wondering; waiting, looking intently

myddes: midst, middle

mynde (v.): to pay attention; to bear in mind; to perceive, notice, be aware of

mynded: intended, had in mind, purposed; contemplated

mynister: agent, representative; servant, attendant; underling

nacion: nation, people, race

name, hath the: has the reputation, is spoken of

naturall: as a noun, natural disposition, inclination, character; as an adj., free from affectation, artificiality, constraint

naturall regyon: native country

neclecte: neglected

nevew: grandson

none: no, none

noones, for the: for the particular occasion; expressly

nothyng: nothing; not at all, in no degree

noughty: immoral, wicked; worthless, vile

noyous: annoying, troublesome

nyce: foolish, stupid, senseless; wanton, lascivious; also *nyse*

nygh: near

obtayn: to arrive at, achieve, reach, succeed

offende: to cause to sin, to transgress

opprest: crushed in battle, subdued, defeated; burdened, troubled, depressed

or: before

orball: sphere, globe, circle

ordeyned: put in order, arranged

oriently: brilliantly, lustrously, clearly

ought: owed

oversome: too quickly, too readily

overwhart: perverse, hostile, unfriendly

parde: pardie, by God; indeed, in truth

parlouse: perilous, dangerous, hazardous

passage: transition from life to death

passe: passage, road, route

passeth: surpasses, excels; crosses, traverses

peax: peace

pensyfe: full of anxious thought; apprehensive, melancholy

peradventure: by accident, by chance

percase: by chance

percial: partial

perlouse: see *parlouse*

persyde: pierced, punctured

perties: parties, groups, factions

perylious: see *parlouse*

playne: entirely, quite, perfectly

pleasaunce: joy, delight, pleasure

polecy: political cunning

porte: deportment, carriage, bearing, demeanor

poynt: point, detail

pray (n.): prey, plunder, booty

prease: crowd, throng, multitude; also *pres, prese, presse*

pretend: proffer, put forth; profess; intend; aspire to; take upon one's self

Glossary

prevy: privy, intimate, personal, private
processe: progress, course
proper: own, particular, personal
proved: gave proof, evidence of
provide: to foresee, make provision or preparation for
purpose (n.): aim, intention, determination
purpose (v.): to propose, speak up, discourse
pussaunt: puissant, mighty, potent, powerful
put . . . from: to remove from
puttes by: thrusts aside, neglects
pycter: picture
pytie: grief, repentance, remorse; compassion; piety; also *pytye*

quadrant: quadrangle, square:
quyte (v.): to be set free; to be released, delivered, freed of

rabidouse: furious, raging, violent; also *rabidus*
rage (n.): madness, insanity, mania
rage (v.): to go mad, to be mad, to act madly or foolishly
ragyouse: furious, mad
rate: speed, pace, measure
rath: quick, speedy, prompt, eager, earnest, vehement
raunge (n.): row, line, file, rank, order
reason (v.): to argue, discourse, converse
reason, out of: inordinate, in opposition to what reason directs
reasonynge: arguing, discoursing, conversing
rede: to read
rede (v.): to advise, counsel
regard (n.): look, glance, gaze; habit or manner of looking
regarde (v.): to look at, gaze upon, observe
rehearsall: recital, recounting, narration
rehearse: to recite, repeat, give account of, narrate, recount
removed: remote, distant, long dead
rennyng: running, rapid, hasty; continuous
renowmed: famous, celebrated
repent: to regret, to cause to feel regret

reprehencion: reproof, censure, rebuke, reprimand
repreve: reproof, shame, disgrace; also *reprove*
respecte, to the: with respect to; in comparison with
reversyd: overthrew, overturned, upset; opposed, resisted, turned back
revolved: considered, thought over, pondered
riall: regal, royal; also *ryall*
rodye: ruddy, rosy
route: company, band, troop of persons
routing: snoring

sadde: steadfast, firm, constant; grave, serious
salutyd: greeted in words; hailed
sapiently: wisely, sagely
scant: scarcely, hardly
scape: to escape
sclaunder (n.): discredit, disgrace, shame
sclendre: slender, slim, weak
scorned: derided, ridiculed
scornes (n.): taunts, insults, mockeries, derisions
scrapynge: removing soil by scratching with the feet or claws
selfe (adj.): same, identical
sely: helpless, defenseless, weak, feeble; insignificant, trifling
semblaunt (n.): appearance, demeanor, air
semblaunt (adj.): like, similar
sens, to the: to the quick, to the effect that
sentences: aphorisms, maxims, subjects, themes
sentensiouse: full of meaning, intelligence; aphoristic
set by: valued, esteemed
sheene (adj.): bright, shining; beautiful, fair
short, with . . . words: briefly, in a few words
shot: shut
shote: shoot; rush, be precipitated
shovynge: shoving, pushing, advancing
shytte: shut
slypper (adj.): slippery, unsure; deceitful; light, wanton

smarte: sharp, biting, stinging

smerte (v.): to smart, feel distress, pain

smote: struck, cut

sole: soul, spirit

sometyme: former, formerly

sort: company, band, group

soune: sound

speade: success, prosperity, good fortune; also *spede*

speares: spheres, planets, globes; outward limits of space

spottyd: stained, sullied, tarnished

spoyle: booty, loot, plunder; victory

spye: to discover, notice, observe

spyred: curled, twisted, wound

stacker: to stagger, sway

stall: abide, dwell; come to a standstill; stop, pause

start: to move suddenly

stay: to cause to stand still; to stop, halt

stede: place

storyall: historical

straunge: unfriendly, distant, reserved; unusual

strete: road, path, way

stryvyng: contending, struggling, debating disputing

studiouse: heedful, solicitous, attentive

studye: care, zeal, diligence

suerty: safety, security

suspecte (n.): suspicion

suspyres: sighs

susteyne: to carry, bear; to hold up, bear the weight of

sythyns: since

terme: term, space, limit of time; end, limit

tho: then, after that, upon that

thopasion: topaz

thrall: enthralled, captivated

threateth: threatens, menaces

throw (n.): twist, turn; perverse twist of temper or humor

tone and tother: the one and the other

tone the tother, the: one another

to to: excess, intemperance

towarde: promising, disposed to learn; docile, compliant

trace: path, way, road; line, file, train of persons

travayle (v.): to torment, distress, afflict

travayle (n.): labor, toil, suffering

trone: throne

troubles (adj.): troublous, disturbed, agitated

trowe: trust, believe, think

trueth, for: in fact, truly, really, indeed

tryed: tested, tried out

tryumphing: participating in a triumphal procession; riding triumphantly

turned: returned, went back

twayne: two

tyde (adj.): tied, bound, fastened

tyde (n.): time, hour, season

tymes: leisure or spare time

undertake: dare say, venture to assert

unfayned: honestly, genuinely

ungentleness: harshness, roughness; discourtesy

universall (n.): universe, cosmos

unkynde: unnatural, cruel, ungrateful, devoid of natural goodness

unmete: unequal, unevenly matched; superior

unneth: scarcely, hardly, with difficulty

unprovided: unforeseen

unprudent: imprudent, unwise

unshote: unshut, open, disclosed

unwytty: ignorant, unwise, witless

use: custom, habit, practice, manner

usyd: carry, comport, bear one's self

valure: valor, worthiness, merit, courage

varyable: various, different, diverse

vassalage: prowess in battle, a brave or chivalrous act

vayne: vein, humor, mood.

vayne, with an easy: with gentle speech, language

vesture: garment, vestment, article of apparel

viage: journey, pilgrimage

voyded: avoided, removed, withdrew

voyde from: free, rid of, empty of

vulgar: vernacular

vysage: visage, face

Glossary

warkes: works

was (n.): what was, something past

well doynge: valiant, diligent, well-behaved

wenyng: thinking, supposing, believing, hoping

wexed: waxed, grew, became

whitled: plied with drink, drunk

whyle, in a: at the same time

wise: manner, mode, fashion, style

withstand: to oppose, resist, endure

witty: clever, ingenious, skillful, crafty, cunning

wonder (adv.): wondrously, marvelously

wonderouse (adj.): wondrous, marvelous

woode: mad, angry, wild

worthy: estimable, prominent, courageous

wracke, go to: go to ruin, destruction

wylde: self-willed, resisting control or restraint; licentious, dissolute

wyle: wile, stratagem, trick

wyll (v.): to wish, desire, have a mind to

wyll I, nyll I: willy-nilly

wyse: see *wise*

wyte: understanding, reasoning, intellect: cleverness, skill; also *wytt*

ydressed: arrayed, decorated, adorned

yede: went, proceeded, walked

yssewed: issued, came out

Index of Proper Names
in the *Tryumphes*

The names in brackets are alluded to but not mentioned specifically in the text.

Index of Proper Names in the *Tryumphes*

261

Index of Proper Names in the *Tryumphes*

General Index

Index

Index

Index

Index

Index